The Second Coming of Jesus

Explained So Anyone Can Understand It
Clear Teachings of Jesus and Paul
No Fiction or Fantasies Here

John Ehrlich

Copyright © 2009 by John Ehrlich

The Second Coming of Jesus
Explained So Anyone Can Understand It
by John Ehrlich

Printed in the United States of America

ISBN 9781615793228

All rights reserved solely by the author. The author guarantees all contents are original and do not infringe upon the legal rights of any other person or work. No part of this book may be reproduced in any form without the permission of the author. The views expressed in this book are not necessarily those of the publisher.

Unless otherwise indicated, Bible quotations are taken from The New King James Version. Copyright © 1982 by Thomas Nelson, Inc. Used by permission.

www.xulonpress.com

Cheryl — I hope you enjoy reading this. Take Care.

John

Acknowledgements

First, thanks to my wife, Rosemary, who tolerated my many hours of writing, sometimes, late into the night.

Second, thanks to my father, Norman, with the Lord now for several earthly years, who first got me to thinking along these lines.

Thirdly, thanks to my mother, Connie, who before I was born, prayed that God would use me in the work of the gospel.

Fourthly, thanks to all my premillennial brethren who adamantly and sometimes arrogantly and vehemently asserted the correctness of their position and the error of my position for pushing me into deeper study of the second coming of Jesus.

Preface

"The Second Coming of Jesus Explained So Anyone Can Understand It". What kind of a title is that? An honest one. One that means exactly what it says. Anyone can understand the Second Coming of Jesus. The Bible is clear on that subject. However, so many "prophecy experts" have so distorted and twisted it, that the average Christian is mystified and perplexed by what they teach. They want to believe it because their pastors are teaching it, but they just do not see it taught clearly in God's Word. For many years teaching on prophecy has caused many Christians to scratch their heads wondering what in the world the "expert" is saying. I have had that same problem. Much of what is purported to be Biblical teaching on prophecy is nothing more than a cleverly devised system of man. Bible doctrine is clear on the Second Coming of Jesus. It is not a hodge-podge of nonsense, but it makes perfect sense.

I have always loved writing. When I was in the fifth grade our class had an assignment to write a Christmas story. I do not recall my story – I believe it was something about Christmas on the moon or some such nonsense - but it was voted the best in the class and it was published in our local newspaper. That was my first experience with writing. I began preaching in 1977 – actually, I began teaching in 1967 – so I have written many sermons and Bible studies through the years. I say this for a reason.

Recently I have begun to write as a hobby, not as a profession. A couple of years ago I wrote an article entitled, "Why I am a Republican." Someone I shared it with asked the question, "Why did you write this?" That person never did read it. I also wrote a devotional commentary on the book of Mark and another person asked me, "Why did you write this?" I'm not sure that person ever read it.

The questions were asked in the tone of voice of "Why did YOU write this. What makes YOU think that you have anything to say that anyone would want to hear? You are not well known. You are not a famous writer. I know you, so therefore you must not have anything to say that is worth knowing."

Isn't that the way many people think? "If *I* know you, you just can't have anything to share that is all that important. Don't try to influence me." I'm reminded of the words of Jesus when He spoke concerning the people of Nazareth. "A prophet is not without honor save in His own country." (***Bold and italicized*** for emphasis – so throughout this book.)

Now, do not misunderstand. I know that I am not a prophet. I am not even attempting to imply that in the least. I know my station in life. It is a lowly one. Very few people beyond my family even know who I am. And, very frankly, that's the way I prefer it. Notoriety and fame has many drawbacks and problems the rest of us do not have.

So, why did I write this book? Like the man who climbed the mountain – because it was there. This book has been latent within me for several years, but it just has not worked its way out until now. This subject, in particular, has been stuck in my craw for many years. Every time I hear about the "rapture", I cringe. Not because I do not believe in the Second Coming of Jesus. I do. He is coming again. But, He is not coming again in the manner that is presented by so many good Evangelical Bible preachers and teachers today. The predominate teaching of the "rapture" is founded upon a faulty premise. In fact, it is founded upon many faulty premises.

Right now, I know that many of you are ready to dismiss everything I have written and explained in this book because you have been taught and you believe that the "rapture" is part and parcel of sound theology. Anyone who does not believe in the "rapture" as defined and portrayed by so many popular books, movies, "prophecy experts", teachers and preachers must have a screw loose and may not even be saved.

But, please bear with me. Please give me your ear. I guarantee you that you will not be harmed in any way, shape, or form by reading what I have to say. Any possible harm that can come to you will only come from within yourself if you get so angry with what I am saying that you give yourself a migraine or high blood pressure. Please do not do that to yourself. I say angry because I have witnessed anger first hand when one does not swallow the popular "rapture" teaching hook, line and sinker. Why does failure to accept what is at best a debatable and inferential proposition, one that the church through the centuries knew nothing about, and at present is regarded by many Bible believers to be a false teaching, gender attacks?

If you decide after you have read this – and I hope that you will read it - that I am full of beans, then so be it. At the least, you have given me a fair hearing. And I hope that it is a *fair* hearing in which you will carefully and prayerfully consider the arguments presented in this treatise and not simply read this with an antagonistic, Pharisaical, critical attitude, only wanting to find fault and to protect the "system" at all costs.

I have no delusions of grandeur or of having the talent to sway those who are convinced in their minds that the system they have been taught is true. No one who *wants* to believe in the "rapture" will have their minds changed by what I write. I know that up front. Turn on any Christian radio or TV station and there are a multitude of teachers who adamantly declare the virtues of the "rapture" theory and of the entire Dispensational, Pre-Tribulation, Pre-Millennial position. I am convinced that the hard core Dispensational, Pre-Tribulational, Pre-Millennial teachers and disciples will simply pooh – pooh everything I write without giving it much - if indeed any - thought whatsoever. "Who does this guy think he is?" It is *not* my intention to change *their* minds. It is already set in granite. They were taught this system – so it must be true - and no one can or will change their minds on it. They have accepted it as truth, and not even dynamite can alter their positions. Really. Honestly. I do not mind that I cannot influence them. That is their choice. It is not a proper choice, but it is theirs to make.

Unfortunately, I do not have the exact quote or the reference for the quote, but I remember the gist of it. When I was doing a Master's thesis on the rapture many years ago, I came across a quote by Dr. Harry Ironside, the pastor of Moody Church in Chicago from many years ago. He was one of the foremost Dispensational, Pre-Tribulational, Pre-Millennial teachers of his time, having written many books on the subject. When he was elderly, he was being interviewed by a writer and was asked about his Dispensational leanings and whether he still held to them. His answer was (and I'm paraphrasing here) that he had written too many books and preached too many sermons on the subject to publicly renounce it, but he knew that the "system had too many holes in it". (I remember that much of the quote). He knew it was a very shaky system, but if he renounced it, it would cause a lot of confusion among those who had heard him and read his books.

There it is! "Full of holes." Well, he was honest in so far as he took it, but he should have gone further with it. He should have publicly renounced it, even if doing so would have caused confusion. It would not have been any more confusing than the system he had taught for many years.

I have no desire to debate this with anyone. If you disagree with my arguments, write your own book to set forth what you believe. I'll read it. My problem with debating any issue on which Christians disagree is that all too often, harsh words are spoken, attacks become personal, and the cause of Christ is harmed.

I am writing this primarily to set forth - in as logical a manner as I can - my thoughts on the Second Coming of Jesus so I will have them recorded. Secondarily, I am writing this for those who question the Dispensational, Pre-Tribulational, Pre-Millennial doctrine, who just can't for the life of them figure it out, who are having a hard time reconciling it with what they see the Bible teaching, who thinks it sounds entirely too complex and complicated for the average man or woman to figure out on their own. As others have told me, it all just sounds "fishy" to them. It just doesn't sound right.

Bingo! That is the problem with it. It does not even *sound* right to people. The average person just cannot see it taught in the Bible unless they have been indoctrinated into it. The reason they can't see it is because…it just is not there. The Biblical doctrine of the Second Coming of Jesus Christ is simple. It is not complicated. The average Christian can sit down with his or her Bible and figure it out for his or her self. The Scriptures were written, not for the well schooled or brilliant, but for the common man. Jesus Himself said in Matthew 24: 15 in what is known as the Olivet Discourse, a prophecy that has been misunderstood by many, "Whoso reads, let him understand." Therefore, let everyone understand this basic premise - all we need in order to understand the Second Coming of Jesus is contained in the Bible itself. We do not need the New York Times or Newsweek or any TV news program to interpret or help us to explain the Bible, nor do we need any hype-filled "prophecy" seminar or conference. And it is the Bible that we will go to for understanding.

Hopefully, this book will give anyone who reads it an insight that has been withheld from them due to false teaching. I have tried to keep the arguments simple because the Biblical doctrine on the Second Coming of Jesus is simple. What Jesus said and what Paul said is very clear. There can be no misunderstanding of their doctrine. The only complicated part of this book is trying to explain and counteract the Dispensational, Pre-Tribulational, Pre-Millennial system. That is what will confuse those who have never heard it before and will cause them to scratch their heads.

Introduction

Ever since the apostles stood and watched Jesus ascend into Heaven, believers have been waiting for Jesus to return to Earth. We have all prayed earnestly just as the Apostle John prayed, "Even so, come Lord Jesus." Two thousand years have passed since He ascended and still the promise is fresh to us – Jesus will come back and receive us unto Himself that where He is there we may be also.

There are hundreds of Bible passages that promise that He will return to Earth one day. Of His certain return, there is no doubt. All true Christians believe that truth and are waiting for that day when we are all together with Jesus for eternity. But, what exactly does the second coming of Jesus involve – will there be a rapture of the Christians and tribulation for those left behind, or is it a simple one day event and what will transpire during that momentous event? Will there be a 1000 year reign of Christ on the Earth, or does His Second Coming usher in eternity? There are many opinions – all claiming to be right – each supported by Scripture – whether rightly or wrongly interpreted. Many Godly men and women believe one school of thought or the other and believe that all others are wrong. And this has caused much dissent and name calling among God's people. It seems that there can be disagreement on many other doctrines, but if there is disagreement on this one, many Christians just cannot tolerate others who disagree with them and their understanding of the Second Coming of Jesus. Everyone wants to be right.

Here is the problem. Not every belief system concerning the Second Coming of Jesus can be right. There are three main belief systems concerning the Second Coming of Jesus; Pre-Millennialism, Post- Millennialism, and A-Millennialism, each with various offshoots that further distinguish them from others. Assuming that one is correct in totality, then that means all the others, of necessity, are wrong. Who is right? Does each of these three main systems hold truths that the others overlook? What do the Scriptures really teach about the Second Coming of Jesus? Is what I believe the truth or is what I believe to be a wrong teaching really the truth? How can I tell? Are the details of what I believe about the Second Coming of Jesus as important as the fact that I believe He is coming again? Is what I believe about the return of the Savior vital to my salvation?

Let me say at the beginning that I believe the Scripture is clear – crystal clear as to the Second Coming. I do not believe that it is complicated, complex, or hidden. I do not believe that in order to understand the Second Coming of Jesus that we need 50 foot charts and diagrams stretched across the front of the church. The Scriptures were written so the common man – not only the highly educated - could understand them. It does not take a seminary degree to understand the basic tenets of the faith, of which the Second Coming is one. It does not take a teacher who "specializes" in "prophecy" to make it clear. It does not take books or movies or weekend conferences to understand. It takes a simple reading and believing of the Word of God.

The Bible is clear on all vital doctrines. Anyone can read the Bible and understand that Jesus was born of a virgin, lived a sinless life, was crucified, buried, and raised from the dead on the third day. Anyone can read the Bible and understand how to be saved by trusting in Jesus as their Savior. Anyone can read the Bible and understand the truth about the six days of creation, that God created the heavens and the earth. Anyone can read the Bible and understand that God wants us to live lives that are pleasing to Him. The only qualification in understanding the particular doctrine is – do you choose to believe it or not. If you choose not to believe the Bible teaching on any doctrine, then you are defining it your own way and you will be wrong in your belief. You believe that your way is better than the Bible way. You name the doctrine or teaching, and the Holy Spirit gives understanding to those who humbly and honestly read the Bible with the desire to learn and conform to it. The same holds true for the Second Coming of Jesus. The Bible is clear and can be understood by anyone – even a novice - who humbly, carefully and prayerfully reads it with the desire to understand and accept it as written.

Yes, there are some teachings in the Scriptures that are harder to understand than others. Yes, some "meat" of the Scriptures does take time and study to come to grips with and comprehend. Many obscure or prophetic portions of Scripture need help from someone who has studied them in order for us to understand. God does use teachers whom He has chosen and gifted to instruct others. By prophetic I mean those passages that use symbolic language or figures of speech that the original readers may have understood because they were living in those times, but today have become obscure due to lack of historic perspective. I mean language that was used by the prophets, not necessarily passages dealing with prophecy as the foretelling of events, but prophecy as the forth-telling of God message that used parables or symbolic language. But passages that are clear, plain in their words, and unambiguous in their meaning do not need special instructors to bring out their meaning to us. Anyone who believes in Jesus and in His Word can understand precisely what is being taught.

The mistake many teachers have made is to take clear teachings of Scripture and interpret them by using obscure passages or hard to understand ones, ones that are not clear in their meaning. They have been taught certain theological systems, and therefore everything that they teach must line up with their system. The system must be protected and defended at all costs, even if the clear teaching of Scripture contradicts it.

It reminds me of the Pharisees of Jesus' time who refused to believe truth because it interfered with and contradicted their system of belief. They were the experts and this upstart Jesus was not going to tell them differently. Who did He think He was to say the things He said and do the things He did that did not conform to what they taught the masses? They had the schooling, He did not. He was a mere carpenter. They were the ones who were trained. They had been taught certain doctrines by their teachers, and what they learned had to be right because it was taught in the local synagogues and schools by men they respected. What they believed and taught was the widely accepted teachings of the day. The entire Jewish nation followed their teachings and accepted them as truth. Only those who were looking for trouble would dare to disagree with them.

But...what if what they were taught was wrong? What if what how they interpreted Scripture was not the way God intended it to be interpreted? What if they were teaching as truth the doctrines of men, invented by men, rather than the truth of God? No matter how sincere they were in what they taught, if their interpretation and their doctrine was wrong, then what they were teaching was wrong. They would not accept the fact that they were wrong when confronted by Jesus. In fact, they hated Him because He challenged their cherished belief system.

An example that Evangelicals can relate to is that of our Roman Catholic friends. They sincerely believe that Mary and their saints can intercede for them with Christ. They were taught that and they believe that, but they cannot find Scripture to back it up. Just because they were taught that and believe that does not make it right. It does not mean that they do not love Jesus or do not believe in Him as Savior. It simply means that they were taught wrong in this regard. They would defend vigorously their belief, thinking that we who do not believe the same way were wrong. Many would be angry with us for daring to challenge that belief system. I know this first hand. So do many of you. How can anyone challenge what they hold dear, what every good Catholic believes to be truth? They were taught certain doctrines since youth, so what they were taught by those whom they respect must be right.

That, unfortunately, is how many theologians, preachers and teachers think today. How can anyone disagree with the widely held complex and complicated eschatological system that they believe and teach? Professors and pastors have studied and learned and taught this system (and they are legion who really are experts in the system), and they are widely respected men, so what they say must be right. They are Godly men who are concerned with winning the souls of others for Jesus. No doubt about that at all. Practically the whole of the evangelical community accepts what they teach about the Second Coming of Jesus as truth because they are right about salvation and winning the lost and other essential doctrines of the faith. So, if they are right about the essential doctrines, who does anyone think he is to disagree with them about the Second Coming? Unfortunately, their reaction to those who do not accept their teaching – in many cases, not all – is the same as the Pharisees. They want nothing to do with those who disagree with them. So, again I ask, what if the system of eschatology they were taught was wrong? What if it is a doctrine of man – as the Pharisees were guilty of - rather than Biblical truth? Where does that leave their teaching? It leaves it vacant and hollow, lacking Scriptural support.

One question I have asked of people who believe in the popular teachings of the Second Coming of Jesus is whether or not they discovered it by reading the Bible for themselves or if they were taught it by others. Immediately their defense shields go up. Most do not like that question because they know the answer. That question in and of itself reveals the truth. Of course, the only answer that can honestly be given is that they were taught it by others. There is no other way for anyone to believe it because the Bible simply does not teach it. No Christian – who I know anyway - can just sit down with the Bible and read it – allowing the Bible to speak for itself - and discover this system on their own with no outside help. It cannot happen because it just is not there. The whole system is entirely too complicated and complex. They need to hear it from someone else. They need to have it spoon fed to them. Ask yourself right now how you came to believe in the "rapture." Were you simply reading your Bible one day and saw the intricacies of the "rapture", or did someone else teach it to you? Be honest in your answer. No one discovered it all by themselves. Yes, there are well known teachers who have further developed the system and have added many more intricacies and complexities to it, but they did not discover the basic system on their own. Even they were taught it by someone else.

Some people I know have gotten huffy and angry because I have dared to question their dearly held belief. I want them to show me where the Scripture clearly – repeat - clearly and unambiguously

– teaches what they say it does. The fact that they get angry presupposes error on their part. Anyone who believes the truth will not be angry when others do not see the truth they are presenting. They will bear patiently with them. It has been my experience that only those who believe error get angry with those who do not agree with them. Biblical truth should never be argued in anger.

I am the first to state that I do not have all the answers. In fact, I do not even know all the questions. (I know. You've heard that before). Neither does anyone else - even if they think they do. No one has all the answers because no one knows all the questions. I readily admit that I cannot give an answer as to what every passage in the Bible does mean, but I can recognize error when I hear it. One does not need to know what an obscure passage *is* teaching to know what it is *not* teaching. Either truth or error may be readily evident in the explanation of any given passage. Sometimes both are. Once one's imprimatur is stamped upon a certain passage, it is extremely hard to give up that particular interpretation. It is far better to have no explanation of a difficult passage than to have a wrong one.

But, anyone can read Scripture and understand the clear teachings it sets forth. There are many passages that are clear concerning the Second Coming of Jesus, and I do know what they are saying. I understand them. And so can anyone else who is saved, who is trusting in the Lord for their salvation and who relies on the Holy Spirit for help in understanding Scripture, who is not reading it with a predetermined interpretation in mind. If the passage is not crystal clear and unambiguous, do not base interpretation of the clear passage on the misinterpretation of the obscure one.

One of the important rules of interpretation is called the analogy of Scripture. In other words, Scripture must interpret Scripture. Whatever is needed to clarify a passage will be found within the Scriptures. The clear meaning of a passage must be used to interpret the obscure and hard to understand passages. Do not take the unclear passage and use it to interpret the clear passage. That just does not make sense, but that is precisely what many interpreters have done in the subject before us. Many will take passages from the Old Testament prophets or from Revelation - passages that are not clearly understood – they are symbolic in nature - and use those passages to make a passage that is very easy to understand mean something that it does not mean. If you do this, you will be wrong in what you interpret. Also, what many have done in their attempt to show their knowledge of Scripture is to make assertions as to what a passage means without offering Scriptural proof. They believe themselves to be such authorities on the Bible that whatever they say, one is obligated to believe. Such are many of the so called "prophecy experts."

Now, something must be said here. Those good Christians who believe in the Pre-Millennial return of Christ claim that they use a literal hermeneutic – a literal interpretation of Scripture while they accuse those of different persuasions of "spiritualizing" the Scriptures, not using literal interpretations. I remember years ago hearing some Pre-Millennial preachers say: "Those who spiritualize tell spiritual lies because they have no spiritual eyes."

Well now, the problem with that is that Pre-Millennialists do not interpret all Scripture in a literal sense. Of course not. Much Scripture must be interpreted in a symbolic way if it is to make any sense at all. Pre-Millennialists, Post-Millennialists, and A-Millenialists *all* interpret Scripture literally *and* symbolically. All believe that the Word of God is infallible and is to be believed and trusted in its entirety. They just disagree at to what Scripture is to be interpreted literally and which symbolically. One is not an unbeliever if he disagrees with the other interpretation.

But it goes beyond that. There is another saying, "God says what He means and means what He says." Usually it is those who profess "literalism" that use that phrase. No one who believes that the Bible is the inspired Word of God would dare dispute that, for it is "impossible for God to lie", and "He cannot deny Himself." God used earthly objects and principles to express spiritual realities. When He used these objects, did He limit what He said to the mere literal earthly meaning, or did He go beyond that to a more spiritual meaning?

We have all heard the expression, "the New is in the Old concealed, the Old is by the New revealed." What God said in the Old Testament is given His real meaning in the New Testament. There are many examples to give, but I will limit them to a few.

We know that Abraham had two sons by two different women. Abraham, because of his lack of faith in God's promise to give him a son through which He would bless the world, fathered a son through Hagar, the Egyptian servant of Sarah, his wife. Thirteen years later he fathered a son, Isaac, by his wife, Sarah. This was the son God had promised to him many years before. This is the literal account of what happened.

Is there any further instruction in this? Does it carry further meaning other than what literally happened? The Apostle Paul in Galatians 4:24 specifically says that the birth of these two boys was symbolic. So, the literal birth of Ishmael and Isaac – and nothing can be more literal than the birth of a son – was literally symbolic. Unless the Apostle was telling spiritual lies because he had no spiritual eyes. The symbolism of the birth of these two boys was the two covenants, the covenant of law and the covenant of grace. The old and the new. God meant what He said in the Old Testament, but revealed what He meant in the New Testament.

In Isaiah 7: 14, it is prophesied that a virgin will bear a Son and His name will be called "Immanuel."

14 Therefore the Lord Himself will give you a sign: Behold, the virgin shall conceive and bear a Son, and shall call His name Immanuel.

Yet, in Matthew 1: 21, the angel announced that the name of the Son that the Virgin Mary would bear would be Jesus.

21 And she will bring forth a Son, and you shall call His name JESUS, for He will save His people from their sins."

He was called Jesus when He was born and not Immanuel. Two different names are given in the two testaments. God meant what He said in Isaiah – His name shall be Immanuel – and He explained what He meant in Matthew – His name shall be called Jesus. The name Immanuel indicated the presence of God among His people, but His people were sinners and God could not dwell among them, so He sent Jesus to "save His people from their sins." God can now have fellowship with them as Immanuel because Jesus saved them from their sins, making it possible for people to be in His presence. God meant what He said in the Old Testament, but revealed what He meant in the New Testament.

In Deuteronomy 25 Moses gives a command not to muzzle an ox that is treading out the grain or plowing a field.

4 "You shall not muzzle an ox while it treads out the grain.

God meant exactly what He said. The ox deserves to partake of his labor, but in 1 Corinthians 9, Paul gives God's spiritual meaning behind that command.

9 For it is written in the Law of Moses, "You shall not muzzle an ox while it treads out the grain." Is it oxen God is concerned about? 10 Or does He say it altogether for our sakes? For our sakes, no doubt, this is written, that he who plows should plow in hope, and he who threshes in hope should be partaker of his hope.

God's meaning goes beyond the literal meaning of the law and shows that He was speaking of support for those who preach the Gospel.

So, for anyone to say that all Scripture must be taken "literally", we must then determine whose definition of "literal" will be used. Will we take merely the earthly literal meaning, or will we use the analogy of Scripture to determine God's meaning behind any given passage. The New Testament interpretation, how the apostles interpreted Scripture should be our guide today.

What I will do in this writing is take clear teaching of Scripture to show the Second Coming of Jesus. Believe me, there are many verses that clearly teach – in other words, there is no way to misunderstand what they are saying unless it is misunderstood or twisted deliberately - what the Second Coming of Jesus is all about. I will also take other Scriptures that are used (misused) by others and show what they really mean.

Again, they are clear in what they mean. Anyone can do this. I will not read into them anything that they do not clearly state. We will use exegesis – we will take out of the verse what it says. We will not use eisegesis – we will not read into the verses what is not there. We will not look at any verse through the lens of any eschatological system in order to force a meaning into it. We will simply let the Bible speak for itself. Anyone who will be a faithful interpreter of Scripture must decide that he will not allow anything into his interpretation that is not clearly and evidently inherent in the passage.

In 1 Corinthians 4, Paul warns against forcing interpretation into the Word of God. In verses 1 and 2 he says that he is a *"...steward of the mysteries of God. Moreover, it is required in stewards that one be found faithful."* Paul says that he – and we also – are stewards of what has been revealed. We are not owners. We do not have the right to alter it or to read more or less into it than what it says. We must be faithful to what the Scriptures say. He sternly warns in verse 6 that his readers are to *"learn...not to think **beyond** what is written."*

We are to take the Bible for what it says, not for what we imagine it to say or what we would like it to say in order to suit our fancy. We are not to think beyond – add to or insert into any passage of Scripture – anything other than what is there, what is being taught by the speaker or the author. At times, what is being taught holds both a literal and a symbolic meaning. But, no one, the Apostle Paul instructs, has the right to ***force*** an interpretation into a passage just so a certain theological method or system can be supported. We must seek the counsel of the apostles and how they interpreted Scripture.

We will use Biblical theology - no passage disagrees with or contradicts other passages - to interpret passages rather than a predetermined systematic theology where every passage must conform to the system – even if it is not clearly understood from the context or obvious in its meaning. When we do this, the Second Coming of Jesus will be clearly understood. When we let the Bible speak for itself, we will wonder why the Second Coming of Jesus has become so complex and complicated that it takes charts and books and conferences and specialized teachers to understand. The early church and church through the ages did not have all of this; why do we need it today?

What I perceive has happened in this phenomenon of modern day "prophetic" teaching is that it has turned into a huge profit machine. People are making enormous amounts of money off of it.

The Second Coming of Jesus has become spectacular and sensational in its presentation. Books, novels, movies, conferences, charts and diagrams, bumper stickers, tee shirts, hats, etc. are being sold by the thousands to those who have been caught up in it. Christians want to be in the know – and they want others to know that they know - so they spend their money to get the goods that will give them the inside track. Those selling these items evidently do not believe in what Jesus said in *Matthew 10:8 "Freely you have received, freely give."* Oh no. The side show must continue so the profits keep coming in.

What's wrong with this picture? It does remind me of the money changers and those who sold animals in the Temple. Jesus threw them out twice. Money was their motive. I wonder if the Lord is pleased with what He sees happening today?

We will also briefly look at the origin of the modern day prophecy movement. The origin really does need to be examined and understood. There have been many scholarly works written on this subject, so what I include will be minimal but to the point.

It will not be my intention to make mockery of what others believe nor to make any personal attacks. Of necessity, some negative comments must be made, but they are not made in order to deride others, or in an antagonistic manner; they will be given merely to explain the Biblical position as I understand it. *(This was my original intent, but the more I wrote, the more and more I saw the utter foolishness of the Dispensational, Pre-Tribulation, Pre-Millennial position – which I have known for quite some time now - and I just couldn't help myself with some of my comments. I know. I know. If I really had tried, I could have not said some of the things I said, but... My comments, although sarcastic at times, in all seriousness, are not meant to be hostile or to cause harm to anyone, but to get us all to think about what we say we believe. Why do we believe it? Did I discover it from reading the Bible or from what I heard someone say or write in a book?)* I know that there are many good and Godly people who do not agree on all the aspects of the Second Coming of Jesus; they agree on the fact that He is coming again. That is the important issue.

But, on the other hand, when opinions are stated, some will take it personally if it does not agree with them, and their feelings will get hurt. How can it possibly hurt us to know what others believe about the Second Coming of Jesus? Who knows, maybe there is something we all can learn from each other. If we will all not be defensive about our preference and offensive toward other preferences, but will conscientiously study the Word of God for what it is saying – not with a presupposed knowledge of the passage – not with preconceived notions and systems of interpretation - then we will all be the better off for it.

As you read this do so critically – as the Bereans did - to make sure the Scriptures that are used are clearly understood and interpreted properly. Do not criticize antagonistically or hatefully – as the Pharisees did – just because what is stated is not the system you believe or your preference. God can change your heart if what I am saying is true. God can change my heart if I am wrong in what I am saying. He has changed my view of the Second Coming of Jesus already.

I have been a Christian for over 50 years and have been teaching the Bible either as a teacher or pastor for over 40 years. I was taught the pre-millennial position by pastors and professors. For several years I also taught it to my congregation. When I taught it, I found that it was very complicated and difficult to understand and to teach so others could readily grasp it. It did not flow easily for me. I took all I said from what others had either preached or written. I did not get my ideas from the Bible because I could not figure out how the Bible taught what I was saying. I remember clearly saying on one occasion while I was teaching the complicated order of events that some people say must occur before Jesus returns for good – I say "for good" as opposed to the part way second coming or the first phase of the two phases of His Second Coming that some imagine – "I know all this sounds like a fairy tale…"

Whoa! Did I really say that? What made me say that? Did I really believe what I was preaching? **Why** was I preaching something that did not make Biblical sense to me? I was taught this particular systematic theology and because I respected the men who taught it, then it must be right. But, I had to admit to myself that I was having a hard time with this position. It took several weeks of careful examination before I was ready to admit that this system was wrong. I could not back it up Scripturally. I could back it up using popular books that had been written and by what others were saying. I could back it up by forcing interpretation into certain verses, but I could not rightfully and honestly say that the verses really meant what I was saying they meant.

I prayed and asked God to help me come to an understanding of the Second Coming. I knew that no matter what view I took, it did not affect my salvation – I knew I was saved eternally. But I still wanted to have a proper view of this important doctrine. It was a struggle to accept the simple teaching of Scripture over the popular teaching because I was essentially standing alone. This just was not what others were saying. I had to make sure that what I discovered was correct.

Other pastors had unkind things to say because I had rejected as untrue the pre-millennial view, in particular, the so called two phased second coming of Jesus. Just saying it sounds wrong. One two phased – the phases separated by seven years – second coming. If you think about the words, it makes you scratch your head and say, "Huh?"

Unfortunately in the seventies and eighties – and it still may be true today in some circles – the view one took on the Second Coming of Jesus determined for others whether or not they would even speak with the "offender." The view that one held on eschatology seemed to have more significance and influence on others than any other doctrine in determining whether or not a man was saved or not. I've heard it said on more than one occasion that if anyone did not believe in the pre-millennial return of Jesus, then he was not saved. Period. No questions. No if ands or buts. That is why I made reference earlier to the Pharisees. You either believe our way or you are an outcast. Not all pre-millennialists believe this, but many do. I know many good people who hold the pre-millennial view who readily admit that it is not a doctrine that is essential to salvation or holiness.

Having said all of this, my purpose in writing this is to explain as simply as I can, without negativity as much as is possible, what I see the Bible teaching about the Second Coming of Jesus. I will not even attempt to give answers to every conceivable question regarding the second coming. I won't even attempt to answer all obvious questions. That is not the purpose of this writing. The purpose is to give a Biblical overview of what the Lord Jesus Christ and the apostles taught concerning the second coming of Jesus. It is my hope and prayer that what you read will cause you to study the Bible for yourself. Let the Bible speak to you concerning the "simplicity that is in Christ" (2 Corinthians 11:3) – even the simplicity that is in His Second Coming.

Chapter 1

The Necessity of the Second Coming of Jesus

The fact that the Lord Jesus Christ will return to earth one day is not in question. Every believer holds to His promise to return to earth. Even many unbelievers recognize that truth. It will not be my purpose to show that Jesus will one day return, but it will be to show the manner of His return. As important as it is to know that Jesus is returning one day, it is just as important to know why Jesus must one day return. In order to more fully understand why Jesus must return to earth we must understand why He had to come here the first time.

Creation

When God created the heavens and the earth, He made them "very good." God created not only the heavens, sun, moon, stars, and the earth, but also all of creation on the earth including fruits, vegetables, animals, sea life, birds and man, both male and female. All of creation was in harmony with itself and with its Creator. Nothing disruptive occurred, nothing to cause any interference with God's order. They were perfect in their creation and in their obedience to God, their Creator. The man and the woman had free reign in the garden where God placed them. He provided all they needed or could even want. He visited with them, walked and talked with them and taught them what He wanted them to do. There was only one negative command that they must obey. Do not eat of the tree of the knowledge of good and evil. God strictly warned them that if they did eat of it, the day that they did, they would surely die. No second chances. No excuses. Death was their immediate punishment for disobedience. Doesn't sound too difficult to understand, does it?

Then the unthinkable happened. Sin entered the perfect order. Satan, in the form of the serpent, tempted man to disobey God. He told them that God was holding out on them, that He did not want them to be like Him, knowing good and evil. But, if they would only eat of the tree of the knowledge of good and evil, that God had forbidden them to eat of, then they would be like God. Eve listened to the serpent and ate of the tree then gave the fruit to Adam to eat. 1 Timothy 2: 14 sheds some light on this event.

Adam's Sin

1 Timothy 2:14 And Adam was not deceived, but the woman being deceived, fell into transgression.

It is important to understand that Adam was not deceived by the serpent, but sinned deliberately. Eve was deceived. She swallowed Satan's lie hook, line and sinker. She believed his lie that God was holding out on them. Adam sinned willfully. He walked into his sin with his eyes wide open. The significance of this fact is that Adam is the federal head of the human race, and because he sinned, the entire human race was plunged into sin. Eve's sin did not plunge the race into sin. Her sin affected Adam in that it enticed him to sin, but it had no effect on the human race as a whole. Adam was not deceived as to the consequences of his sin. He knew the effects of his sin. He in all likelihood knew God better than Eve did since he was created first and God made him the head of his wife. It is not conceivable that Adam did not know his position as the federal head of the human race and that what he did affected all humans for all time.

Since the Bible does not spell this out specifically, my following statements are speculation, but I think they extend beyond speculation into probability rather than mere possibility. I believe that they follow the logic of the Word of God. Eve did not fully understand the terrible consequences of her sin although God had promised death to them if they did sin by eating the fruit of the tree of the knowledge of good and evil. Maybe it just did not register with her. In any case, she was deceived. Her sin was one of at least partial ignorance through her blindness to the serpent's deception, although it was inexcusable ignorance. She had been warned by God not to eat of the tree.

Adam's sin, on the other hand was deliberate. He was not deceived. He understood exactly what God had commanded and he understood the far reaching consequences for disobedience. Why did Adam, therefore, sin as he did? Why did he deliberately plunge himself and all of his descendants into the horrible misery and terrible consequences of sin and the fiery displeasure and anger of God?

Adam's Sin and Us

Before we attempt to give an answer to that question, let's examine briefly why we suffer the consequences of Adam's sin. So many have asked that question in an accusatory manner, charging God with wrong doing by placing everyone under the condemnation of His judgment just because Adam sinned. Romans 5: 12 gives us some insight.

Romans 5: 12 Therefore, just as through one man sin entered the world, and death through sin, and thus death spread to all men, because all sinned—

This verse does not mean that we die because eventually we all commit sins, although that is true – we all have committed sins and it does result in death according to *James 1: 14 But each one is tempted when he is drawn away by his own desires and enticed. 15 Then, when desire has conceived, it gives birth to sin; and sin, when it is full-grown, brings forth death.*

What Romans 5:12 means is that when Adam sinned, we also sinned. How did all men sin when Adam sinned, thus having death as the consequence for all men? The unwritten words that are beyond the hyphen at the end of verse 12 are "in Adam." We all sinned in Adam. We, as yet unborn, were in Adam – literally – when he sinned. We were contained in his seed. Every human being that has been born on the earth is a direct descendant of Adam and was in his body at the time he chose to sin. Adam's sin, therefore, directly affected us while we were still in him. Am I off base here? Am I guilty of going beyond what is written? Am I guilty of reading into verse 12 what is not there? Consider what the writer of Hebrews says concerning Levi who paid tithes to Melchizedek while he was still in Abraham's loins.

Hebrews 7: 8 Here mortal men receive tithes, but there he receives them, of whom it is witnessed that he lives. 9 Even Levi, who receives tithes, paid tithes through Abraham, so to speak, 10 for he was still in the loins of his father when Melchizedek met him.

It is stated clearly that Levi was present when his great-grandfather met Melchizedek and paid tithes to him. The same genetic principle is true of each of us. We were present in our father Adam when he sinned. Therefore, the consequences of his sin were passed on to us because we sinned in Adam. We were infected with sin and given a sin nature the very moment Adam sinned.

*1 Corinthians 15: 22 For as **in Adam** all die, even so in Christ all shall be made alive.*

This verse further explains why human beings die. We are in Adam. We were a part of him when he decided to disobey God. Human nature was degraded from "very good" to "sin" in an instant. Sin became the nature of all of humanity. It was passed from one generation to the next and to the next through the father's seed, specifically through the blood that was contained in the father's seed. As a result, death became our destiny.

Psalm 51: 5 Behold, I was brought forth in iniquity, and in sin my mother conceived me.

David states that he – and that includes every one of us – was born in iniquity, with a sin nature. Sin is our nature from the very moment we were born. Some people want to believe that babies are innocent. They are not. They may be innocent in that they have not deliberately – with knowledge of what they were doing – and with malice - sinned. Every child is born with a sin nature. They do not have to be taught to do wrong, but they need direction and guidance to do what is right. They need discipline to teach them God's way of living.

Psalm 58: 3 The wicked are estranged from the womb; They go astray as soon as they are born, speaking lies.

Again the Psalmist shows that we are born with a sin nature in that the moment we are born we begin to lie. Come on, now. That's stretching it a bit, isn't it? How soon after being born does a baby learn how to get its own way? Not long. They learn that by crying they get what they want. Their crying is their lying. Not always, of course. Sometimes there really is something wrong, but many times they just want to be held so they cry like something is wrong.

Sin Nature in the Blood

The sin nature is passed to all offspring through the father's seed. It is a medical fact – and I believe that most of you know this anyway – that the baby's blood does not mingle with the mother's blood unless there is a serious health problem. There are hundreds of medical papers and books that verify this. The baby's blood is wholly contained within the infant. The father's seed supplies the blood for the infant.

Although there is much scientific proof of this fact, Genesis 3: 15 provides all we need to understand and believe this. It shows us the Biblical proof of this fact.

15 And I will put enmity between you and the woman, and between your seed and her Seed; He shall bruise your head, and you shall bruise His heel."

Speaking to the serpent, God declares that the Seed of the woman would crush the head the serpent's seed. That would not at all be possible if the blood of the woman mixed with the blood of the Christ. His blood would have been contaminated then, and be sinful blood, and unable to cleanse us from our sin. Yes, the woman does have sin nature, but she does not transmit that sin nature to her offspring. The father does. The sin nature is in the blood, and it is passed down through the seed of the father.

The Word of God has much to say concerning blood and the fact that it is the life of the man or the animal under consideration.

Genesis 9: 4 But you shall not eat flesh with its life, that is, its blood.

God told Noah that when he ate the flesh of an animal, he was to do so without the blood. It was forbidden to eat the flesh with the blood. Why? It showed honor to the Lord who created the animal that they understood He was the source of life and man had no right to disregard that fact and think he could do whatever he wanted to do. Adam disobeyed God and the world suffered. God was setting the standard for all men to regard God and His commands. God is in charge of life, not the individual. All life is to be regarded as a gift from God, and that life is not to be consumed by man.

Leviticus 17: 11 For the life of the flesh is in the blood, and I have given it to you upon the altar to make atonement for your souls; for it is the blood that makes atonement for the soul.'

The main reason man was not to eat the blood was that blood was God's method for making atonement for man's sin. Verses 13 and 14 give further instruction.

13 "Whatever man of the children of Israel, or of the strangers who dwell among you, who hunts and catches any animal or bird that may be eaten, he shall pour out its blood and cover it with dust; 14 for it is the life of all flesh. Its blood sustains its life. Therefore I said to the children of Israel, 'You shall not eat the blood of any flesh, for the life of all flesh is its blood. Whoever eats it shall be cut off.'

God was serious. He would not have man taking for his own use what He had sanctified to Himself. It was His blood. He gave it as life to all living flesh. He then gave the blood of certain animals as a sacrifice for the sins of man. It was God's gift to man for their atonement (verse 11) that He gave to Himself as payment for sin. No one had the right to take it to himself.

So, the life is in the blood. It is passed down through successive generations by the father's seed. It also contains the sin nature that we all have. Our fathers gave us our blood – our life - but also our sin - our death. We will be getting back to this thought later in this chapter.

Why Did Adam Deliberately Sin?

So, why did Adam sin deliberately and by so doing condemn himself and all future offspring – which includes everyone who has ever been born – as sinners? Because – and here is my speculation that I believe to be in line with the Bible – Adam knew God well enough to believe that God would provide forgiveness for him and his family. Had Adam refused to sin as Eve sinned, she, most likely would have died physically as well as spiritually immediately, and would have been eternally condemned without forgiveness, but Adam would have continued to live in a perfect state forever. Had she not immediately died physically, then the two could not live together with this horrible spiritual distinction. They could not have offspring or any type of life together. Eve would be a sinner and Adam would be perfect. The two could not mix. Adam understood this immediately. In order to protect Eve and God's purpose for humans to populate and have dominion over the earth, Adam sinned, believing that God would provide forgiveness for them – somehow.

And of course, God did provide atonement for their sin. He shed the blood of an innocent animal and made coats of its skin to cover their nakedness. The coats covered both the nakedness of their bodies and their souls. The animal, perhaps a lamb, an innocent lamb, a sinless lamb died, shed its blood, its life, so that God could make atonement for the sin of Adam and Eve. However, it did not atone for original sin or the sin nature that Adam possessed and passed down to his descendants and they passed down to theirs and so on. Each person after Adam had to realize their own sin and offer an atoning sacrifice for their own sins. Each sacrifice pointed to the Lamb of God who would one day make atonement for sin in its original form for all who would trust in Him. Animal sacrifices would atone for sins (what we commit), but only a sinless Human - Jesus - could atone for sin (sin nature, what we are).

Hebrews 9: 9 It was symbolic for the present time in which both gifts and sacrifices are offered which cannot make him who performed the service perfect in regard to the conscience...13 For if the blood of bulls and goats and the ashes of a heifer, sprinkling the unclean, sanctifies for the purifying of the flesh, 14 how much more shall the blood of Christ, who through the eternal Spirit offered Himself without spot to God, cleanse your conscience from dead works to serve the living God?

The blood of Jesus cleanses our conscience of dead works, of sin, so we can serve God with a pure heart. The blood of bulls and goats could never do that. The blood of Jesus is infinitely more efficacious than that of animals. His blood alone washes away sin and its consequences.

All of Nature Under Sin Curse

Another consequence of Adam's sin was that nature itself was now under the curse of sin. God created all things "very good" but when Adam sinned, his disobedience caused sin to contaminate nature, the rest of God's good creation.

Romans 8: 19 For the earnest expectation of the creation eagerly waits for the revealing of the sons of God. 20 For the creation was subjected to futility, not willingly, but because of Him who subjected it in hope; 21 because the creation itself also will be delivered from the bondage of corruption into the glorious liberty of the children of God. 22 For we know that the whole creation groans and labors with birth pangs together until now.

The physical earth became affected by sin. The earth, which was "very good", which contained no thorns or any unpleasant growth or non productive ground, became cursed. Plants, trees, grass, and all vegetation began to die. They were cursed with death also. Farmers have to work hard to produce a crop. Man would have to labor by the sweat of his brow in order to maintain his life. People wonder why there are hurricanes, tornadoes, earthquakes, floods and other severe and destructive weather. Sin. Weather was pleasant prior to sin entering the world. In fact, there wasn't even rain. Water came up from the earth to give nourishment to the soil. Even nature died because of sin. God's perfect world suffered a catastrophic death. It was no longer what God had intended for man. It would fight man at every turn. Everything in the universe was adversely affected by sin.

Animals were affected by Adam's sin. Some became fearful of man, others became antagonistic and aggressive towards man and each other. They began to suffer hurts and pains and death also. If you have pets, you know that they get hurt, sick and eventually die. It is because of sin in the world. They are innocent as far as sin is concerned. They do not know right from wrong, but they suffer none the less. Because they are innocent of sin, God chose certain ones to be a substitute for man's required death because of sin. Only sinless blood can atone for the sins of sinners. One must have no sin of their own if he is to pay for the sin of another.

Atonement Provided

Because everything in all of God's creation was contaminated by sin, everything in nature dies. But, God has provided atonement for man's sin in the death, burial, and resurrection of His Son, our Lord Jesus Christ. Under the Old Covenant God gave man certain animals to use as a substitute for their sins. The lamb would be sacrificed upon an altar according to God's requirements and He accepted it as payment for sins. God gave requirements for how to sacrifice and those requirements must be followed exactly for the sacrifice to be accepted. If those requirements were not followed, the sacrifice was rejected.

Nadab and Abihu, the sons of Aaron, the High Priest, decided to offer a sacrifice their own way and God killed them.

Leviticus 10: 1 Then Nadab and Abihu, the sons of Aaron, each took his censer and put fire in it, put incense on it, and offered profane fire before the LORD, which He had not commanded them. 2 So fire went out from the LORD and devoured them, and they died before the LORD.

God has commanded that He be worshiped in a certain way and no other way is acceptable to Him. No, we cannot worship God any way we choose. It is not worship if it is not according to God's commands – regardless of what men call it. Beginning with Cain, man has thought to worship God in his own way, but that only leads to further isolation from God in this life and separation from Him eternally in death. Since God is the offended party in our sin, He has the right to set the terms for reconciliation with Himself. When Japan surrendered to the United States to end World War Two on the deck of the battleship USS Missouri, it was not Japan who dictated the terms of surrender and of peace, but it was America, the victor in the war. In the same way, we cannot dictate the terms of our surrender to God and our peace with Him. Those terms, under the New Covenant, is repentance from our sins and faith in Jesus Christ. No other way is acceptable to God. Jesus said that all who attempt to come to the Father any other way are "thieves and robbers" (John 10:8).

Of course, the verse everyone quotes is *John 14: 6 Jesus said to him, "I am the way, the truth, and the life.* ***No one*** *comes to the Father except through Me."*

Faith in Jesus Christ, and Him alone – not the works of our hands or intellect, not good works, but faith alone in the blood that was shed by Jesus – is what God demands for our redemption from sin. Jesus, the Lamb of God, died so we could be reconciled to God, so we could be forgiven of our sin and become a new man in Him. We must believe that when Jesus shed His blood, He shed it for our sin.

Reconciled to God by the Blood of Jesus

How does the death of Jesus reconcile us to God? If everyone is guilty of sin in Adam, how can Jesus, who was born of Mary, a human woman, pay for our sin? Didn't He also have a sin nature? The answer, of course, is no. He did not have a sin nature because God was His Father. He had an earthly mother, the virgin Mary, but He had a Heavenly Father. There was no human who supplied His blood. It must be stressed that Mary was a virgin when Jesus was conceived by the Holy Spirit. No man could claim to be the father of the Lord Jesus Christ, for no man had had an intimate relationship with Mary. The Holy Spirit was His Father and supplied the blood to His body. His blood did not mix with Mary's blood. It was totally uncontaminated by sin. It was therefore, sinless blood, the only blood that could pay for the sin of the world. He was God in the flesh – the God Man - totally God and totally man. There was no sin nature passed on to Him. It is His blood that gives us life, access to the Father, and forgiveness of sins.

John 6: 53 Then Jesus said to them, "Most assuredly, I say to you, unless you eat the flesh of the Son of Man and drink His blood, you have no life in you.

The eating of His flesh and drinking His blood means the appropriation of His substitutionary sacrifice to ourselves, the taking of

His death, burial, and resurrection as our only means of salvation and applying it to our sin.

Under the Old Covenant, those offering a sacrifice would eat of it, thus indicating that they were appropriating the vicarious death of the animal to himself. He was trusting in God that the death of the lamb – the sinless lamb - would be applied to his sins.

Paul warns the Corinthians not to eat of meat that was sacrificed to idols, for in so doing, they were participating in fellowship with demons. Any sacrifice to an idol was in reality worship of demons. If a Christian knew a certain piece of meat was offered to an idol, he was not to eat of it. Eating of it meant that he was trusting in that idol, that demon, to save him; he was appropriating that demon to himself; he was, in essence, worshiping a demon. He was turning his back on Jesus in favor of a demon.

*1 Corinthians 10: 14 Therefore, my beloved, flee from idolatry. 15 I speak as to wise men; judge for yourselves what I say. 16 The cup of blessing which we bless, is it not the communion of the blood of Christ? The bread which we break, is it not the communion of the body of Christ? 17 For we, though many, are one bread and one body; for we all partake of that one bread. 18 Observe Israel after the flesh: Are not those who eat of the sacrifices partakers of the altar? 19 What am I saying then? That an idol is anything, or what is offered to idols is anything? 20 Rather, that **the things which the Gentiles sacrifice they sacrifice to demons** and not to God, and I do not want you to have fellowship with demons. 21 **You cannot drink the cup of the Lord and the cup of demons; you cannot partake of the Lord's table and of the table of demons.***

The illustration of eating His flesh and drinking His blood is the same thing. It is by trusting in Him and His work on the cross, by trusting that what God promised He will do, that God will apply the blood of Jesus to our sin that saves us. By doing that, we have life.

We have been brought into a covenant relationship with God through the blood of Jesus and now have peace with God.

Ephesians 2: 12 that at that time you were without Christ, being aliens from the commonwealth of Israel and strangers from the covenants of promise, having no hope and without God in the world. 13 But now in Christ Jesus you who once were far off have been brought near by the blood of Christ. 14 For He Himself is our peace, who has made both one, and has broken down the middle wall of separation,

The blood of Jesus gives us boldness in our approach to the Father. We have access to the Holiest place, the presence of God, through the blood of Jesus shed for us.

Hebrews 10: 19 Therefore, brethren, having boldness to enter the Holiest by the blood of Jesus

The blood of Jesus is what grants us forgiveness of all of our sin.

1 John 1: 7 But if we walk in the light as He is in the light, we have fellowship with one another, and the blood of Jesus Christ His Son cleanses us from all sin.

Jesus died not only for our sins – that which we have committed – but also for our sin – that which we are – our sin nature - through our relationship to Adam. He died to restore in us the image of God which was lost when Adam, and we, in Adam, sinned.

When we receive Jesus as our Lord and Savior, we are baptized into Him. His death, burial and resurrection are credited to us. The death that we owe God for our sin has been paid in full by Jesus, and His payment becomes our payment. He graciously has taken our death, our sins, our sin nature, placed them on Himself, gone to the cross, and was crucified there so we, through trusting in His atoning death, may be reconciled to God and have eternal life. We have been raised from the death of sin and given a new nature and a new life to be lived, one that is abundant (John 10:10), one that is no longer under the dominion of sin.

Romans 6: 3…Or do you not know that as many of us as were baptized into Christ Jesus were baptized into His death? 4 Therefore we were buried with Him through baptism into death, that just as Christ was raised from the dead by the glory of the Father, even so we also should walk in newness of life. 5 For if we have been united together in the likeness of His death, certainly we also shall be in the likeness of His resurrection, 6 knowing this, that our old man was crucified with Him, that the body of sin might be done away with, that we should no longer be slaves of sin. 7 For he who has died has been freed from sin. 8 Now if we died with Christ, we believe that we shall also live with Him, 9 knowing that Christ, having been raised from the dead, dies no more. Death no longer has dominion over Him. 10 For the death that He died, He died to sin once for all; but the life that He lives, He lives to God. 11 Likewise you also, reckon yourselves to be dead indeed to sin, but alive to God in Christ Jesus our Lord.

2 Corinthians 5: 17 Therefore, if anyone is in Christ, he is a new creation; old things have passed away; behold, all things have become new.

This is a fact. This has been done for us. We have a new life – resurrection life – a new nature from God. All things are new. Yet, we are still subject to sin and its consequences while we live here. Jesus has given us a new life, yet we still struggle with the old nature, the sin nature. Why? Because, although our redemption has been paid for in full by the blood of Jesus, our salvation is not yet complete in reality, as far as we have experienced. It is completely paid for, but we have received only the down payment. We have been delivered from the penalty of sin – we have forgiveness. We have been delivered from the power of sin – it no longer has dominion over us – we are no longer a slave to it, but it still rears its ugly head in our lives and makes our lives miserable because of it. We have yet to be delivered from the presence of sin. That will happen when Jesus returns. Our salvation will be complete then.

Total Redemption

God does not do things half way. He completes what He sets out to do. He will restore His perfect creation to where it was prior to sin entering the world. This is all inclusive; redeemed man, animal, plant, inanimate creation – the heavens and the earth, the entire universe. All must be brought back to its original condition. Jesus has paid for this total salvation from sin by shedding His blood. It will happen. It is necessary. It will happen when Jesus returns to earth.

When Jesus returns, we who are His own will be changed into His likeness. We will drop the corruptible robe of mortal flesh and put on the incorruptible robe of immortality.

1 Corinthians 15: 50 Now this I say, brethren, that flesh and blood cannot inherit the kingdom of God; nor does corruption inherit incorruption. 51 Behold, I tell you a mystery: We shall not all sleep, but we shall all be changed— 52 in a moment, in the twinkling of an eye, at the last trumpet. For the trumpet will sound, and the dead will be raised incorruptible, and we shall be changed. 53 For this corruptible must put on incorruption, and this mortal must put on immortality. 54 So when this corruptible has put on incorruption, and this mortal has put on immortality, then shall be brought to pass the saying that is written: "Death is swallowed up in victory."

When Jesus returns, we shall be like Him. We will have the same bodily characteristics that He has now. We will still have a recognizable body, but it will not be fleshly as we know it now. It will not have blood. We do not know what it will be like, but we know it will be far better than the one we have now. All effects of sin will be erased, gone forever – "death is swallowed up in victory."

1 Corinthians 15: 42 So also is the resurrection of the dead. The body is sown in corruption, it is raised in incorruption. 43 It is sown in dishonor, it is raised in glory. It is sown in weakness, it is raised in power. 44 It is sown a natural body, it is raised a spiritual body...

1 John 3: 2 Beloved, now we are children of God; and it has not yet been revealed what we shall be, but we know that when He is revealed, we shall be like Him, for we shall see Him as He is.

Revelation 21: 4 And God will wipe away every tear from their eyes; there shall be no more death, nor sorrow, nor crying. There shall be no more pain, for the former things have passed away." 5 Then He who sat on the throne said, "Behold, I make all things new."

These are only a few Biblical references that explain the change that happens to believers when Jesus returns, but they are sufficient to show that those who have trusted in Jesus for salvation will be restored to God's original state of perfection when Jesus returns.

What about the heavens and the earth? Will they be changed also? As we have previously seen, Paul explains that all of creation has been made subject to sin, not willingly, but because of sin, and is eagerly waiting for the day when Jesus returns and makes all things new, including creation.

Romans 8: 19 For the earnest expectation of the creation eagerly waits for the revealing of the sons of God. 20 For the creation was subjected to futility, not willingly, but because of Him who subjected it in hope; 21 because the creation itself also will be delivered from the bondage of corruption into the glorious liberty of the children of God. 22 For we know that the whole creation groans and labors with birth pangs together until now.

Isaiah prophesied of the new heavens and new earth. When they are created, the former heavens and earth will no longer be remembered by those inhabiting them. Since they are free from sin and its consequence of death, they will remain forever.

Isaiah 65: 17 "For behold, I create new heavens and a new earth; And the former shall not be remembered or come to mind.

Isaiah 66: 22 "For as the new heavens and the new earth which I will make shall remain before Me," says the LORD, "So shall your descendants and your name remain.

Acts 3 tells us that when Jesus returns, all things will be restored. All things include heaven and earth all that dwell therein.

Acts 3: 20 and that He may send Jesus Christ, who was preached to you before, 21 whom heaven must receive until the times of restoration of all things, which God has spoken by the mouth of all His holy prophets since the world began.

Although not mentioned in all of the writings of the prophets, Peter states with certainty that all of the prophets since the beginning of time spoke concerning the restoration of all things that sin had destroyed. From Adam onwards, God's people have known of the new heavens and new earth and have anxiously looked for them.

Abraham in particular is mentioned in Hebrews 11 as looking for the restoration of all things.

Hebrews 11: 10 for he waited for the city which has foundations, whose builder and maker is God. 16 But now they desire a better, that is, a heavenly country.

Peter instructs us that God will destroy this old heaven and earth with fire and create new ones in which only righteousness can dwell. This creation of a new heavens and earth does not mean that the old is annihilated and the new is created out of nothing as was the original, but it means that the old is purified by fire and restored to original state once it has been purified. Just as the earth which perished in the flood was not recreated from nothing – as it was when originally created - but rebuilt so to speak, so is the new heaven and earth.

2 Peter 3: 12 looking for and hastening the coming of the day of God, because of which the heavens will be dissolved, being on fire, and the elements will melt with fervent heat? 13 Nevertheless we, according to His promise, look for new heavens and a new earth in which righteousness dwells.

Hebrews has much to say about the new heavens and new earth. Quoting Psalm 102: 25-27, Paul says in *Hebrews 1: 10 "You, LORD, in the beginning laid the foundation of the earth, and the heavens are the work of Your hands. 11 They will perish, but You remain; And they will all grow old like a garment; 12 Like a cloak You will fold them up, and they will be changed. But You are the same, and Your years will not fail."*

Since the heavens and the earth are mere creations from the hand of Jesus Christ, and have been subjected to sin, they are showing the signs of a slow death by growing old and will one day experience death and rebirth – they will be changed into the original state of creation.

Another verse that teaches us of the total restoration of all things and that all things will be put under the feet of the Lord Jesus is found in Hebrews 2.

Hebrews 2: 8 You have put all things in subjection under his feet." For in that He put all in subjection under him, He left nothing that is not put under him. But now we do not yet see all things put under him.

This is the "everlasting dominion which shall not pass away" (Daniel 7:14). This subjection is not yet completed, but will come to fruition when Jesus returns. This subjection of all things takes place in "the world to come" (Hebrews 2:5), the new Heavens and New Earth. It was at His ascension that He was given His "everlasting dominion which shall not pass away."

Daniel 7: 13 "I was watching in the night visions, and behold, One like the Son of Man, coming with the clouds of heaven! He came to the Ancient of Days, and they brought Him near before Him. 14 Then to Him was given dominion and glory and a kingdom, that all peoples, nations, and languages should serve Him. His dominion is an everlasting dominion, which shall not pass away, and His kingdom the one which shall not be destroyed.

This present world, it appears from Scripture (this is not an adamant declaration as fact, but a humble opinion on my part), is subject to angels to some degree or another. I cannot declare with certainty to what extent this is so, but my understanding of some Scriptures leads me to believe this.

The Scriptures make a distinction between this present inhabitable world, calling it "this present age", and the world to come, "the age to come." This present age, this whole world, according to 1 John 5: 13 "lies *under the sway of* the wicked one."

How did that happen, that the wicked one, Satan, got control, or power, over the whole world? This is what we discussed at the beginning of the chapter. When Adam sinned, the entire creation was thrown into a state of sin, and Satan gained the dominion of the world which God had given to Adam. Adam relinquished his authority in and over this present world to the devil. God still has ultimate authority and dominion over His creation – He never abdicated His authority - but God did grant to man certain authority in this world, and it is that authority that has been usurped by "the wicked one." Every person born into this world knows firsthand that Satan and his demons can and does disrupt lives.

It is these fallen angels that have this world in subjection. However, the Bible makes clear that the holy angels also have power and authority in this world. They are sent out to minister to those who are the heirs of salvation.

Hebrews 1: 14 Are they not all ministering spirits sent forth to minister for those who will inherit salvation?

Acts 7: 53 ...who have received the law by the direction of angels and have not kept it."

Galatians 3:19 What purpose then does the law serve? It was added because of transgressions, till the Seed should come to whom the promise was made; and it was appointed through angels by the hand of a mediator.

Hebrews 2: 2 For if the word spoken through angels proved steadfast, and every transgression and disobedience received a just reward,

Angels were involved in the giving of the law, of the old covenant. What exactly they did is not clearly specified, but they had a hand in the administration of the law in the Old Testament. So therefore, they have authority in this present world.

Hebrews 13: 2 Do not forget to entertain strangers, for by so doing some have unwittingly entertained angels.

Angels have manifested themselves to men in this world, but have not made themselves known as angels. They have aided the heirs of salvation in many ways that are not known, but will be revealed one day. Their authority in this world is to help Christians in their journey.

Angels, both holy and evil, have authority in this world, but in the world to come, they do not have authority over it.

Hebrews 2: 5 For He has not put the world to come, of which we speak, in subjection to angels.

When Jesus returns, all things will be made new, and He shall have "all power in Heaven and Earth" and will rule "forever and ever." Not a mere one thousand years, but His kingdom is without end. Eternal.

In Chapter 12, Paul quotes Haggai 2:6.

Hebrews 12: 25 See that you do not refuse Him who speaks. For if they did not escape who refused Him who spoke on earth, much more shall we not escape if we turn away from Him who speaks from heaven, 26 whose voice then shook the earth; but now He has promised, saying, "Yet once more I shake not only the earth, but also heaven." 27 Now this, "Yet once more," indicates the removal of those things that are being shaken, as of things that are made, that the things which cannot be shaken may remain.

When God spoke on Mount Sinai, the mountain shook. God promises that the earth will again be shaken, and when it is, the earth, which is being shaken by God, will be removed, and the eternal things, the new heavens and earth, will remain forever. They cannot be removed because they will be totally free from the contamination of sin.

John in Revelation 21 had a vision of the new heaven and earth.

Revelation 21:1 Now I saw a new heaven and a new earth, for the first heaven and the first earth had passed away. Also there was no more sea.

God will restore all things to their original – or better – condition. Since we have never been in a perfect environment or have ever been perfect, we cannot even begin to envision the grandeur and glory of the new heavens and new earth. But we will experience it – forever. Jesus has paid for this renewal of all things – man and nature – with His blood. It is necessary and will be accomplished when Jesus returns to this earth.

But, a second reason Jesus must return to earth is to punish the wicked. Their punishment is an everlasting punishment, not merely a seven year one. When the Lord returns, not only will the righteous be glorified and enter into eternal joy in the presence of Jesus, the unrighteous will be punished with eternal destruction from the presence of the Lord because they did not obey the gospel of Jesus Christ. Scripture appears to teach that not only will the angels execute judgment upon the workers of evil, but also all the redeemed will aid in this judgment. John Calvin and Matthew Henry agree with this interpretation of the word "saint" to apply to both angels and redeemed men. To Enoch this truth was revealed that the Lord Jesus would come the second time to judge the ungodly.

Jude 1: 14 Now Enoch, the seventh from Adam, prophesied about these men also, saying, *"Behold,* **the Lord comes with ten**

thousands of His saints, 15 to execute judgment on all*, to convict all who are ungodly among them of all their ungodly deeds which they have committed in an ungodly way, and of all the harsh things which ungodly sinners have spoken against Him."*

*Psalm 149: 5 **Let the saints be joyful** in glory; Let them sing aloud on their beds. 6 Let the high praises of God be in their mouth, and a **two-edged sword in their hand**, 7 **To execute vengeance on the nations**, and **punishments on the peoples**; 8 To bind their **kings** with chains, and their **nobles** with fetters of iron; 9 **To execute on them the written judgment**—This honor have all His saints. Praise the LORD!*

It may be hard to visualize this scene of executing judgment upon the ungodly, but the Word of God assures us that all of God's people will have a part in doing this. God is not forgetful. He knows every sin against His people, every time an ungodly person has willfully attacked, harmed, accused, or killed one of His saints, whether that person was a neighbor, employer, or government representative. Not even governments, kings, or nobles can harm God's people in any way and not be held accountable for such actions. God will have His vengeance upon them and He will use those who were meek, gentle, and mild, who were the ones attacked and harmed on earth to execute His vengeance. What one sows, he reaps. But he reaps infinitely more than he sows. Sow the wind, reap the whirlwind.

Paul the apostle gives instruction to us that those who trouble Christians today will deeply regret doing so when Jesus returns in glory.

*2 Thessalonians 2: 6 since it is a righteous thing with God to repay with tribulation those who trouble you, 7 and to give you who are troubled rest with us when the **Lord Jesus is revealed from heaven with His mighty angels**, 8 **in flaming fire taking vengeance on those who do not know God, and on those who do not obey the gospel of our Lord Jesus Christ. 9 These shall be punished with everlasting destruction from the presence of the Lord** and from the glory of His power, 10 **when He comes, in that Day**, to be glorified in His* *saints and to be admired among all those who believe, because our testimony among you was believed.*

Trouble for God's people may last until Jesus returns, but in that day, we shall have our rest while those who appear to be in control of the situation today by harassing God's people will suffer beyond all that they have required from Christians through the ages. Flaming fire, vengeance, punished with everlasting destruction are the words used to describe what will happen to them on the day the Lord Jesus Christ is revealed from Heaven.

And their destruction will occur suddenly, as a thief in the night. They will not expect it when it comes upon them. It is sudden and it is sure. It comes with such power and speed that escape from it is impossible.

*1 Thessalonians 5: 2 For you yourselves know perfectly that the **day of the Lord** so comes as a thief in the night. 3 For when they say, "Peace and safety!" then **sudden destruction** comes upon them, as labor pains upon a pregnant woman. And **they shall not escape.***

Again, the words of our Lord Jesus emphasize the truth of the coming judgment upon those who reject His as Lord and Savior. The judgment is inevitable and will occur on the last day, the day of His return.

*John 12: 48 He who rejects Me, and does not receive My words, has that which judges him—the word that I have spoken will **judge him in the last day.***

Why would anyone continue through life without receiving Jesus, not obeying the gospel, not knowing God when His promise of certain judgment looms before them? Do they think that they shall escape the judgment, that it is only for others who they determine to be worse than them? The criteria for judgment is likeness to Jesus, not comparison to others. Only those who have confessed and repented of their sin and trusted in the atoning, sacrificial death of Jesus on the cross and believed that God has raised Him from the dead will be saved from this sudden and irrevocable and eternal judgment. It is not a joke nor is it to be taken lightly.

Many reject the judgment today as "outdated", something that belongs in the middle ages or before, but certainly not in this "enlightened age." How foolish. Is your pride or anything else in this world worth chancing eternal destruction? Are you willing to take the chance that your beliefs will stand up to God's pronouncement? What God has declared in His Word is truth that needs to be believed if you have not done so previously. Your eternity depends upon it.

Chapter 2

Last Day, Last Trumpet, Last Enemy

We have seen that the necessity of the Second Coming of Jesus Christ is based on the promise of God to restore all things that sin has influenced and contaminated and placed under the sentence of death. This includes all of creation – the heavens and the earth and those of the human race who have trusted in Jesus Christ as Lord and Savior. Man has been redeemed in that the blood of Jesus has paid the penalty of his sin, but man has not yet fully realized the extent of his salvation. When Jesus returns, all things will be made complete.

We now come to a crucial part of our study. Just what is the manner of the Second Coming of Jesus? What happens when He returns? As was mentioned in the introduction, there are many opinions concerning the events that surround the Second Coming. In this chapter I will not be addressing some of the errors that I see in the popular teachings of the day. I will address some – not all – of the notorious errors that I see in Pre-Millennialism in a subsequent chapter. In this chapter I will show some simple Bible verses that really need no commentary in that they are self explanatory. Anyone who can read and understand simple words can grasp what these verses are saying.

Yet, I dare say that there will be many who read this who will immediately find fault with it because it is so simple and that it does not line up with what they have been taught. Many will think that these verses do not mean what they say. They will want to add to or subtract from these verses. Most evangelicals of this day and age have been taught a complicated system, one that is not readily seen in the pages of Scripture by the average Christian. In fact, no one that I personally know can tell me honestly that they discovered Pre-Millennialism – and the intricacies that it presents - all by themselves. They were taught it by others who were taught it by others, who read it in books or in "study Bibles."

I want to present what I see as the simple teaching that Jesus returns, resurrects the dead – saved and unsaved alike – a general resurrection, the saved rise to meet Him in the air and escort Him to Earth, He judges the lost and throws them into Hell, the righteous shine forth in His eternal kingdom as He turns the kingdom over to His Father - all in one day. Not over anywhere from seven to one thousand and seven years as some portend. We will let the Word of God speak for itself. We will not force a theological system into it.

The Last Day

One of the easiest concepts to grasp in understanding the Second Coming of Jesus is what He said concerning it. **Four times** between verses 39 and 54 of John chapter 6 our Lord Jesus said emphatically that He would raise up all believers on the *last day*. To me, that is very easy to understand. The resurrection occurs on the last day. Some may ask "Yeah, but what does the word 'last' mean? Huh?"

The reason I say it that way is I have had people ask me exactly that. It reminds me of when President Clinton said, "It all depends on what the meaning of the word 'is' is." If you were reading these verses for the first time, never having heard the Pre-Millennial point of view, what would you think the word "last" means? Would you think that it meant something other than what it sounds like it means? Just so you know what it means, the Greek word translated "last" is "eschatos" from which we get the word "eschatology", the study of the last things – which is what we are studying in this book. The meaning of "eschatos" is exactly what you think it means - last in time or in place, last in a series of places, last in a temporal succession. It simply means the last, referring to time, of space, the uttermost part, the end, of the earth, of rank, grade of worth, last i.e. lowest (Strong's Concordance #2078).

This word is the identical word the Jesus used to describe Himself in Revelation 1:11, 17; 2:8, 22:13 when He called Himself the First and the Last. He is the First, the "protos" (Strong's Concordance # 4413), and the Last, the "eschatos." Would anyone dare to say that these words do not mean exactly what Jesus thought them to mean? In 1 Corinthians 15:45 Jesus is called the "Last Adam." When viewing the first Adam, was there any human being before him? None. He was the first human, so therefore, there was no one prior to him. Jesus is the "Last Adam", therefore, there is none after Him.

It is our Lord Himself who called the day of the resurrection the last day, the "eschatos" day. If Jesus is literally the First and the Last, if He is the "Last Adam" as He says He is, then is it not reasonable to believe that He knows what the word means and He used it correctly and that the day of resurrection is literally the last day, as He says it is? The word "last" has the same meaning in respect to time, days, hours, trumpets, and enemies.

Here are the verses that Jesus Himself spoke. Now, if Jesus said these words, do you think that He would intentionally confuse His disciples by saying words that He did not mean or that He did not use in a way they would understand? Did He know exactly what He meant by them and is He able to preserve them for us today with His exact meaning intact? If so, how can others say that He did not mean what He said? Some say that these words really mean that He will not really return on the last day, but depending on which form of Pre-Millennialism one believes, He returns either seven years or one thousand and seven years after the resurrection. To use an overused expression, "What part of 'the last day' do you not understand?"

John 6: 39 This is the will of the Father who sent Me, that of all He has given Me I should lose nothing, but should **raise it up at the last day.** *40 And this is the will of Him who sent Me, that everyone who sees the Son and believes in Him may have everlasting life; and I will* **raise him up at the last day.**"

*44 No one can come to Me unless the Father who sent Me draws him; and **I will raise him up at the last day.***

*54 Whoever eats My flesh and drinks My blood has eternal life, and **I will raise him up at the last day.***

It is self-evident that what He was saying is that the resurrection from the dead occurs on the last day. He will raise up His own on the last day. On the last day. Not before. Paul, in 1 Corinthians 15: 22, discourses at length concerning the resurrection. He explains that the resurrection occurs at the time of the Lord's Second Coming.

*1 Corinthians 15: 22 For as in Adam all die, even so in Christ all shall be made alive. 23 But each one in his own order: Christ the firstfruits, afterward **those who are Christ's at His coming.***

Other verses are in 1 Thessalonians 4 that unequivocally state that the resurrection – on the last day - is when Jesus returns.

1 Thessalonians 4: 15 For this we say to you by the word of the Lord, that we who are alive and remain until the coming of the Lord will by no means precede those who are asleep. 16 For the Lord Himself will descend from heaven with a shout, with the voice of an archangel, and with the trumpet of God. And the dead in Christ will rise first. 17 Then we who are alive and remain shall be caught up together with them in the clouds to meet the Lord in the air. And thus we shall always be with the Lord.

How many days can there possibly be after the "last day"? The "eschatos" day? The final day in time? Not trying to sound condescending, but I cannot for the life of me understand why so many Christians teach something other than the simple teaching of Jesus. I guess that the "literalists" are not being true to their claim. They are not adhering to their boast of taking the Bible literally, but are adhering to their system of eschatology, which obviously takes precedence over what Jesus literally said.

When Lazarus died and Jesus went to see Mary and Martha, Jesus told them that Lazarus would rise again, and Martha responded in *John 11: 24 Martha said to Him, "I know that he will rise again in the **resurrection at the last day."***

Jesus went on to explain to her that He was the resurrection and the life and that anyone who believes in Him would never die. Both Mary and Martha knew that the resurrection would occur on the last day, so they were at least comforted by that knowledge. If, as the Pre-Millennialists teach that the resurrection is not on the last day, but many years prior to the last day, then our Lord was mistaken in what He taught, and He missed a great opportunity to correct Martha's misconception of when the resurrection would occur.

Is it not much easier to believe what our Lord Jesus Christ said and taught rather than believe a sincere, but misguided system that either finds His words confusing or hard to understand, or ignores His words completely, or refuses to believe that they mean exactly what they say and deliberately twists them to conform to their doctrine? These are clear teachings. They cannot be unintentionally misunderstood.

Judgment on the Last Day

Not only did Jesus teach that the resurrection would occur on the last day, but He also taught that the judgment of those who reject Jesus would occur on the last day.

*John 12: 48 He who rejects Me, and does not receive My words, has that which judges him—the word that I have spoken will **judge him in the last day.***

Those who reject our Lord and the gracious words He has spoken through His prophets, apostles, and ministers through the years will be judged, found guilty, and cast away into everlasting punishment. When Jesus returns, the sentence on unbelievers that has already been passed because of their unbelief will be administered. He will gather everyone from all ages together. He will place them into one of two groups, sheep which He will put on His right hand or goats which He will put on His left hand.

Matthew 25: 31 "When the Son of Man comes in His glory, and all the holy angels with Him, then He will sit on the throne of His glory. 32 All the nations will be gathered before Him, and He will separate them one from another, as a shepherd divides his sheep from the goats. 33 And He will set the sheep on His right hand, but the goats on the left...46 And these will go away into everlasting punishment, but the righteous into eternal life."

There will be no waiting for over one thousand years for God to punish those who have rejected His Son, have lived selfish and self-centered lives, living only for what they can get out of life and the world. When He returns, the ungodly, those who chose not to obey the gospel, will be punished with everlasting destruction from the presence of the Lord. To reiterate, He comes – in that day – that last day - a singular day, not two second comings separated by seven years.

2 Thessalonians 1: 7 and to give you who are troubled rest with us **when the Lord Jesus is revealed from heaven** *with His mighty angels, 8 in flaming fire taking vengeance on those who do not know God, and on those who do not obey the gospel of our Lord Jesus Christ. 9 These shall be* **punished with everlasting destruction** *from the presence of the Lord and from the glory of His power, 10* **when He comes, in that Day,** *to be glorified in His saints and to be admired among all those who believe, because our testimony among you was believed.*

The punishment of unbelievers and the reward of believers both occur on the day of the Lord - that day - when Jesus comes to save his people. Confusion regarding the timing of the day of the Lord was a major problem in Thessalonica because of false teaching, just as it is for many today. But, Paul's description of the day of the Lord's return should have helped to alleviate the crisis. But, somehow, it is overlooked in the Dispensational scheme of things.

I will refrain from belaboring the point. I think this Biblical evidence is sufficient to prove that Jesus returns on the last day of time and that there are no more days following His return.

The Last Trumpet

The last day is not the only "last" the Bible mentions in conjunction with the Lord's Second Coming and the resurrection. The resurrection not only occurs on the last day, but also at the last trumpet.

*1 Corinthians 15: 51 Behold, I tell you a mystery: We shall not all sleep, but we shall all be changed— 52 in a moment, in the twinkling of an eye, at the **last trumpet**. For the trumpet will sound, and the dead will be raised incorruptible, and we shall be changed. 53 For this corruptible must put on incorruption, and this mortal must put on immortality.*

Again, this should be crystal clear to all who read it. The resurrection from the dead, the catching up of the saved to meet the Lord in the air, occurs when the last trumpet sounds. As with the last day, the word "last" in this verse is also "eschatos." The final trumpet. The "eschatos" trumpet. No trumpet to follow. The last trumpet sounds on the last day. This is the trumpet sound of 1 Thessalonians 4 that calls forth the dead in Christ to rise up and meet Him.

1 Thessalonians 4: 15 For this we say to you by the word of the Lord, that we who are alive and remain until the coming of the Lord will by no means precede those who are asleep. 16 For the Lord Himself will descend from heaven with a shout, with the voice of an archangel, and with the trumpet of God. And the dead in Christ will rise first.

No, the seven trumpets of Revelation do not follow this trumpet. How could they if the Apostle Paul – inspired by the Holy Spirit - meant what he said about the last trumpet calling forth the dead from their graves on the last day? It is obvious, is it not, that the trumpets of Revelation must refer to something else? The verse before us is clear. It means exactly what it says. Therefore, the seven trumpets of Revelation cannot possibly sound after this trumpet sounds regardless of what the popular explanation is. They must hold an entirely different meaning than what has been taught by so many. I will touch on them in a later chapter.

How hard is it to see what the Bible teaches? When we look at these verses after having been subjected to wrong teaching, it is difficult to accept the simple truth. No one wants to admit that they have been taught wrong doctrine. We love our pastors and teachers and do not want to believe that they taught us wrongly. I will be the first to say that their teachings on the Second Coming have not been with the intent to deceive. They were taught wrong doctrine and there are very few who have been taught Pre-Millennialism who can see the errors in that system. Everything concerning the Second Coming is seen through those lens that distort true teaching. It is hard to overcome.

The Last Enemy

There is another "last" that Paul mentions in 1 Corinthians 15, and that is the last enemy that will be destroyed.

*1 Corinthians 15: 26 The **last enemy** that will be destroyed **is death**.*

The last enemy that is destroyed when the last trumpet sounds on the last day is death. Of course death is destroyed by the resurrection from the dead. Again, the word is "eschatos." Death is the "eschatos" enemy. No more enemies beyond the resurrection. No, not even the multitude of enemies that Revelation speaks of. If Paul really meant that death is the final enemy of man – no more enemies possible afterwards - and that it is destroyed when Jesus returns and resurrects the dead - then someone has misinterpreted Revelation – deliberately misinterpreted I might add - as occurring after the resurrection and placed it where is does not belong. You will see who that someone was in another chapter. It may surprise you to find out who and for what reason.

Again I ask, what is the clear teaching of Scripture, and what is obscure due to its symbolism? Should we use a book that is replete with symbols and has many methods of interpretation to negate the clear and impossible to misunderstand teaching of Scripture, or should we use the clear teaching to find the truth concerning the not so clear?

After our resurrection, Paul emphatically states that "then comes the end."

1 Corinthians 15: 22 For as in Adam all die, even so in Christ all shall be made alive. 23 But each one in his own order: Christ the firstfruits, afterward those who are Christ's at His coming. 24 **Then comes the end, when He delivers the kingdom to God the Father, when He puts an end to all rule and all authority and power.** *25 For He must reign till He has put all enemies under His feet. 26* **The last enemy that will be destroyed is death.**

Then - the next event in succession - that is what the word "then" means, is the end, the "telos", the termination, the limit at which a thing ceases to be, that by which a thing is finished, its close, the end to which all things relate, the aim, its purpose (Strong's Concordance #5056). Time is finished. It has run its course. It is complete. No more time. The goal has been reached. This is the last day when the last trumpet sounds and Jesus destroys the last enemy. Jesus delivers the kingdom to His Father and eternity is all there is.

The purpose of the Lord's Second Coming, the "telos", the ultimate goal, as we have seen before, is the restoration of all things, the creation of the new heavens and new earth. When He returns and resurrects the dead and destroys the last enemy, when the new heavens and new earth come into existence, what further need is there of time?

Paul uses clear language to set forth the doctrine of the resurrection, when it occurs (at the Second Coming), and the subsequent end of time and our entrance into eternity. What he teaches cannot be misunderstood unless it is done so intentionally. Both our Lord and the Apostle Paul use words and language that are precise and to the point. Why not take them for exactly what they are saying?

Acts 3: 20, 21

*20 and that He may send Jesus Christ, who was preached to you before, 21 whom **heaven must receive until the times of restoration of all things**, which God has spoken by the mouth of all His holy prophets since the world began.*

Here is another simple teaching that specifically and categorically states that Jesus will not leave Heaven until the time when all things are restored – the time of the new heavens and the new earth – the time of His return. Peter preaches that Jesus *must* (it is necessary, there is need of, it behooves, is right and proper - necessity established by the counsel and decree of God, especially by that purpose of his which relates to the salvation of men by the intervention of Christ and which is disclosed in the Old Testament prophecies [Strong's Concordance # 1163]) ***stay in Heaven*** until He returns to make all things new. He will not leave temporarily to snatch away His people from the world and meet them in the air. He stays in Heaven until it is time to return to earth. Is not this verse clear?

Parable of the Tares

24 Another parable He put forth to them, saying: "The kingdom of heaven is like a man who sowed good seed in his field; 25 but while men slept, his enemy came and sowed tares among the wheat and went his way. 26 But when the grain had sprouted and produced a crop, then the tares also appeared. 27 So the servants of the owner came and said to him, 'Sir, did you not sow good seed in your field? How then does it have tares?' 28 He said to them, 'An enemy has done this.' The servants said to him, 'Do you want us then to go and gather them up?' 29 But he said, 'No, lest while you gather up the tares you also uproot the wheat with them. 30 Let both grow together until the harvest, and at the time of harvest I will say to the reapers, "First gather together the tares and bind them in bundles to burn them, but gather the wheat into my barn."'"

This parable is another teaching of our Lord that clearly explains truth about the Second Coming of Jesus. To recap it, a farmer found tares, weeds, in the crop of wheat he had planted that were put there by one of his enemies. The weeds, if not controlled, had potential to take over his field and do harm to his crop of wheat. His servants came to him asking how the tares got there, which he answered. They then requested that they be allowed to pull up the tares, but the farmer said no, that by doing so they would also pull up the wheat, and he would lose part of his crop. He told them to let both grow until the time of the harvest and then the harvesters were to first pull up the tares so they could be bundled and burned, but the wheat was to be gathered into his barn.

The disciples came to Jesus later asking for an explanation of the parable.

36 Then Jesus sent the multitude away and went into the house. And His disciples came to Him, saying, "Explain to us the parable of the tares of the field." 37 He answered and said to them: "He who sows the good seed is the Son of Man. 38 The field is the world, the good seeds are the sons of the kingdom, but the tares are the sons of the wicked one. 39 The enemy who sowed them is the devil, the harvest is the end of the age, and the reapers are the angels. 40 Therefore as the tares are gathered and burned in the fire, so it will be at the end of this age. 41 The Son of Man will send out His angels, and they will gather out of His kingdom all things that offend, and those who practice lawlessness, 42 and will cast them into the furnace of fire. There will be wailing and gnashing of teeth. 43 Then the righteous will shine forth as the sun in the kingdom of their Father. **He who has ears to hear, let him hear!**

Jesus then explains to His disciples the simple teaching of how at the end of the age, the completion, the consummation of time – the last day, the day of resurrection - the angels will separate the wicked from the righteous and cast them into the furnace of fire. There is a very important doctrine contained in this parable that so many overlook. Who is separated *first* according to Jesus? The wicked, those who practice lawlessness, those who offend Him are separated from the righteous and cast into hell.

Jesus gives a stern warning to those who heard His words at the end of this parable. It is also for every one of us who read these words today. "He who has ears to hear, let him hear." In other words, do not mess around with what He says. Simply believe that what He says is truth.

Using the Bible references that we have looked at already, it is not hard to see that this occurs on the last day. All the wicked and all the righteous of all time will be separated from each other eternally. That, of necessity, implies the resurrection of all who have ever lived.

John 5: 28 Do not marvel at this; for the hour is coming in which all who are in the graves will hear His voice 29 and come forth—those who have done good, to the resurrection of life, and those who have done evil, to the resurrection of condemnation.

This verse does not imply in the least that there are two resurrections, one for the righteous and one for the wicked, separated by years, but it is one resurrection in which all who are in the graves will come forth. It happens "in the hour" that God has appointed, on the last day at the last trumpet, defeating the last enemy. The saved of all the ages will rise from the earth, meet Jesus in the air, and descend to earth with Him, providing a royal escort for their King. More on this later. Everyone is placed either with the sheep on the right hand of Jesus or with the goats on the left hand of Jesus.

It is the wicked who are separated from the righteous first, not the righteous separated from the wicked as is currently taught by Pre-Millennialism. There is no separation of the righteous from the wicked, leaving the wicked on the earth to work further evil. This is another clear teaching from the lips of Jesus. And it occurs on one day, the last day, not over the course of several years. I could hardly believe what I was reading when I saw C.I. Schofield's notes on this verse. He blatantly says that the wicked are merely set aside for burning at a later date and that it is the righteous who are taken first

– just the opposite of what Jesus said. Now, I ask you, who are we to believe, Jesus or those who espouse a different doctrine?

The Parable of the Dragnet

*47 "Again, the kingdom of heaven is like a dragnet that was cast into the sea and gathered some of every kind, 48 which, when it was full, they drew to shore; and they sat down and gathered the good into vessels, but threw the bad away. 49 So it will be at the end of the age. The angels will come forth, **separate the wicked from among the just**, 50 and cast them into the furnace of fire. There will be wailing and gnashing of teeth."*

Again, Jesus says that the angels will come and separate the wicked from the just, not the just from the wicked. They will be cast into the furnace of fire.

Matthew 24: 38- 41 gives even more light on the subject. This is not the righteous being taken away in the "rapture", but the wicked being taken away to be burned.

*38 For as in the days before the flood, they were eating and drinking, marrying and giving in marriage, until the day that Noah entered the ark, 39 and did not know until the flood came and **took them all away**, so also will the coming of the Son of Man be. 40 Then two men will be in the field: one **will be taken** and the other left. 41 Two women will be grinding at the mill: one **will be taken** and the other left.*

Clearly Jesus connects those of Noah's day who were taken away in judgment by the flood to those who will be taken away to be burned in the everlasting fires of hell when He returns with His holy angels who will gather the wicked from among the just. They will be taken away by the angels just as the unrighteous in Noah's day were taken away by the flood. Now, lest some scholar points out that the Greek words are different between the two phrases, they still mean the same. Taken away. Anyone can see that Jesus is connecting the two events – the evil people are taken away in both cases.

These parables, these other verses we have looked at leave no room at all for the current doctrine of the "rapture." It is a man-made doctrine, not to be found in the pages of Scripture.

These have been short explanations, but adequate. I do not believe that one must be complex and lengthy to make a point. Let us all let the Bible speak for itself without forcing our own interpretation into it. If when the Lord returns and we find that I have misunderstood what the Lord and the Apostles are teaching in the pages of Scripture, I will apologize to each and every one of you who are offended by what I have written here. And apologize to our Lord for not having ears to hear what He says. If you will not give up the "rapture" doctrine for what the Bible clearly teaches, will you be willing to do the same?

Chapter 3

Where Did the Two Phased Second Coming of Jesus Originate?

Search the Scriptures, and you will not find anything within them to even hint at the possibility that there are two Second Comings of Jesus Christ, or if you wish, one two phased Second Coming of Jesus Christ, or to put it another way, one Second Coming for His saints, and one Second Coming with His saints. However you wish to word the idea that Jesus appears in the clouds to "rapture" His people then take them to Heaven, then waits for three and a half years or seven years – depending on your theological system – then returns to earth with them to set up a one thousand year kingdom on earth during which time Satan is bound in the bottomless pit and Jesus reigns with a rod of iron, destroying all enemies just is not seen on the pages of Holy Scripture. That is unless you have been indoctrinated with this system previously and cannot read anything in the Bible pertaining to the Second Coming of Jesus without seeing it. As I have stated before, so say I again; if you read the Bible for what it is really saying, not for what your systematic theology dictates, you will not see this supposed scenario.

I realize that this sounds harsh and totally unbiblical to those who have been indoctrinated into the Pre-Tribulation rapture system, who have been taught not to question this system, but to accept it as taught. *(I use the word "indoctrinated" deliberately, because that is exactly what has happened. This false doctrine has been forced into the minds of people who have not had the strength to resist it).* But all I ask is that you consider what the pages of Scripture are saying. This entire system *(I use the word system because that is exactly what it is, a system of belief that disregards any teaching that contradicts itself. The system is a whole. It cannot be broken up into bite sized chunks. It must be taken in its entirety.)* is so complicated and complex that no one who is reading the Bible devotionally or exegetically, letting it speak for itself, can possibly see it and ascertain it as truth. The reason this is so is that the Pre-Tribulation rapture doctrine had a definite historical beginning – born amid an influx of destructive cults - that can be shown. Although many Christians believe that it was taught by Jesus and the apostles, specifically Paul, it is not a doctrine that has been taught since the time of Jesus or the time of the apostles. It cannot be traced back to the early church or even to the time of the Reformers. It can only be traced back to the early 1800's. That is the time of its birth.

I will not be going into much detail with this because there are many good and scholarly works that explain the origin of the "rapture" in much detail, and should I write of it in detail, I would only be taking from these other works and rewriting them and paraphrasing them. I do not wish to do that. So, I will draw from my memory, using the other works only to verify what I write. I did do an extensive work on the rapture for my Master's thesis 25+ years ago, so I have done original research on the subject. Through the years I have changed my mind on some particulars of the Second Coming, but not in regard to the "rapture." Unfortunately, I do not have a copy of my thesis available, but my memory is still functioning relatively well. OK. Enough of that.

Ribera and Lacunza

There are many researchers who believe that the "rapture" as taught today goes back to a couple of Jesuit priests named Francisco Ribera (1537-1591) and Emmanuel Lacunza (1731-1801). Ribera began it during the time of the Reformation in order to combat the teaching of the Reformers that the Roman Catholic Church was the great whore of Revelation and that the pope was the beast of Revelation, the anti-christ. Ribera taught that Revelation was not relevant to their day, but it was to be fulfilled in the future, and that it would occur during the time the anti-christ was in power, and he would come to power somewhere down the line. He was rejecting the traditional interpretation of Revelation which applied it to every generation of believers – as all Scripture must be done – and placed it somewhere a long ways off in his future. He was diverting attention from the Reformation and its teachings of living by faith, not by the edicts of the pope. The scope of his teachings was known as futurism. He had to take the focus off of Rome and put it somewhere else. He could not otherwise refute the Reformers, so he made Revelation, which was the basis of the Reformers anti-Rome teaching, a future event with different enemies of the church.

Lacunza, who followed Ribera, wrote a book entitled, "The Coming of the Messiah in Glory and Majesty."[1] He did not use his own name, but a pseudonym of Rabbi Ben Ezra in order to divert attention from the fact that he was a Jesuit, which would automatically alienate him from Protestants. He taught that in order for God's people to escape that anti-christ of Ribera's teaching, they would be "raptured" away. They would not be on earth during that time. Because he used a Jewish pseudonym, his book was readily more readily accepted by Protestants than it would have been otherwise. Both of these men were successful to some extent in diverting attention from the anti-christian activities of Rome that the Reformers saw and condemned, and their teachings and writings made the focus of Revelation some future world dictator.

Rise of Cults in England

Although the church of Jesus Christ has always been under attack by Satan, it seems that in the eighteenth and nineteenth centuries in England she was more susceptible than at other times. It was a time of religious tolerance and textual criticism that cast doubt as to the inerrancy of Scripture. It was also a time of greater scientific discovery that made man believe that his knowledge outweighed the truth of God's Word. Man was fulfilling Romans 1: 21.

21 because, although they knew God, they did not glorify Him as God, nor were thankful, but became futile in their thoughts, and their foolish hearts were darkened. 22 Professing to be wise, they became fools

When the church allows even a little leaven to be mixed in the loaf, it will soon permeate the entire loaf. Tolerance of false teachers and teachings is extremely dangerous to the church. It allows "doctrines of demons" (1 Timothy 4:1) to creep in and gain a foothold. Tolerance is deceptive. It is destructive to solid Biblical doctrine. Setting the stage in England for the inception and acceptance of the Pre-Tribulation "rapture" teaching was the warped doctrines of Emmanuel Swedenborg (1688-1772). There were those who actually accepted his teachings as a revelation from God, and they started several "churches" based upon his errant teachings. He had done a study on Revelation and had concluded based on current events in England and France, that the final judgment had occurred in 1757, and that he and his contemporaries were in the final days of time. He had identified Napoleon as the anti-christ. These interpretations are not so far removed from what many "prophecy experts" of today imagine. Look at the newspaper so you can interpret Scripture.

But, his other writings were so farfetched that no one who was in control of his faculties could possibly believe them. An example of his "revelations" is that every planet has inhabitants that are human. He goes into great detail about each planet, describing their appearance and manner. The best spirits, says he, are those who inhabit Mars. Now we know where the idea of Martians comes from. He traveled to other planets by means of astral projection and spirit travel. He traveled many times to Heaven and Hell. He had thousands of conversations with angels who used to be men.[2] OKAY.

Following on his heels in England was Richard Brothers who called himself "The Prince of the Hebrews" and wrote a book entitled Revealed Knowledge of the Prophecies and Times. The signs of his times such as increased pestilence, earthquakes and wars led him to believe that he was living in the final days. Because of his teachings he was committed to an asylum.

Joanna Southcott came along claiming the powers of the angel in Revelation 7 who seals the servants of God in the forehead. Those whom she sealed would at the Second Coming of Jesus be taken alive into Heaven. She also presented herself as the woman in Revelation 12 who bears the Child who is to rule the nations and be caught up into Heaven. She, however died childless in a few short years. Her position was assumed by another who very shortly was imprisoned for blasphemy.[3]

Edward Irving

Because these false teachers were tolerated, the door for more intense and more widely accepted millennial teachings was opened and many there were who pranced right on through, knowing that they would be tolerated and even accepted and held in esteem by some. Sometime during the late 1820's Edward Irving, who at one time had been an assistant to Thomas Chalmers, the most well known and respected preacher in Scotland, discovered Lacunza's book and picked up on its theme of a secret rapture. He translated it into English in 1827. In his rather lengthy preface, in which he set forth his own views on prophecy, he states that when he began preaching his new views on unfulfilled prophecy, he *"did not know of one brother in the ministry who held with him in these matters."* (*Please* *hear his own words*) He stated that he was resolved to hold to his new convictions no matter who disagreed with him.[4]

Irving was a Presbyterian minister who was a great orator and crowd motivator. He was a friend of Henry Drummond (1786-1860) who was a wealthy banker. They held meetings in Drummond's house discussing unfulfilled prophecy with those interested in the subject. Irving's congregation grew large, but because of his extreme views that speaking in tongues and healing would be signs that preceded and accompanied the Second Coming of Jesus, and because of his new radical teaching on the "rapture" - among other points of contention - he was charged with heresy and was dismissed from the Presbyterian church in England and formed the Catholic Apostolic Church, the forerunner of modern day Pentecostalism.

That the so called "secret rapture" was unknown prior to 1830 is documented by a Bible scholar from that era by the name of Tregelles. He was a well known and well respected New Testament scholar. He was present at the 1830 "Powerscourt Conferences of Prophecy" when this doctrine first surfaced. Here is a quote from him. "I am not aware that there was any definite teaching that there should be a secret rapture of the Church at a secret coming until this was given forth as an utterance in Mr. Irvings's church, from what was then received as being the voice of the Spirit. But whether anyone else asserted such a thing or not, it was from that supposed revelation that the modern doctrine and the modern phraseology arose."[5]

Tregelles further states that this utterance was given in tongues and that it was interpreted by someone else as being a "revelation."[6]

Irving's most damning heresy that was the final straw for the Presbytery that ordained him was that he began teaching that the Incarnate Christ had a sin nature.[7] He died at age forty two with very few friends. There is much more that could be said concerning Irving and Drummond and their eccentricities and heresies, but I believe the little I have included here will be sufficient to show that this "father" of the Pre-Tribulation "rapture" teaching was on very shaky theological ground and his ideas should be dismissed as the heresy that it is.

John Darby and Friends

John Darby was a contemporary of Irving in England. He was influenced by Irving although their backgrounds were different. Where Irving was highly emotional, Darby was from the Brethren movement, and was highly intellectual, a lawyer. He became dissatisfied with the Church of England, by whom he was ordained, because of some errors in the church that he perceived. While recuperating from a leg operation, he meditated on the state of the church and reached some conclusions. He decided that *all* organized churches were apostate and that *all* genuine Christians should leave them and meet together as members of the Body of Christ, not as members of any church. It was during this time of recovery that he came to a new belief concerning the people of God through the ages. *(I wonder if he was taking medicine that caused him to hallucinate.)* He came to believe that there were not one people of God through the ages but two, the earthly people and the heavenly people. This new concept drastically affected his understanding of prophecy. He took Irving's teaching and, and along with his "new revelations" concerning the distinction between the Jews and the Church, he developed what became known as Dispensationalism, a radical form of Pre-Millennialism that systematized it based upon the foundation of the Pre-Tribulation "rapture."

He was not of the same nature and spirit of the Apostle Paul as he describes himself in 1 Thessalonians 2.

*6 Nor did we seek glory from men, either from you or from others, when we might have made demands as apostles of Christ. 7 But **we were gentle** among you, just as a nursing mother cherishes her own children.*

Darby was of such a nature and disposition that anyone who disagreed with him and his points of view were attacked viciously – the identical attitude of Irving. Does this attitude sound familiar concerning many Pre-Millenialists today? When he came to higher power within the Brethren movement, he excommunicated not only individuals but entire churches who did not see eye to eye with him concerning the state of the church during the "tribulation period." His actions among the churches are exactly what Paul warned the Ephesians would happen after he left them in Acts 20.

*29 For I know this, that after my departure savage wolves will come in among you, not sparing the flock. 30 Also from among yourselves men will rise up, **speaking perverse things, to draw away the disciples after themselves.***

He taught that the church would be "raptured" while others taught that the church would go through the "tribulation." But the major debate centered on the difference – as he defined it and bifurcated it – between the Jews, the Old Testament saints, and the church, the New Testament saints. As with all those who have espoused perverse new doctrines through the years – as the apostle warned - Darby sought others to join him in his distorted way of thinking, and rejected all who did not follow him.

Dispensationalism is the most radical of all Pre-Millennial, Pre-Tribulation "rapture" teachings in its approach to Scripture. Without getting into many details – this is not meant to be an exhaustive critique of Dispensationalism – there are many available should you desire to avail yourself of them - it breaks down history into seven ages, or dispensations as they are referred to, in which God tested – and is currently testing in the present dispensation and will test in the future dispensation - man's obedience to Him in regard to some specific revelation of the will of God. It also dichotomizes just about everything in the Bible between the Jews and the church. They call this "rightly dividing the Word of Truth" (2 Timothy 2:15). I call it hacking up and butchering the Word of God.

Dispensationalists believe that God has two separate and distinct groups of people - Jews and Church. The Jews are the primary people of God, the real chosen people of God. The church, the body of Christ is secondary in God's overall plan for history. The church was merely inserted into God plan for Israel because Israel rejected their Messiah. According to them, the church does not include believers from the Old Testament, and it does not fulfill any of the promises which God gave to Israel in the Old Testament. It is a separate body of believers altogether.

Darby states the distinction between Jews and the Church in the clearest of terms "The Jewish nation is never to enter the church."[8] *WHAT?* Where did he get that idea from? Certainly not the Bible. He taught that God has two peoples in redemptive history who are as different as heaven and earth. The heavenly people, who are as numerous as the stars in the heavens, will spend eternity in heaven. The earthly people, who are as numerous as the dust of the earth, will spend eternity on a new earth.[9] *Oh, Lord, have mercy.*

Charles Ryrie, a modern day leader among Dispensationalists, who, like Schofield – who we have yet to meet in this writing - has added his notes to the pages of Holy Scripture, says that the "basic promise of Dispensationalism is two purposes of God expressed in the formation of two peoples who **maintain their distinction throughout eternity."**[10] ***HUH??*** (See Acts 15: 9, 11; discussed later in this chapter). Such nonsense really does not require an answer, but let's let the Bible answer Darby and Ryrie. Only a few passages are needed to put them to silence, although I seriously doubt that their disciples will be silenced by Scripture. *(It has been my unhappy discovery that most people who believe this system are quite satisfied with it and do not desire to even listen to anything that would contradict it – even truth. They adamantly declare that anyone who disagrees with their interpretation does not believe the Bible.)* There are many more passages that reiterate and reconfirm Biblical truth, not Dispensational error.

Jesus speaks in *John 10: 16 And other sheep I have which are not of this fold; them also I must bring, and they will hear My voice; and there will be **one flock and one shepherd.***

*John 11: 52 and not for that nation only, but also that He would **gather together in one the children of God** who were scattered abroad.*

*Romans 12: 4 For as we have many members in **one body**,*

One flock, one Shepherd, one body, gather together in one the children of God. What can be misunderstood here? If these are not sufficient, then listen to what the Apostle Paul writes in Ephesians.

*Ephesians 2: 14 For He Himself is our peace, who has made both one, and has broken down the middle wall of separation, 15 having abolished in His flesh the enmity, that is, the law of commandments contained in ordinances, so as to create in Himself **one new man from the two**, thus making peace, 16 and that He might **reconcile them both to God in one body through the cross,** thereby putting to death the enmity. 17 And He came and preached peace to you who were afar off and to those who were near. 18 For through Him we both have access by one Spirit to the Father.*

Jesus made peace between Jews and Gentiles in His death on the cross. He has broken down the wall of separation and has brought us all together into one body. These are clear statements by Jesus, John and Paul. I know that I am not the most profound thinker or scholar, and I do not qualify as brilliant by anyone's standards, but these statements are not difficult at all to understand – not even for me. Now, if Jesus and the apostles teach one thing and Darby, Schofield, Ryrie, Chafer and a host of other Dispensationalists teach something contrary, who am I – and who are you – to believe?

Another one of their tenets of belief that is based on the eternal separation of Jews and the church is that God has *two plans of salvation* – one for Jews and another for Gentiles. Read their own words. Here are two quotes, one from the 1909 Schofield Reference Bible notes on John 1:17.

"As a dispensation, grace begins with the death and resurrection of Christ....The point of testing is *no longer legal obedience as the condition of salvation*, but acceptance or rejection of Christ, with good works as a fruit of salvation"

Lewis Sperry Chafer, the founder of Dallas Theological Seminary, an avowed student of Schofield, writes in his eight volume Systematic Theology,

"With the call of Abraham and the giving of the Law... there are *two widely different* standardized, *divine provisions* whereby man, who is utterly fallen, might *come into the favor of God.*"[11]

How dare they! Can they be serious? Or are they simply testing our Bible knowledge to see if we will believe a deception? Or, do they not know Scripture, especially Acts 15? Or, are they simply rejecting truth in order to defend the system?

*Acts 15: 9 (God) made **no distinction between us and them**, purifying their hearts by faith... 11 But we believe that through the grace of the Lord Jesus Christ **we shall be saved in the same manner as they.**"*

Peter, speaking to the Jerusalem council concerning the conversion of Gentiles lays it out in clear, unambiguous language that cannot possibly be misunderstood. Jews and Gentiles are saved in the same way. There is no distinction between them, then, now and forever. What is so hard to understand about this? How do you answer that, Mr. Ryrie?

The apostle Paul, in Galatians 2 destroys, in the strongest possible voice, the Dispensationalist's unholy, vile doctrine that Jews are saved by keeping the law while Gentiles must trust in Jesus.

*Galatians 2: 15 We who are Jews by nature, and not sinners of the Gentiles, 16 knowing that a **man is NOT justified by the works of the law** but by faith in Jesus Christ, even we have believed in Christ Jesus, that we might be justified by faith in Christ and not by the works of the law; for by the **works of the law NO FLESH shall be justified**. (If common sense serves me here, no flesh also means Jews).*

*Galatians 3: 11 But that **NO ONE is justified by the law** in the sight of God is evident, for **"the just shall live by faith."*** (Do you think that also means Jews?)

How much clearer can the Word of the Almighty God be on this subject? Why do they continue to insist that there are two ways of salvation, one for the Jews and one for the rest of mankind? Why do people today continue to believe that the church must be taken out of the way so God can restart His work with the Jews, which is the *only* reason for the "rapture"?

It is because of this false teaching of the eternal distinction between the Jews and the Gentiles that the Pre-Tribulation "rapture" came into being. Were it not for Darby's and Schofield's insistence that Jews are saved by law keeping rather than by the blood of Jesus, there would be no "rapture" teaching that insists that the church must be taken out of the way so God can continue "plan A", offering the kingdom to the Jews through keeping the law.

Here are Darby's own words as to the necessity of the "rapture." "It is this conviction, that the Church is properly heavenly, in its calling and relationship with Christ, forming no part of the course of events of the earth, which makes the rapture so simple and clear; and on the other hand, it shows how the denial of its rapture brings down the Church to an earthly position, and destroys its whole spiritual character and position."[12]

This particular distinctive of Dispensationalism borders on, if indeed it does not absolutely qualify it as a non–Christian cult. That particular doctrine is anti the blood, the precious blood of Jesus Christ. To even suggest such a damnable thought is "treading underfoot the blood of Jesus." Dispensationalists believe that God's promises to Israel are entirely earthly, that they belong entirely to Israel and must be fulfilled on the earth, and that God's promises to the church are spiritual. It is because of this argument of the Dispensationalists that I gave the illustrations of God meaning what He said and saying what He means in the introduction to this writing. It is important to realize God's spiritual application to His earthly laws. The Old Testament law and prophets are spiritually interpreted in the New Testament as having application to the church. So saith the apostles. So saith our Lord.

The proponents of Dispensationalism believe that since the Jews rejected Jesus as their King, He had to go to the cross. **_WHAT??_** From eternity it was God's plan for the redemption of man – Jews and Gentiles alike – for Jesus to be crucified on the cross. "Without the shedding of blood, there is *no* remission of sin."

According to them, becoming the King of Israel was God's plan A, but since Jesus was rejected, God implemented plan B, the cross. If they would have accepted Him when He came the first time, and crowned Him as King, the cross would have been avoided, and Jesus would have ushered in the Kingdom of Heaven – their definition of it. What do they do with John 6:15 when the people want to take Jesus by force and make Him their king? They tried to make Him king, but He rejected it. The cross was His and His Father's plan from eternity.

So, in order to give the Jews another chance to accept Jesus as their Messiah, He will "rapture" the church and the Jews will immediately see that He is indeed their Messiah, their King, and will begin to evangelize the world – without the aid of the Holy Spirit, who has been taken out of the world with the church in the "rapture." The two thousand year New Testament church age is seen as an interruption of God's plan for Israel. The time period between the rejection of Christ by Israel and the "rapture" of the church is called a parenthesis – God inserts the church into history, but stops His "prophetic clock" (their phrase, not a Biblical one) while the church is present. God's time table is halted for the length of the church age and will not begin again until the church is "raptured" away and Israel is again the focus of God's dealings with the world. The church has to be taken out of the way so God can continue His plan for Israel, His real chosen people.

If you have not been taught the system of Dispensationalism, then this sounds to you exactly like what it is – outrageous and heretical – something that must have been dreamt up on a funny farm somewhere. You have to wonder what someone was thinking? drinking? eating? just before they went to bed. (I wanted to say smoking, but I didn't) when they came up with this. Yet, many Christians believe it and cling to it as truth. They were taught it, so it must be true.

What is especially disturbing in this heresy of two ways of salvation is that it mandates that Jews "keep the law" – which is impossible – if they are to be saved. Dispensationalism and Pre-Millenialism prides itself on being the friends of Jews, making them "special" to God. *(The Jews are special in that God chose them to be the earthly family of our Lord Jesus Christ and to be the ones to receive His law and be the first ones to have the gospel preached to them. But they are not special in that they get their own way of salvation. All must come through the blood of Jesus if they are to see God.)* Anyone who disagrees with their placement of Jews as "special" to God is attacked as being anti-Semitic. Unregenerate Jews, not knowing any differently, think that they are "special" to God and that the Christians who make them feel "special" are their friends. How is it being friends with Jews to let them continue to think that their religion based on Old Testament Law – as they understand it – not as interpreted in the New Testament by the Lord and the Apostles - will earn them a place in God's favor and the manifestation of His grace? Dispensationalists are the real anti-Semites in that they encourage Jews to keep the law as a means of salvation instead of including them in God's plan of salvation by grace through faith in the Lord Jesus Christ. Of course, just because they say there are two plans of salvation in absolutely no way makes it true. They are deceiving Jews and Christians alike by feeding them lies.

Darby's new views were contrary not only to the theology of his day, but were also contrary to the historic teaching of the church over the centuries. Darby knew this. His assumption was that the teaching of the church since the days of the apostles had been marked by apostasy. He as an individual was trying to recover apostolic truth.[13]

He is another example of one individual who thought he knew more than the aggregate wisdom of the Church. Anyone who desires to teach the Word of God should not work in isolation from the church and its historic teachings, but should be in agreement with the church "fathers." He should not believe that he is the first and only person to whom the Holy Spirit has granted significant illumination into the meaning of Scripture since the age of the apostles. But, Irving and Darby thought they were the sole repositories of the wisdom and revelation of God. Do you still want to be a Dispensationalist and Pre-Tribulationist?

Margaret MacDonald

During the time of Irving and Darby, a young Scottish girl named Margaret MacDonald had a "revelation" of a secret coming of Jesus for His saints. She was sick in bed at the time and she was overcome with dreams and visions (hallucinations because of her sickness and fever?). The main thrust of her "revelation" was that only Christians would know about this first appearing of Jesus. She had a vision of Jesus returning in two stages. I have included her "revelation" in appendix A should you desire to read it in its entirety.

It is believed that John Darby built his system using not only Irving's writings, but Margaret MacDonald's dreams and visions also. I do not doubt that she was a godly young girl who loved the Lord, but just because she was in no way makes what she had "revealed" to her a correct interpretation of Scripture. Each of us has had dreams and hallucinations when feverish. Would you base Christian doctrine on what you experienced during those times? I didn't think so. Neither would I. And we should not base doctrine on Miss MacDonald's, either.

Cyrus Ingersol Schofield

While many people credit Darby with the implementation of Dispensationalism, it is C.I. Schofield who made it popular. He is the one who is most often quoted when Dispensationalism and the Pre-Tribulation "rapture" is taught. He was a Congregational minister from Dallas, Texas, who later became pastor of the Moody Church in Chicago, who added his own notes to the pages of Scripture – many notes contained within the text of Scripture itself. I believe that this serious aberration of placing man's thoughts within the Holy text itself has been the cause of much doctrinal error. He truly is guilty of adding to the Scriptures. It became so popular among Bible believers that many Christians through the years have equated his notes with the inerrancy of Holy Spirit inspired Scripture. I have personally heard people quote his notes by saying, "My Bible says..."

What kind of man was C.I. Schofield? The following is a quote from The Daily Capital, the newspaper from Topeka, Kansas, dated August 27, 1881.

Cyrus I. Schofield in the Role of a Congregational Minister

Cyrus I. Schofield, formerly of Kansas, late lawyer, politician, and shyster generally, has come to the surface again, and promises once more to gather around himself that halo of notoriety that has made him so prominent in the past. The last personal knowledge that Kansans have had of this peer among scalawags, when was about four years ago, after a series of forgeries and confidence games he left the state and a destitute family and took refuge in Canada. For a time he kept undercover, nothing being heard of him until within the past two years he turned up in St. Louis, where he had a wealthy widowed sister living who has generally come to the from and squared up Cyrus' little follies and foibles by paying good round sums of money. Within the past year, however, Cyrus committed a series of St. Louis forgeries that could not be settled so easily, and the erratic young gentleman was compelled to linger in the St. Louis jail for a period of six months.

Among the many malicious acts that characterized his career, was one particularly atrocious, that has come under our personal notice. Shortly after he left Kansas, leaving his wife and two children dependent upon the bounty of his wife's mother, he wrote his wife that he could invest some $1,300 of her mother's money, all she had, in a manner that would return big interest. After some correspondence, he forwarded them a mortgage, signed and executed by one Chas. Best, purporting to convey valuable property in St. Louis. Upon this, the money was sent to him. Afterwards, the mortgages were found to be base forgeries, no such person as Charles Best being in existence, and the property conveyed in the mortgage fictitious...[14]

It seems that every one who was instrumental in establishing Dispensationalism and Pre-Millennialism had more than a few character quirks and flaws. Not to say that we all are not sinners – we are – but their particular character defects were of such a nature that they cared not what others thought of them personally as long as they achieved their objectives, which were to get as much as they could from others and to have others join them in their strange new doctrines.

Most Evangelicals today think that the "rapture" has historically been a part of Christian doctrine since the beginning. It has not. It is a relatively new doctrine that should be viewed with suspicion, especially when it is realized that it is of recent origin and that it came into being amid many cults and the liberal view of tolerance for all religious doctrines, and that those who espoused it originally did so without regard for historic theological interpretation. They arrogantly placed themselves above their contemporary peers.

Warnings Against Heresy

Why has the "two staged Pre-Tribulation rapture" not been taught through the ages if it is as clearly portrayed in the Bible as some people tout? Well, that is the question that needs to be answered, is it not? It has not been taught through the years because, very simply, it is not in the Bible. There is an old saying that bears repeating here; "If it is new, it is not true; if it is true, it is not new." We need to be reminded of what Jude exhorts us to do in verse 3 of his epistle.

*"3 Beloved, while I was very diligent to write to you concerning our common salvation, I found it necessary to write to you exhorting you to **contend earnestly for the faith which was <u>once for all</u> delivered to the saints.***

Although not in the category of soul damning heresy or of denying the faith, the "rapture" is not a doctrine of the faith that was "once for all delivered to the saints." It is, however, heretical in that it does cause schisms within the body of Christ. As has been stated before, and as many of you know from experience, there are many within the community of adherents to the Pre-Tribulation "rapture" who are militant in their attacks on those who do not subscribe to it. They viciously attack anyone who does not believe in their system – they must have inherited this trait from Irving, Darby, and Schofield – even those who are orthodox in their belief in Jesus.

In many circles, Pre-Millennialism – specifically the Pre-Tribulation "rapture" - is equated with a fundamental belief in the Bible. One is simply not a fundamentalist – one who believes in the fundamentals of Scripture - unless they accept the Pre-Millennial system. Perhaps you have seen, as I have, signs in front of many churches that proudly proclaim, "Fundamental, Independent, Pre-Millennial." In other words, they proclaim that in order to be fundamental in your Biblical doctrine, you must be Pre-Millennial. And independent.

Titus 3:10 and Romans 16:17 are appropriate here. Paul warns us to reject those who are heretics, those who bring in divisive doctrines that were not taught by the apostles. This Pre-Tribulation "rapture" is one such doctrine that has caused much division within the body of Christ. Just before my father became the pastor of church on the Eastern Shore of Maryland, it had gone through a split over this very issue. Those who clung tenaciously to the "rapture" took their ball and went and started a new church based on that doctrine, and for years there was animosity directed from the new church toward the old one. "How dare they not accept the Pre-Tribulation "rapture!" Many other such church splits have occurred over this issue. It is best, I suppose, that those in disagreement form a new body, but I do not think the Lord is pleased with this, do you? Paul gives excellent advice concerning those who attempt to force others to accept their particular form of doctrine.

Titus 3: 10 Reject a divisive man after the first and second admonition,

Romans 16: 17 Now I urge you, brethren, note those who cause divisions and offenses, contrary to the doctrine which you learned, and avoid them. 18 For those who are such do not serve our Lord Jesus Christ, but their own belly, and by smooth words and flattering speech deceive the hearts of the simple.

1 Timothy 1 gives added warnings against teaching any doctrine that causes disputes among the church. The "rapture" teaching caused much dissent when first taught and it still is causing dissent within the Body of Christ.

*3 As I urged you when I went into Macedonia—remain in Ephesus that you may charge some that they teach **no other doctrine, 4 nor give heed to fables** and endless genealogies, **which cause disputes** rather than godly edification which is in faith. 5 Now the purpose of the commandment is love from a pure heart, from a good conscience, and from sincere faith, 6 from which some, having strayed, have turned aside to idle talk, 7 desiring to be teachers of the law, **understanding neither what they say nor the things which they affirm.***

Yes, it is taught by many today, but no one can show where the apostles clearly taught a two stage Second Coming of Jesus or where the early church taught it or where the Reformers taught it. If it were the important doctrine that it is presented as, then the Bible would clearly and unambiguously reveal it. It would be plainly taught in words that anyone could see and understand. But, it is not clearly taught – in fact it is not even unclearly taught. This doctrine must be forced into a passage – a square peg into a round hole - in order for it to be taught.

Those who began this teaching – as Darby's attitude toward those who did not accept it clearly demonstrates – did so to serve their own purposes as Romans 16:18 states. They deceived the hearts and minds of the simple – those who were not grounded firmly in the Word.

Also 1 Timothy 6 gives instruction concerning the originators of this system, and also many of its modern day disciples.

3 If anyone teaches otherwise and does not consent to wholesome words, even the words of our Lord Jesus Christ, and to the doctrine which accords with godliness, 4 he is proud, knowing nothing, but is obsessed with disputes and arguments over words, from which come envy, strife, reviling, evil suspicions, 5 useless wranglings of men of corrupt minds and destitute of the truth... From such withdraw yourself...20 O Timothy! Guard what was committed to your trust, avoiding the profane and idle babblings and contradictions of what is falsely called knowledge

It had its beginning in the latter part of the sixteenth century by a couple of Jesuits and in the early part of the nineteenth century in England and Scotland by those who had been severely reprimanded – and even tried for heresy - by their contemporaries and equals, those who knew the Word of God and would not be swayed from its truth.

These are facts that are not in question. It is confirmed and verified by history. These facts may be denied or altered by hardcore disciples of the "rapture" in an attempt to protect the system at all costs, or rejected by others because they have never heard them before, but these facts are true none the less. Too much research by many scholars has proven these facts to be true.

It is also interesting to note that during the time period when the "rapture" theory was being born in England amid the birth of many cults and heresies, several cults were being formed in America. Joseph Smith was having his "revelations" and forming the cult of Mormonism. Ellen White was having her "revelations" that formed the basis of Seventh Day Adventism. Howard Russell began the Watchtower Bible and Tract Society, better known as Jehovah's Witnesses. Kate and Margeretta Fox, sisters that were 12 and 15 years old began Spiritism, the supposed communication with the dead through a medium. (These two, by the way, read Swedenborg.) Mary Baker Eddy began the Christian Science belief system during this time frame of the nineteenth century.

It seems like Satan was determined to undermine the "faith once delivered to the saints" by making these people believe that God was giving them "extra revelation" that was (according to them) equivalent to or superior to the revealed Word of God. This phenomenon appears to have been epidemic during the eighteenth and nineteenth centuries. So many people with "new revelations." All of them advanced their doctrines as being inspired of God, but if we read Scripture, they are all found wanting, including those of Irving, Darby, and Schofield. Those who propose to speak for God had better make sure they are speaking truth that can be clearly verified and supported by His Word.

There is danger when anyone proposes to speak for God through revelations, dreams, visions etc., and it is even more dangerous when the church receives as truth a teaching that has never been taught before. Evangelicals today – with the exception of some extreme Pentecostal groups - would reject them immediately, especially those spoken in "tongues." Yet, when these "new revelations" about the "rapture" occurred in the 1800's, they are accepted today. Why? Do not the same standards apply for then as they do today? Are those "new revelations" that occurred then still not heretical today, as they were then? It must be noted again that only extremists accepted any of these "revelations" then, not the church as a whole.

Just to reiterate, what details one believes about the Second Coming of Jesus Christ has no bearing on their salvation providing that they are trusting in the blood of Jesus shed on Calvary as payment for their sin. I hope that all Godly men and women can agree on that. That is the primary issue in Christianity. But, it is still important, I believe, to make sure that we believe truth rather than error. If we believe error over the truth, what might prevent us from further doctrinal error? We should never – ever – believe something

just because we were taught it, but we should be good Bereans and search the Scriptures to see if it is so. If what we were taught does not line up with the clear, unambiguous teaching of the Word of God, it needs to be rejected as a doctrine that causes heresy with the church. And if it takes over 1800 years to surface, it must be viewed as false. There are no new doctrines being revealed by God. His revelation is complete. It has been since John received the final installment on Patmos. Anyone declaring "new revelation" from Scripture must be rejected along with their teaching.

Whenever a new doctrine surfaces that had never been taught in over eighteen centuries of church history, it should cause a great deal of suspicion, and should be rejected. If something is taught in Scripture, is it not reasonable to expect that at least a few theologians and exegetes to have discovered it somewhere in the preceding centuries? The teaching of a secret pre-tribulation "rapture" is a doctrine that never existed before 1830. It definitely did not come to be known through careful study and exegisis of the Word of God.

The "rapture" should be carefully examined against the Scriptures we have used in the previous chapter and against its beginnings. How can there possibly be a "secret rapture" that leaves the world to the anti-christ if all enemies, of which death is the last, are eliminated on the last day? Those verses used previously are all that are really needed to disprove the "rapture." But, we will examine other "proof texts" that are used to show the two stage Second Coming of Jesus in another chapter.

Chapter 4

The Seventy Weeks of Daniel

The seventy weeks of Daniel is another passage that has caused much confusion with its twisted prophetic interpretation by those professing the Dispensational, Pre-Tribulation "rapture." Somehow it has been knocked completely off track of God's original intent and meaning when Gabriel announced this prophecy to Daniel. It has been ripped from its context and forced into a convoluted system of interpretation that is so ridiculous that, were it not taught with such sincerity by its adherents, it would be seen as having been taken right off the pages of the latest Looney Tunes comic book.

I know I said that I would refrain from negative comments as much as is possible, but this deserves to be shown for absolutely how ridiculous it is. The Pre-Tribulation, Dispensational interpretation of Daniel 9 is so farfetched that even those who accept it have to stretch their minds beyond its natural capacity in order to begin to believe it. Were it not for the misinterpretation of this passage, the Dispensational, Pre-Tribulation "rapture", Pre-Millennial system would crumble – there would be no "rapture" teaching. This is the mortar that holds its foundation together.

No New Temple or Reestablished Animal Sacrifice

Somehow this passage has been reinterpreted to mean something that was never intended. Instead of a prophecy of the coming

Messiah and His work for the redemption of Israel – in answer to Daniel's prayer - and the destruction of the temple and the Old Covenant, which it is, as will be explained in this chapter, it has been twisted to prophesy a coming anti-christ and his desecration of a rebuilt temple and reestablished animal sacrificial system that for some reason God accepts as atonement for sins, even after the Bible specifically states that there is no other sacrifice acceptable to God other than the blood of His Son, our Lord Jesus Christ.

The entire book of Hebrews deals with this subject. It is Paul's treatise on the superiority of the New Covenant over the Old Covenant, of Jesus over angels and Moses, of the blood of Jesus over the blood of animals. Many of the first century Jews who had trusted in Jesus for salvation were rethinking their belief system and were reverting to the old ways, so Paul wrote his letter to encourage them to maintain their faith in Jesus and not to give into the Judaizers who would discourage them and drag them back into the bondage of the law. At least thirty four times in his letter, Paul exhorts the Hebrews to "hold fast, endure, give heed, hold firm, be diligent, have confidence, lay hold of" and other phrases that carry the meaning of diligence and steadfast commitment to what they had learned from him and the other apostles. He warns them against giving in to the desire of others to destroy their faith and bring them back into bondage.

In fact, Hebrews 10: 29, in no uncertain terms states that those who believe in the efficaciousness of animal sacrifice after having known of the establishment of the New Covenant and the supreme power of the blood of Jesus are literally trampling underfoot the blood of Jesus Christ and are insulting the Spirit of Grace, and is worthy of greater punishment than those who rejected Moses and his law.

Hebrews 10: 29 Of how much worse punishment, do you suppose, will he be thought worthy who has trampled the Son of God underfoot, ***counted the blood of the covenant by which he was sanctified a common thing****, and insulted the Spirit of grace?*

In Hebrews 10, Paul teaches in detail that the old animal sacrifice is no longer acceptable to God and that only the blood of Jesus will cleanse our hearts and consciences from sin. He exhorts us in verse 23 to "hold fast to the confession of our hope without wavering." In other words, do not even think about going back to the old way of sacrifice because it is now willful sin to do so.

How dare anyone, no matter how sincere they are in their belief, even begin to think that God will be well pleased with any sacrifice for sin other than the blood of Jesus Christ? How dare they trample underfoot the blood of Jesus and count His precious blood a common thing by advocating animal sacrifice in order to expiate sin? Do they not understand this, or is this another example of protecting the system at all costs? It is unthinkable that Christians today, who have never been under the sacrificial or ceremonial law of the Old Covenant, who know the truth of the New Covenant in the blood of Jesus, would want to reestablish the Old Covenant, the temple and its sacrifices and subject others to it. There is no other sacrifice for sin remaining other than the blood of Jesus – not even for Jews.

This supposed scenario of the rule of the anti-christ and reestablished animal sacrifice in the rebuilt temple – howbeit for only three and a half years until he decides to put an end to the sacrifices - takes place in what is referred to as Daniel's Seventieth Week, which, according to the Dispensational, Pre-Tribulation system, has been separated from the other sixty nine weeks by over two thousand years as of this writing, although the context of the prophecy – and common sense - knows no such separation or gap or lack of continuity in the seventy weeks. This seventieth week is called the Time of Jacob's Trouble, or the Great Tribulation Period by those who adhere to this system of belief.

Instead of picking apart everything the Dispensational theory presents in this chapter, I will show that what God is doing is encouraging Daniel, and hence, those in captivity in His explanation of the seventy weeks. The Dispensational theory gives nothing but doom and gloom, foreboding and destruction, but God gives hope and encouragement to Daniel and to the children of Israel who were in Babylon. As is always the case, the context of the passage must be understood if we are to get to the meaning of it. The context is Daniel's prayer of confession of the sins of Judah and their release from captivity in Babylon.

The Broken Covenant

Before we examine this chapter, we must understand why Judah was in captivity in the first place. Why had God sent the Babylonians to take the Jews captive? The answer is found in 2 Chronicles 36.

*15 And the LORD God of their fathers sent warnings to them by His messengers, rising up early and sending them, because He had compassion on His people and on His dwelling place. 16 But they mocked the messengers of God, despised His words, and scoffed at His prophets, until the wrath of the LORD arose against His people, till there was no remedy. 17 Therefore He brought against them the king of the Chaldeans, who killed their young men with the sword in the house of their sanctuary, and had no compassion on young man or virgin, on the aged or the weak; He gave them all into his hand. 18 And all the articles from the house of God, great and small, the treasures of the house of the LORD, and the treasures of the king and of his leaders, all these he took to Babylon. 19 Then they burned the house of God, broke down the wall of Jerusalem, burned all its palaces with fire, and destroyed all its precious possessions. 20 And those who escaped from the sword he carried away to Babylon, where they became servants to him and his sons until the rule of the kingdom of Persia, 21 **to fulfill the word of the LORD by the mouth of Jeremiah, until the land had enjoyed her Sabbaths. As long as she lay desolate she kept Sabbath, to fulfill seventy years.***

The simple answer as to why the Jews were in captivity is so that the land of Israel could enjoy its Sabbath rest in accordance with the covenant God had with Israel. God has always had a covenantal relationship with His people. Under the Old Covenant, He fulfilled His part of the covenant and He required His people to fulfill their part. There were blessings to be enjoyed when the covenant was kept and consequences to be suffered when the covenant was broken.

When God gave the land to the children of Israel, among other requirements of His law was the command to give the land rest every seventh year. They were to work the land for six years, then on the seventh, let it rest. No planting. No farming it.

*Exodus 23: 10 "Six years you shall sow your land and gather in its produce, 11 but the **seventh year you shall let it rest** and lie fallow, that the poor of your people may eat; and what they leave, the beasts of the field may eat. In like manner you shall do with your vineyard and your olive grove. 12 Six days you shall do your work, and on the seventh day you shall rest, that your ox and your donkey may rest, and the son of your female servant and the stranger may be refreshed.*

It correlated with the Sabbath day each week that men were to enjoy for rest. Work six days, rest on the seventh. This is not hard to grasp. One would think that Israel would be more than willing to take a day off every week and a year off from farming every seven years. God said the land needed to rest for one year out of every seven. But, as is so often the case, man thought he knew better than God. Greed set in, and Israel refused to obey the covenant. Having an extra year of crops to sell became their way of life. Money became their god. They failed to trust God to provide for them as He promised to do if they would but obey Him. They just could not conceive that God was serious and would take action against them. After all, they were His chosen people. As 2 Chronicles 36 points out, God sent prophets and messengers to them to warn them of their disobedience and of consequences for their disobedience, but they refused to listen and "shot the messenger." They beat and killed the prophets and those who preached God's message.

Blessings for Obedience

God gave a very clear message to Israel in Leviticus 26.

2 You shall keep My Sabbaths and reverence My sanctuary: I am the LORD. 3 'If you walk in My statutes and keep My commandments, and perform them, 4 then I will give you rain in its season, the land shall yield its produce, and the trees of the field shall yield their fruit.

God lists many other blessings He would grant to them if they would but obey Him – abundant crops, safety in the land, peace in the land, no wild beasts, no fear, no enemies would attack them.

9 'For I will look on you favorably and make you fruitful, multiply you and confirm My covenant with you... 12 I will walk among you and be your God, and you shall be My people.

Sounds to me like a pretty good deal. Who would not want this kind of life? What else could possibly be more important to anyone than this? Having God Himself dwell among us and be our God and us be His very own people?

Consequences for Disobedience.

14 'But if you do not obey Me, and do not observe all these commandments, 15 and if you despise My statutes, or if your soul abhors My judgments, so that you do not perform all My commandments, but break My covenant, 16 I also will do this to you: I will even appoint terror over you, wasting disease and fever which shall consume the eyes and cause sorrow of heart. And you shall sow your seed in vain, for your enemies shall eat it. 17 I will set My face against you, and you shall be defeated by your enemies. Those who hate you shall reign over you, and you shall flee when no one pursues you.

God adds extreme consequences if they do not repent and conform to His covenant. This is so important to understand. If we do not grasp this, then we will not understand God's dealings with Israel. God lovingly warns His people of dire consequences for disobedience, just as He lovingly warns people today of eternal consequences for rejecting His Son, our Lord Jesus Christ. When people choose to disobey God, and to reject His offer of grace and salvation, choosing rather to live life their own way, thinking they know what is best for themselves rather than trusting their Creator, then they will suffer the dire consequences for willful disobedience. God has no other choice but to let their decision to disregard Him play out to its logical conclusion. Just as God allowed the Jews to willfully disobey Him in the Old Testament and to suffer the consequences, so He also allows people today to make choices as to obey Him or reject Him. Read and listen to the words of the Lord as He spells out to the Jews in the clearest of language what would happen if they disobeyed in these things.

18 'And after all this, if you do not obey Me, then I will punish you seven times more for your sins. 19 I will break the pride of your power; I will make your heavens like iron and your earth like bronze. 20 And your strength shall be spent in vain; for your land shall not yield its produce, nor shall the trees of the land yield their fruit. 21 'Then, if you walk contrary to Me, and are not willing to obey Me, I will bring on you seven times more plagues, according to your sins. 22 I will also send wild beasts among you, which shall rob you of your children, destroy your livestock, and make you few in number; and your highways shall be desolate. 23 'And if by these things you are not reformed by Me, but walk contrary to Me, 24 then I also will walk contrary to you, and I will punish you yet seven times for your sins. 25 And I will bring a sword against you that will execute the vengeance of the covenant; when you are gathered together within your cities I will send pestilence among you; and you shall be delivered into the hand of the enemy. 26 When I have cut off your supply of bread, ten women shall bake your bread in one oven, and they shall bring back your bread by weight, and you shall eat and not be satisfied.

After this warning, you would think that no one would disobey God, but would be more than willing to conform to His commands. But, God knew that they would not live in obedience to Him, so He gives them further warning.

*27 'And after all this, **if you do not obey Me**, but walk contrary to Me, 28 then **I also will walk contrary to you in fury**; and I, even I, will chastise you seven times for your sins. 29 You shall eat the flesh of your sons, and you shall eat the flesh of your daughters. 30 I will destroy your high places, cut down your incense altars, and cast your carcasses on the lifeless forms of your idols; and My **soul shall*** *abhor you. 31 I will lay your cities waste and bring your sanctuaries to desolation, and I will not smell the fragrance of your sweet aromas. 32 **I will bring the land to desolation**, and your enemies who dwell in it shall be astonished at it. 33 **I will scatter you among the nations** and draw out a sword after you; your land shall be desolate and your cities waste. 34 **Then the land shall enjoy its sabbaths** as long as it lies desolate and you are in your enemies' land; then the land shall rest and enjoy its sabbaths. 35 As long as it lies desolate it shall rest—**for the time it did not rest on your sabbaths when you dwelt in it.***

Here is God's word that He would bring Israel to desolation by having them taken captive by their enemies until all of the years that He was due for Sabbath was fulfilled. God's Sabbath was not to be neglected. If they did, it was at their own peril. It was His Sabbath and man did not have the right to make it his own, to do his own thing with it. Again, wouldn't you think that Israel would have been more than willing to live in compliance to God's covenant with them that they ratified at Mount Sinai and receive the promised blessings of obedience? They swore they would keep their word to Him. I can't for the life of me figure out what they were thinking when they decided that they knew better than God.

Not only did God warn the Jews in this passage in Leviticus what would happen if they failed to keep His Sabbaths, He warned them time and time again, especially by the mouth of Jeremiah as the time drew near that His anger with them was reaching the reaching the point of no remedy.

*2 Chronicles 36: 15 And the LORD God of their fathers sent warnings to them by His messengers, rising up early and sending them, because He had compassion on His people and on His dwelling place. 16 But they mocked the messengers of God, despised His words, and scoffed at His prophets, until **the wrath of the LORD arose against His people, till there was no remedy.***

Listen to Jeremiah's warnings to Judah.

*Jeremiah 25: 1 The word that came to Jeremiah concerning all the people of Judah, in the fourth year of Jehoiakim the son of Josiah, king of Judah (which was the first year of Nebuchadnezzar king of Babylon), 2 which Jeremiah the prophet spoke to all the people of Judah and to all the inhabitants of Jerusalem, saying: 3 "From the thirteenth year of Josiah the son of Amon, king of Judah, even to this day, this is the twenty-third year in which the word of the LORD has come to me; and **I have spoken** to you, rising early and speaking, but **you have not listened. 4 And the LORD has sent to you all His servants the prophets, rising early and sending them, but you have not listened nor inclined your ear to hear.** 5 They said, 'Repent now everyone of his evil way and his evil doings, and dwell in the land that the LORD has given to you and your fathers forever and ever. 6 Do not go after other gods to serve them and worship them, and do not provoke Me to anger with the works of your hands; and I will not harm you.' 7 Yet you have not listened to Me," says the LORD, "that you might provoke Me to anger with the works of your hands to your own hurt. 8 "Therefore thus says the LORD of hosts: 'Because you have not heard My words, 9 behold, I will send and take all the families of the north,' says the LORD, 'and Nebuchadnezzar the king of Babylon, My servant, and will bring them against this land, against its inhabitants, and against these nations all around, and will utterly destroy them, and make them an astonishment, a hissing, and perpetual desolations. 10 Moreover I will take from them the voice of mirth and the voice of gladness, the voice of the bridegroom and the voice of the bride, the sound of the millstones and the light of the lamp. 11 **And this whole land shall be a desolation and an astonishment, and these nations shall serve the king of Babylon seventy years.***

The captivity in Babylon was the fulfillment of God's promised "vengeance of the covenant" (Leviticus 26:25; see above). Those are frightening words, are they not? Yet, Israel had every opportunity to obey God and escape His vengeance. They chose their own way and suffered the vengeance of God for disobedience in their captivity and destruction of Jerusalem. One more time they would suffer God's vengeance (Luke 21:22 "these are the days of vengeance…") when Jerusalem would once again be leveled and Jews killed by the tens of thousands when the Romans attacked them in fulfillment of a portion of the very prophecy we are considering in this chapter.

Let's take a look at Daniel 9.

1 In the first year of Darius the son of Ahasuerus, of the lineage of the Medes, who was made king over the realm of the Chaldeans— 2 in the first year of his reign I, Daniel, understood by the books the number of the years specified by the word of the LORD through Jeremiah the prophet, that He would accomplish seventy years in the desolations of Jerusalem.

Daniel was reading in Jeremiah that Judah would serve the king of Babylon for seventy years, then be released from that captivity. He realized that the seventy years were completed, but he also realized that as a nation Judah had not confessed the sin that had caused their captivity to God (verse 13). Daniel humbled himself before God with fasting, sackcloth and ashes and began his prayer of confession.

Daniel's Prayer

3 Then I set my face toward the Lord God to make request by prayer and supplications, with fasting, sackcloth, and ashes. 4 And I prayed to the LORD my God, and made confession, and said, "O Lord, great and awesome God, who keeps His covenant and mercy with those who love Him, and with those who keep His commandments, 5 we have sinned and committed iniquity, we have done wickedly and rebelled, even by departing from Your precepts and Your judgments.

He immediately confesses that God is great and awesome and that He keeps His covenant with those who love Him and who keep His commandments which are contained in His covenant with them.

He knows that God has never broken His word with them and that all of His promises are merciful. He then confesses that Judah was entirely at fault in the situation and circumstances that they were in. They had sinned and committed iniquity. They had done wickedly and had rebelled against God by rejecting His covenant and His commandments. They deserved the punishment they had received.

6 Neither have we heeded Your servants the prophets, who spoke in Your name to our kings and our princes, to our fathers and all the people of the land. 7 O Lord, righteousness belongs to You, but to us shame of face, as it is this day—to the men of Judah, to the inhabitants of Jerusalem and all Israel, those near and those far off in all the countries to which You have driven them, because of the unfaithfulness which they have committed against You. 8 "O Lord, to us belongs shame of face, to our kings, our princes, and our fathers, because we have sinned against You. 9 To the Lord our God belong mercy and forgiveness, though we have rebelled against Him. 10 We have not obeyed the voice of the LORD our God, to walk in His laws, which He set before us by His servants the prophets.

He confesses that Judah had rejected the word of the Lord that the prophets had spoken to them. Kings, princes, leaders, and all the people had not listened to the warnings to repent, and because of that, they deserved the shame they were enduring because of their unfaithfulness to God and His covenant. They deserved the shameful treatment by the Babylonians because of their rebellion and sin against God and His commands. The Babylonians were not to be blamed, and God certainly was righteous in His actions toward them. They were entirely to blame for their own punishment.

11 Yes, all Israel has transgressed Your law, and has departed so as not to obey Your voice; therefore the curse and the oath written in the Law of Moses the servant of God have been poured out on us, because we have sinned against Him. 12 And He has confirmed His words, which He spoke against us and against our judges who judged us, by bringing upon us a great disaster; for under the whole heaven such has never been done as what has been done to Jerusalem. 13

"As it is written in the Law of Moses, all this disaster has come upon us; yet we have not made our prayer before the LORD our God, that we might turn from our iniquities and understand Your truth. 14 Therefore the LORD has kept the disaster in mind, and brought it upon us; for the LORD our God is righteous in all the works which He does, though we have not obeyed His voice.

Daniel confesses that they had been warned in the law of Moses that should they choose to disobey God that disaster would come upon them, this very disaster. And furthermore, the nation had not confessed their sin to God until this point. God is righteous in everything that He has done to us. We are to blame.

15 And now, O Lord our God, who brought Your people out of the land of Egypt with a mighty hand, and made Yourself a name, as it is this day—we have sinned, we have done wickedly! 16 "O Lord, according to all Your righteousness, I pray, let Your anger and Your fury be turned away from Your city Jerusalem, Your holy mountain; because for our sins, and for the iniquities of our fathers, Jerusalem and Your people are a reproach to all those around us. 17 Now therefore, our God, hear the prayer of Your servant, and his supplications, and for the Lord's sake cause Your face to shine on Your sanctuary, which is desolate. 18 O my God, incline Your ear and hear; open Your eyes and see our desolations, and the city which is called by Your name; for we do not present our supplications before You because of our righteous deeds, but because of Your great mercies. 19 O Lord, hear! O Lord, forgive! O Lord, listen and act! Do not delay for Your own sake, my God, for Your city and Your people are called by Your name."

He continues his prayer of confession by acknowledging the Lord's goodness to them in bringing them out of Egypt, then asks that He turn His fury away from them and from Jerusalem, confessing once again that it was for their sin that He punished them. He pleads with God to open His ears to His prayer and open His eyes to see their desolate condition and the desolation of Jerusalem, not because of their righteousness, but because of His great mercies. He begs

God to answer his prayer for forgiveness and not to delay. God must act for His own sake, for His name's sake, for His own glory because of His promise to keep the captivity for seventy years, which was now complete.

There is no disagreement among anyone as to these first nineteen verses. Everyone realizes that Daniel was confessing the sin of Judah and asking God for forgiveness and speedy action for their release from captivity.

20 Now while I was speaking, praying, and confessing my sin and the sin of my people Israel, and presenting my supplication before the LORD my God for the holy mountain of my God, 21 yes, while I was speaking in prayer, the man Gabriel, whom I had seen in the vision at the beginning, being caused to fly swiftly, reached me about the time of the evening offering. 22 And he informed me, and talked with me, and said, "O Daniel, I have now come forth to give you skill to understand. 23 At the beginning of your supplications the command went out, and I have come to tell you, for you are greatly beloved; therefore consider the matter, and understand the vision:

God's Answer

As Daniel was praying Gabriel reached him about the time of the evening prayers and began to speak to him. He told Daniel that God had sent him to him because God greatly loved him and wanted to give him understanding of the things that concerned him and of the vision he was about to reveal to him.

It is the next four verses that have caused much disagreement among God's people. The reason for the disagreement is that the prophecy of the seventy weeks and the activities that are described by Gabriel have been misinterpreted by some – and I believe that the originators of Dispensationalism did so deliberately - in order to squeeze them into their new system of belief, their "new revelation." I say that with absolute assurance of being correct, not arrogantly, but because of what the passage is really saying.

I must also admit that those today who have been taught the Pre-Tribulation "rapture" theory and Dispensationalism believe it honestly. There is no intent on their part to deceive others or to be deceived in their belief. They just have not taken the time to study what the Bible is really teaching. Yes, they have studied the Bible, but they have been conditioned only to see what they have been taught previously and taught not to question it. I was there once; I know how it all works. If they have read any literature on opposing points of view, it is literature that has been written in a negative context by those espousing pro "rapture" teachings. It is much easier to believe what has been taught by others than it is to dig out truth yourself. Besides, making waves can be dangerous to your reputation and standing in certain churches. Not everyone, of course, but a great majority fall into this category.

It is similar to political ads. If all you hear is the Democrats tell you what the Republicans are all about, and you never hear the Republicans tell you what they believe, then everything you think you know about the Republicans will be negative and you will believe the worst about them. The same is true in this case. If all you read about the Second Coming is from the pen of those who teach the Pre-Tribulation "rapture", if they tell you what others who do not believe their way teach, then it will all be negative, and in many, if not all cases, will not be the truth.

The Seventy-Weeks Prophecy

24 "Seventy weeks are determined for your people and for your holy city, to finish the transgression, to make an end of sins, to make reconciliation for iniquity, to bring in everlasting righteousness, to seal up vision and prophecy, and to anoint the Most Holy. 25 "Know therefore and understand, that from the going forth of the command to restore and build Jerusalem until Messiah the Prince, there shall be seven weeks and sixty-two weeks; The street shall be built again, and the wall, even in troublesome times. 26 "And after the sixty-two weeks Messiah shall be cut off, but not for Himself; And the people of the prince who is to come shall destroy the city and the sanctuary. The end of it shall be with a flood, and till the end of the war desolations are determined. 27 Then he shall confirm a covenant with many for one week; But in the middle of the week He shall bring an end to sacrifice and offering. And on the wing of abominations shall be one who makes desolate, even until the consummation, which is determined, is poured out on the desolate."

Now, keeping in mind the context of Daniel's prayer, which is his confession of the Jew's sin of breaking God's covenant and of their utter contempt for His commands and of the just punishment they had received, and for forgiveness of those sins, it makes the interpretation of these four verses much easier to understand. God was well pleased with Daniel's prayer and confession, and immediately He dispatched Gabriel with the **answer to his prayer**. Gabriel immediately lets Daniel know that he is greatly loved by God and that God desires for him to have the answer that he seeks.

God is pleased when men pray. He loves to answer prayer, as so many passages of Scripture show. Daniel 9 is a great example of answered prayer. But, there is another important principle here, and that is that God answers prayer which is according to His Word. God loves to have us pray His Word. When we know God's Word, and pray according to it, He is pleased and must answer our prayer. We wonder sometimes why our prayers go unanswered. It is because we are not praying according to God's will, which is revealed in His Word. We must know His Word in order to pray properly.

Daniel prayed according to what he knew Scripture revealed. He knew the requirements of the covenant, that the Jews had forsaken their God and had rebelled against His commands. He knew that Jeremiah had foretold the desolation of Jerusalem and their captivity and subsequent release after seventy years. He was a man who understood Scripture and the power of prayer that was according to Scripture.

Daniel's concern was for God's glory to be manifest in the restoration of Jerusalem and the forgiveness of the Jews that were in captivity which God had promised to fulfill by the mouth of Jeremiah. God's glory depended on Him keeping His promise to restore Jerusalem. God had promised, so Daniel had absolute confidence that He would do as He had spoken. His confidence was anchored in God's great mercies that were based in His character, not in their actions. God now explains to Daniel through Gabriel exactly the steps He would take to fulfill His word.

He begins his explanation by stating that seventy weeks had been determined, or marked out, settled upon by God for the Jews and for Jerusalem. No commentator disagrees on the fact that the seventy weeks are seventy weeks of years, or seventy sevens, or 490 years no matter how they interpret the rest of the passage. But, for those who may not understand how seventy weeks can mean 490 years, I'll explain.

The context of the captivity was failure to keep God's Sabbath years, or one year out of each seven. For 490 years, the Jews had failed to keep the covenant of Sabbath years, so therefore, they must spend seventy years in captivity so the land could enjoy its God ordained rest, one year for each of the years they had neglected to keep. God uses the word "week" in this passage, which is translated as "seven" (seven, period of seven (days or years), heptad, week. Strong's Concordance #7620). In this context, it certainly means years as opposed to days. Seventy weeks of years. This principle of a year for a day is set forth in Numbers 14 when Israel refused to enter the Promised Land because of fear, and God punished them by making them wander in the wilderness for forty years, a year for each day that the land was spied out.

Numbers 14: 34 According to the number of the days in which you spied out the land, forty days, for each day you shall bear your guilt one year, *namely* forty years, and you shall know My rejection.

So, seventy weeks of years, 490 years had been marked out by God in order to deal with the Jews and Jerusalem. What God is going to do during those 490 years is exactly what Daniel prayed for – to restore Jerusalem, to grant reconciliation to the Jews and to provide forgiveness for their sins.

Before we discuss how God will bring about reconciliation and forgiveness, let's look a little closer at these seventy weeks and the divisions that are evident there, and one division that is expounded by Dispensationalists that is definitely not there. We are skipping over the rest of verse 24 for the time being and going to verses 25 and 26.

Gabriel tells Daniel that there will be a command given to restore and build Jerusalem. Beginning with that command there would be seven weeks and sixty two weeks until Messiah the Prince. There would be a group of 49 years and another group of 434 years, or a total of 483 years. At the end of those 483 years, Messiah would be recognized – "until Messiah the Prince." The appearance of the Messiah starts the seventieth week, which we will look at shortly. This is an exact prophecy as to when the Messiah would appear on the scene. The scribes, Pharisees, priests and other rulers in Jerusalem had absolutely no excuse for not recognizing Jesus when He appeared and began to preach the gospel and work miracles.

Gabriel breaks these 483 years into two groups, one of 49 years and another of 434 years. Why? In order to mark events that would take place during that time. These were 483 consecutive years, no separations or gaps in this time, and not even the Dispensationalists teach that there was. It was during the first 49 years that the Jerusalem was restored and rebuilt. It took exactly 49 years from the time Cyrus gave the command to rebuild Jerusalem and to release the captivity that the city was rebuilt.

The prophecy that Cyrus would give the command to restore and rebuild Jerusalem is found in Isaiah 45.

Isaiah 45: 1 "Thus says the LORD to His anointed, to Cyrus, whose right hand I have held...13 I have raised him up in righteousness, and I will direct all his ways; He shall build My city and let My exiles go free,

The fulfillment of Isaiah's prophecy is found in Ezra.

Ezra 1: 1 Now in the first year of Cyrus king of Persia, that the word of the LORD by the mouth of Jeremiah might be fulfilled, the LORD stirred up the spirit of Cyrus king of Persia, so that he made a proclamation throughout all his kingdom, and also put it in writing, saying, 2 Thus says Cyrus king of Persia: All the kingdoms of the earth the LORD God of heaven has given me. And He has commanded me to build Him a house at Jerusalem which is in Judah. 3 Who is among you of all His people? May his God be with him, and let him go up to Jerusalem which is in Judah, and build the house of the LORD God of Israel (He is God), which is in Jerusalem.

To use the expression that so many have used concerning this prophecy, God's "prophetic clock" began ticking when this command was issued. It would tick for 490 consecutive years – no gaps or separations or stoppage of prophetic time during those years.

It took 49 years for the completion of the rebuilding of Jerusalem. Gabriel told Daniel that the city would be rebuilt in "troublesome times." The Jews met with violent opposition. In Ezra and Nehemiah we read how their enemies opposed them with deceit and violence. They had to build with tools in one hand and a sword in the other. When the city was rebuilt, it was at the end of the "seven weeks," the first 49 years. That is the event that marks the first division as stated by Gabriel.

Then immediately, the sixty two weeks began. This began the four hundred silent years between the Old and the New Testaments. The only events recorded in Scripture pertaining to this time period between the completion of the rebuilding of Jerusalem and the appearance of Jesus as the Messiah are the events surrounding His birth and His brief appearance at age twelve.

At the end of the sixty two week segment, the third segment of the prophecy, the seventieth week began immediately. So says Gabriel. He plainly says that **AFTER** the sixty two weeks - that was inseparably connected to the seven weeks - some important events would take place. We will cover them all, but the one that inseparably connects the seventieth week to the other sixty nine weeks is what he says happens to the Messiah. He is cut off. The Messiah is crucified. In the ***middle*** of the seventieth week. *(I'll explain this shortly. Although the middle of the week is mentioned in relation to making an end of sacrifice and offering, it is connected to His being cut off.)* After the sixty two weeks which is after the seven weeks. He is cut off – crucified - after He is anointed as the Messiah by His Father and recognized as such by the Jews during the course of His public ministry, and especially at the Triumphal Entry into Jerusalem when He was proclaimed as Messiah by the public.

Why am I emphasizing the fact that all of the seventy weeks are connected to each other? If you are familiar with the Dispensational, Pre-Tribulation "rapture" theory, then you know why. If you are not familiar with it, then I will explain what they teach regarding the seventieth week. Their teaching regarding the seventieth week of Daniel is that it has been separated from the other sixty nine weeks by over two thousand years as of this writing. There is a "gap" between week sixty nine and week seventy.

What is the basis for thinking that there is a gap of some 2000+ years between the sixty ninth week and the seventieth week? Logic or common sense certainly does not dictate that. Seventy follows sixty nine immediately. There are not some 2000 numbers between the two. Saying that there is an extended gap between the sixty ninth week and the seventieth week is tantamount to saying the following. Suppose I'm a mechanic working on your vehicle. I tell you that it will take me eight hours to do a certain repair. If I begin the work at eight in the morning, when will you expect to have your car returned to you? At four in the afternoon, or five if I take an hour for lunch. But, suppose when you return to pick up your car at four in the afternoon, I tell you, "No. No. You didn't understand me. I did not tell you that your car would be ready at four o'clock. I told you that it would take me eight hours to repair it. I have worked on it for seven hours, but all this other work has come into the shop and I have to do it first. I have put aside your job – indefinitely – so I can do other things. You cannot have the car back until the eighth hour has been completed. There will be an extended gap between the seventh hour and the eighth hour. I may finish next week or next month, maybe next year, or ten years from now. But, it will only take me eight hours to finish." What would you think of that? How much confidence would you have in me as your mechanic? Would I be lying on the floor of the garage with your fist along side of my head? How logical is my explanation of why your car is not ready to you? Well, how much confidence should you have in some Bible teacher who tells you that the seventieth week does not follow the sixty ninth week immediately, but there are several thousand weeks in between the two?

Or, here is another illustration. I live in Naples, FL. Suppose I want to drive to Miami which is 110 miles from here. I get in my car and begin to drive. I drive for 109 miles, one mile from my destination, and my odometer all of a sudden stops. There is a detour sign pointing north on interstate 95. I drive north until I get to Jacksonville, where the detour sign is pointing west on interstate 10. I turn left and drive for another 100 miles until I see interstate 75 with the detour sign pointing north again. So I turn right onto 75 and go north up through several states until I get to Michigan where I am directed to go east across Ohio, Pennsylvania, and New Jersey where I am directed south again through Delaware, Maryland, Virginia, North Carolina, South Carolina, Georgia, and finally back into Florida where I am sent down interstate 95 again. All this time my odometer is not registering any mileage. It is still stopped.

I get to within one mile of Miami and all of a sudden my odometer begins to move again. See? It was only 110 miles to Miami. The other mileage was inserted into the 110 miles, but it really didn't count. There was a "parenthesis", a "gap" between mile 109 and mile 110.

If I – or anyone else – gave you these two scenarios as facts and expected you to believe them – and got angry with you for not believing them – what would you do? You would probably be calling the men in white coats. But, this is *exactly* what Dispensationalists and Pre-Tribulation "rapture" advocates would have us believe concerning the seventy weeks. God just stopped counting time at week sixty nine, inserted 2000 plus years that really do not count at all in God's economy, then He will begin counting time again at some future date when He snatches away those of us who have made up the "parenthesis." Are thinking people really expected to believe this?

God does not play around with His Word and His words. He means exactly what He says. He is not in the habit of deceiving His people with words that do not mean what they say. When He says seventy weeks, He means seventy consecutive weeks. He inserts no gaps or postponements into them. He is totally reliable in what He says. He is not trying to fool us with word games. This is not a riddle or a scrambled word puzzle that we have to figure out.

So, how did these Bible…scholars??? Darby, Schofield, etc., get so twisted in their interpretation of Scripture, in particular, Daniel chapter 9, and insert a 2000 year gap into it? Some people think that it is because the seventieth week is not mentioned until 9:27. This verse follows the prophecy of the destruction of the Temple.

Therefore, according to their logic – or illogic - the seventieth week is to be separated from the other sixty nine weeks. They take the words that Gabriel spoke – in the order that he spoke them - and make that the chronological order in which they are to be fulfilled, much in the same way they interpret Revelation. But, that is not how this passage is to be interpreted. Or Revelation.

Another mistake they make is in understanding grammar. They take the "he" of verse 27 – "and 'he' shall confirm a covenant with many for one week" – and apply "he" to the "prince" in verse 26 - "the people of the prince who is to come."

Since verse 27 sequentially follows the prophecy of the destruction of Jerusalem in verse 26, which destruction occurred in 70 AD, and since the destruction of Jerusalem was done by the "people of the prince who is to come" mentioned in verse 26, then the "prince" must be the anti-christ of Ribera's invention, and must be the "he" of verse 27, who confirms the covenant with the Jews. Complicated, isn't it?

There are several problems with this interpretation. This is not a prophecy of an ***anti***-christ, it is a prophecy of Jesus, ***THE Christ. The Prince. The Savior. The Messiah.*** Where is there an anti-christ mentioned or even assumed in this passage? Where? There must be a noun somewhere in this passage that explicitly states an anti-christ - or at least even vaguely refers to one - in order to make the "he" refer to an anti-christ — but there is not. The anti-christ has been forced into this passage. Whoever did this gets an F in grammar. He fails the course. He has to repeat it until he gets it right. The grammatical problem is with assigning the pronoun "he" to "the prince." Before I explain this, I believe with all my heart that the Godly men who translated the Word of God into English, specifically the KJV, understood English grammar and knew exactly how to write it so it would preserve the meaning of the original, which they also understood perfectly.

Many Dispensationalists and Pre-Tribulation "rapture" advocates are also KJV 1611 enthusiasts. They believe that KJV 1611 is the only inspired English translation of the Word of God. Yet, if they are Dispensationalists, when it comes to believing what Daniel 9 is teaching, and the rules of grammar that must be followed, somehow the translators got it wrong. If we believe that the translators got it right, which I personally do, then we cannot believe that "he" refers to anyone other than the Messiah.

The translators knew what they were writing. They knew just how to translate it perfectly. They were experts in grammar. English grammar does not allow for a personal pronoun to have as its antecedent the object of a modifying clause. The phrase "of the prince" is a modifying clause, and "prince" is the object of it. "Prince" cannot grammatically be the antecedent of "he." Do you remember this from English grammar class in high school or college? The antecedent of "he" is "Messiah"; it is the *only* possible antecedent. The translators got it right; Darby and Schofield and company got it wrong.

Also, the word "Prince" is already used in this passage to refer to the Messiah. In verse 25 Jesus is called "Messiah the Prince." Why would the same word "prince" in verse 26 refer to someone else, an anti-christ, especially when there is no mention of him, not even a hint in this passage that there even is an anti-christ? Well, it wouldn't and it doesn't. It is the same word used in both verses, and it is applied to the Messiah. The subject of the prophecy is the Messiah.

What I fear Dispensationalists have forgotten is that all prophecy is about Jesus. In Luke 24: 25 – 27, Jesus Christ emphatically declares that **all** of the Old Testament writings point to Him

*25 Then He said to them, "**O foolish ones, and slow of heart to believe in ALL that the prophets have spoken!** (pay attention Dispensationalists) 26 Ought not the Christ to have suffered these things and to enter into His glory?" 27 And beginning at Moses and all the Prophets, He expounded to them in **ALL the Scriptures the things concerning Himself.***

*Then in verse 44 Then He said to them, "These are the words which I spoke to you while I was still with you, that **all things must be fulfilled** which were written in the Law of Moses and the **Prophets and the Psalms concerning Me."***

This includes Daniel chapter 9. This prophecy is about Jesus and His redemptive work on Calvary. Bear in mind the reason Daniel was praying. Peter gives further evidence that the "Prince" is none other than Jesus, the Messiah.

*Acts 5: 31 Him God has exalted to His right hand to be **Prince** and Savior, to give **repentance** to Israel and **forgiveness** of sins.*

Peter calls Jesus "Prince", the identical phrase used by Gabriel to describe Him in Daniel 9. He is the Savior, the One who grants repentance to Israel – one of the reasons for Daniel's prayer – and forgiveness of sins - another objective of his prayer. Peter is acknowledging the fulfillment of Daniel's prayer and the prophecy of the seventy weeks by using the identical words of Daniel chapter 9. Jesus is the One to whom all prophecy points, not some anti-christ.

Now, verse 26 states the "people of the prince who is to come" will "destroy the city and the sanctuary." That doesn't sound like something the Messiah would do, does it? Just who are these "people" of this Prince, this Messiah, and why would they destroy Jerusalem and the temple?

This is something that Jesus foretold on a couple of occasions. Because they rejected Jesus, the Jews would suffer the wrath of God on themselves and their city. As Jesus was speaking to the multitude, He scathingly denounced the scribes and Pharisees in Matthew 23. At the end of that pronouncement, He had this to say beginning in verse 34.

*34 Therefore, indeed, I send you prophets, wise men, and scribes: some of them you will kill and crucify, and some of them you will scourge in your synagogues and persecute from city to city, 35 that on you may come all the righteous blood shed on the earth, from the blood of righteous Abel to the blood of Zechariah, son of Berechiah, whom you murdered between the temple and the altar. 36 Assuredly, I say to you, **all these things will come upon this generation**. 37 "O Jerusalem, Jerusalem, the one who kills the prophets and stones those who are sent to her! How often I wanted to gather your chil-*

dren together, as a hen gathers her chicks under her wings, but you were not willing! 38 **See! Your house is left to you desolate.**

In chapter 24: 15 *"Therefore when you see the 'abomination of desolation,' spoken of by Daniel the prophet, standing in the holy place"*

Luke 21: 20 "But when you see Jerusalem surrounded by armies, then know that its desolation is near.

Jesus, without equivocation, says that when Jerusalem was surrounded by the Roman armies that that event was the "abomination of desolation." Jesus Himself says that Daniel's prophecy of the "abomination of desolation" was the destruction of Jerusalem in 70 AD, not some future event 2000 years in the future by some "anti-christ" who sits in the rebuilt temple and makes himself out to be a god. Jesus states that all the things He mentioned in His Olivet Discourse would "come upon this generation."

Dispensationalists, in an attempt to protect their system, feebly force a meaning into the word "generation" that no one reading it – without being indoctrinated differently - would understand it to mean. They try to make "generation" mean "a race of people", namely the Jews, but the Bible defines generation as forty years (Numbers 32: 13). The context demands this interpretation, not a race or nation. Indeed, the destruction of Jerusalem occurred approximately forty years after the Lord spoke these words.

Jesus warns them that the "abomination of desolation" that Daniel foretold would happen to many of those who were alive at that time. The generation that was alive at that very moment. Indeed, did they not cry out to Pilate "His blood be upon us and our children"? Did not the Lord prophecy in Matthew 23: 35 "that on you may come all the righteous blood shed on the earth"?

When Titus besieged Jerusalem and utterly destroyed the temple and the city, it was left completely desolate – not one stone was left upon another - and it was the fulfillment of Daniel's prophecy and the prophecy of Jesus. This has been the traditional view through the centuries. John Calvin wrote regarding this that the prophecy of the "profanation of the Temple, without the slightest doubt, was fulfilled when the city of Jerusalem was captured and overthrown, and the Temple utterly destroyed by Titus the son of Vespasian." Josephus, the Jewish historian, also applied Daniel 9:27 to the AD 70 destruction of Jerusalem in his writings.

The Roman army is "the people" of the "Prince" - Jesus, the Messiah – who was yet "to come" at the time of the prophecy in Daniel. The Romans were used by God to bring judgment on the unbelieving Jews who had rejected Jesus and screamed out for His crucifixion. God had used a foreign army before to destroy the temple and Jerusalem, the Babylonian army, the Chaldeans, because of the failure of the Jews to keep God's covenant, as we have seen. Both times God gave ample warning, and both times His warnings were rejected. Both times the messengers were killed. Both times it was the armies of God who were sent against Jerusalem and the unbelieving Jews. Both times there was massive blood shed and destruction.

The destruction of Jerusalem was "with a flood." The Romans swept through the city and completely destroyed everything in their path. Josephus is very graphic in his description of the destruction of Jerusalem. Josephus, in describing it, uses almost the very words of our Savior in Matthew 24. Here is a partial quote from him.

All the calamities which had befallen any nation from the beginning of the world, were but small in comparison with those of the Jews. (Jewish Wars, book i., preface, 4.)

He has given the following account of one part of the massacre when the city was taken: "And now rushing into the city, they slew whomsoever they found, without distinction, and burnt the houses and all the people who had fled into them. And when they entered for the sake of plunder, they found whole families of dead persons, and houses full of carcasses destroyed by famine; then they came out with their hands empty. And though they thus pitied the dead, they had not the same emotion for the living, but killed all they met, whereby they filled the lanes with dead bodies. *The whole city ran with blood*, insomuch that many things which were burning were extinguished by the blood." (Jewish Wars, book vi. chap. 8, 5; chap. 9, 2, 3.)

He adds, that in the siege of Jerusalem, not fewer than *eleven hundred thousand* perished (Jewish Wars, book vi., chap. 9, 3). In the adjacent provinces no fewer than *two hundred and fifty thousand* are reckoned to have been slain; making in all whose deaths were ascertained, the almost incredible number of *one million three hundred and fifty thousand*, who were put to death. These were not indeed all slain with the sword. Many were crucified. "Many hundreds," says he, (Jewish Wars, book vi. Chap. xi Chap. xi. 1) "were first whipped, then tormented with various kinds of tortures, and finally crucified: the Roman soldiers nailing them (out of the wrath and hatred they bore to the Jews) one after one way, and another after another, to crosses, *by way of jest*, until at length the multitude became so great that room was wanting for crosses, and crosses for the bodies." So terribly was their imprecation fulfilled —" His blood be on us, and on our children," (Matthew 27:25). If it be asked how it was possible for so many people to be slain in a single city, it is answered, that the siege of Jerusalem commenced during the time of the Passover, it is estimated that more than three millions were usually assembled. (Josephus, Jewish Wars, book vi., chap. ix., 3, 4.)

The prophecy is extremely graphic in that it reiterates, using several different phrases, the complete destruction that God had determined upon Jerusalem in retribution for the crucifixion of His Son, even before the actual crucifixion of Jesus, approximately 486 years before it happened. The destruction would be with a flood, a massive amount of Romans pushing their way through the city and destroying it like the flood destroyed the old world. Nothing could stop them. The desolation would be "on the wing of abominations." The Romans would be rapid in their destruction. They would seem to be flying through the city with strength and complete mobility so nothing could even slow them down. They would do so "even until the consummation", until the end, until the utter destruction had been accomplished. And this destruction had been "determined" by God. It was certain. It was sure. It would occur according to God's determined will. All of the destructive fury of an angry God, using His army, would be "poured out on the desolate."

Indeed, Jerusalem and the Jews were desolate. They were stunned, stupefied, utterly amazed that this complete destruction could possibly happen to them. They were immobilized. They could not retaliate. They could not escape the devastation. Only those who heeded the words of Jesus in His warnings of the Olivet Discourse escaped the destruction. No one else thought it even possible. They mocked the warnings. Derided the messengers sent from the Lord. Killed many of them. Tortured others. Threw them to lions. Made sport of their deaths. They laughed and cheered as they died. All the while not giving a second - or first - thought of the desolation that was rapidly approaching them and would destroy them, their city, their temple, their religion, and their way of life.

The destruction of Jerusalem took place after the completion of the seventieth week, in 70 AD. That is a historical fact. It is not a yet future destruction that is in view, even though the placement of the words within the prophecy are not in chronological order. This is easy enough to ascertain when we study what Gabriel states will occur with reference to the Messiah who comes **AFTER**, not in, during or at the end of the sixty ninth week, as Dispensationalists claim.

So, what is prophesied to occur in the seventieth week?

The first thing (in chronological order, not in the order that it was spoken) that is prophesied to occur is the anointing of the Most Holy. There were many people who knew the seventy weeks prophecy and were expecting the appearance of the Messiah as the time drew closer. When John came baptizing there were many who wondered whether he were the Christ, or not. (Luke 3:15). John confessed that he was not the Christ (John 1:20), but was sent to prepare the way for Him. Then right at the exact time that was prophesied - 483 years from the time that the command to rebuild Jerusalem and for the Jews to be released from Babylon and at the beginning of the 484th year, the seventieth week - Jesus came to John and was baptized. The Holy Spirit in the form of a dove descended upon Him. The "Most Holy" was anointed with the Holy Spirit in order to begin his public ministry as the "anointed one" of God, the Messiah, the Christ. The prophecy was fulfilled to the very year. Jesus, in evident reference to the time prophesied in Daniel, said in Mark 1:15, "The time is fulfilled."

When Jesus entered the synagogue of Nazareth He announced in Luke 4: 18 "The Spirit of the LORD is upon Me, because He has **anointed** Me to preach the gospel to the poor; He has sent Me to heal the brokenhearted, to proclaim liberty to the captives and recovery of sight to the blind, to set at liberty those who are oppressed; 19 To proclaim the acceptable year of the LORD."... 21 And He began to say to them, *"Today this Scripture is fulfilled in your hearing."*

In Acts 10:38, Peter mentioned *"how God **anointed** Jesus of Nazareth with the Holy Ghost... who went about doing good, healing all who were oppressed of the devil."*

Dispensationalists have a wrong interpretation of this anointing of the Most Holy. They interpret this anointing as the rebuilding of the Temple and reinstitution of animal sacrifice, which, as we have pointed out, according to Hebrews, will never happen – at least not in fulfillment of Biblical prophecy. It may happen by force of human will (I don't believe even that will happen), but not because God is demanding it and has changed His mind on accepting animal sacrifice again. The entire prophecy of Daniel 9 deals with the coming Messiah, the Prince, so this prophecy refers to the anointing of Jesus Christ – the Antitype of the temple in Jerusalem and all the sacrifices. This anointing of Jesus, the Messiah, according to Matthew 3:16-17, occurred at the beginning of Christ's ministry. At this time He was baptized, and anointed by the Holy Spirit to carry out His Messianic task as Prophet, Priest, and King.

The next event, in chronological order, is that the Messiah would be "cut off." He would be killed, but "not for Himself." This is an obvious prophecy of the crucifixion of our Lord Jesus Christ. It can hold no other meaning. Again, it is important to know when His crucifixion was to occur. **AFTER** the sixty ninth week. That can only be within the seventieth week. It can mean nothing else but that. If Jesus was crucified in the middle of the seventieth week, as Gabriel says, then how in the name of logic can the seventieth week be separated from the other sixty nine by any length of time, much less over two thousand years? This entire idea of a separated seventieth week would be laughable if the same illogic were applied to any other situation. But, there are so many who just cannot see the insanity of such a teaching – because they were taught it, so it must be true. Where in the context is a "gap" demanded? Where? Not there, is it?

Yet, Dispensationalists and those who hold to the Pre-Tribulation "rapture" – all of them are supposedly wonderful Bible teachers with great insight never before known in the history of the church - in an effort to apply the 70th week to an antichrist - say that Christ was cut off within the 69th week, not after it as the Bible says, and that the seventieth week is yet future. They attempt – although it is a futile attempt at best - to teach something that is both inconsistent with their supposedly "literal hermeneutic" and is utterly impossible - that the word "after" does not mean after. To them it means "at the end of" or "during." It is upon this false definition of a word, this neglect of or refusal to accept its "literal" meaning, that a whole nonsensical system of prophetic interpretation has been built.

Messiah was to be cut off **AFTER** 69 weeks, that is, during the 70th week. The crucifixion of Christ took place during the seventieth week. Absolutely no other conclusion can be drawn from the passage. No one, not Darby, Schofield, or anyone else can logically or Scripturally make the seventieth week refer to some future time. Jesus was crucified during the seventieth week.

When exactly during the seventieth week did the prophecy say Messiah would be cut off? "**AFTER** sixty nine weeks – seven plus sixty two - shall Messiah be cut off. And "he (Messiah) shall confirm the covenant with many for one week" - the seventieth week, the only week remaining. "and in the midst of the week" - in the middle of seven years - "he shall cause the sacrifices and oblation to cease."

According to this then, Christ was to confirm (to prevail, have strength, be strong, be powerful, be mighty, be great - Strong's Concordance Hebrew #1396) the covenant - the New Covenant in His blood – the New Covenant of Jeremiah 31: 31 - during the final seven years of the prophecy.

*Jeremiah 31: 31 "Behold, the days are coming, says the LORD, when I will make a **new covenant with the house of Israel and with the house of Judah**—*

Jeremiah says that a new covenant would be made between God and Israel. This new covenant, Jesus said, was "in His blood." His blood made the New Covenant unbreakable, powerful, mighty to the point that it would "cleanse the conscience." No blood offered before to God could do so. Is anyone in doubt as to the strength, the covenant confirming power, of the blood of Jesus?

When Jesus instituted the Lord's supper, representative of his shed blood for the remission of sins, he said, "This is my blood of the new Testament, which is shed for many for the remission of sins" (Matthew 26:28). The word testament means covenant, and is often translated that way.

Jesus is called the "mediator of the new covenant" (Heb. 8:6), the "messenger of the covenant" (Malachi 3:1), and his shed blood is called "the blood of the everlasting covenant" (Heb. 12:24). When He confirmed the New Covenant, He gave it the strength of an "everlasting covenant." No one could ever break it. Make no mistake about it. Our Lord Jesus is truly the one who through His redemptive sacrifice at Calvary confirmed the covenant. And this harmonizes to perfection with what we have already seen.

*Hebrews 9: 13 For if the blood of bulls and goats and the ashes of a heifer, sprinkling the unclean, sanctifies for the purifying of the flesh, 14 how much more shall the blood of Christ, who through the eternal Spirit offered Himself without spot to God, **cleanse your conscience** from dead works to serve the living God? 15 And for this reason He is the Mediator of the **new covenant, by means of death**, for the redemption of the transgressions under the first covenant, that those who are called may receive the promise of the eternal inheritance.*

The confirmation of the covenant is to be with many - those who humble themselves and come to Jesus, receiving Him as their Lord and Savior – Jew or Gentile. They are the recipients of the benefits of the New Covenant, the washing of regeneration, the forgiveness of sins, eternal life, becoming joint-heirs with Christ, being a partaker of the divine nature, knowing God and His Son.

Jesus was to be crucified in the middle of the seven years - that is, at the completion of three and a half years of ministry - and at that time he would cause sacrifices to cease. The crucifixion of Jesus ended all sacrifice for sin. No other sacrifice will ever again be offered for sins. Sacrifice for sins has ended - forever.

*Hebrews 10: 12 But this Man, after He had **offered one sacrifice for sins forever, sat down** at the right hand of God, 13 from that time waiting till His enemies are made His footstool. 14 For by one offering He has perfected forever those who are being sanctified.*

Should anyone ever even think that God desires another sacrifice for sin after knowing of the once for all time sacrifice for sins in the death of Jesus, that person is willfully sinning and is worthy of a much greater punishment than those who disregarded Moses and his commands.

Hebrews 10: 26 For if we sin willfully after we have received the knowledge of the truth, there no longer remains a sacrifice for sins, 27 but a certain fearful expectation of judgment, and fiery indignation which will devour the adversaries. 28 Anyone who has rejected Moses' law dies without mercy on the testimony of two or three witnesses. 29 Of how much worse punishment, do you suppose, will he be thought worthy who has trampled the Son of God underfoot, counted the blood of the covenant by which he was sanctified a common thing, and insulted the Spirit of grace?

It is a terrible insult to the Holy Spirit and to the Lord Jesus Christ and to God the Father to think that the blood of Jesus was not sufficient for sin - forever. Jesus, through His death on Calvary and subsequent resurrection, has caused sacrifice to cease forever.

This all happened exactly as prophesied. Our Savior was crucified after three and a half years of ministry - in the middle of the seventieth week. He confirmed the covenant - the New Covenant - and brought an end to the old system of repeated sacrifices by becoming the sinner's substitute and the eternal sacrifice. The sacrifice of Christ was the ***FINAL*** sacrifice in the program of God. There will be no rebuilt temple and reinstituted animal sacrifice during some imagined future seventieth week. His sacrifice in our place was an exact fulfillment of the seventy weeks prophecy.

It's important to note that the Messiah was to "***confirm*** a covenant" not "***make*** a covenant" as the Dispensationalists teach the anti-christ will do with the Jews of the "tribulation period." There are over 280 references to "covenant" in the scriptures and **not one** of them in any way, shape or form even implies the idea of a covenant being made between the Jews and a future anti-christ. But to listen to or read anything written by Dispensationalists, they want us to believe that their doctrine of the anti-christ "making" this seven year covenant with the Jews is as much a Biblical fact as when God made a covenant with Israel at Mt. Sinai. It jus' tain't so.

They arbitrarily change the word "confirm" to "make" - just another example of their forcing a passage to fit into their system. Or, I should say, forcing their system to fit into a passage of Scripture. There is no anti-christ in this prophecy and no "tribulation period" seen here either. The only way to make a "tribulation period" in this passage is to do exactly what the Dispensationalists have done - insert a gap. They are not "rightly dividing the Word of Truth" as they proudly claim to do - they are maliciously - well, maybe that is too harsh of a word – but then again, maybe not - but at the least they are ignorantly hacking it into pieces in order to protect their system.

We have seen so far that in the seventieth week that the Most Holy would be anointed, that the Messiah would be cut off, that He would cause sacrifice to end, and that He would confirm the covenant with many.

The prophecy also states that the seventy weeks would "finish the transgression." The Jews, during the seventieth week, would "finish the transgression", they would complete their sin, bring to an end the vilest of iniquity in crucifying their Messiah, the One who came to provide atonement for their sin. On many occasions the Lord referred to them as a "wicked generation." They had become so wise in their own eyes that the truth of who Jesus was hidden from them, so "seeing they could not see and hearing they could not hear." When they put to death the Lord of Glory, they made their punishment inescapable.

The Messiah, this Prince, would also "make an end of sins." Here the basic thought of the sacrifice of our Lord is repeated. If we understand the significance of what was accomplished at Calvary, we know that on the cross there truly was an end made of sins. Jesus came "to save his people from their sins" (Matthew 1:21), and He did indeed make an end of sins when he ***put away sin*** by the sacrifice of himself" on the cross (Hebrews 9:26).

All of this does not mean, of course, that when Jesus died, men quit sinning. No one is even suggesting that. But what the Scriptures do mean is that at Calvary the eternal sacrifice for sin was made, so that anyone and everyone who will confess their sin will be forgiven of all their sin - past, present, and future sins - because our Lord's death made an "end of sins." He abolished them by nailing them to the His cross. When He died, we died, our sins died.

*Colossians 2: 13 And you, being dead in your trespasses and the uncircumcision of your flesh, He has made alive together with Him, having forgiven you **all** trespasses, 14 having wiped out the handwriting of requirements that was against us, which was contrary to us. And He has taken it out of the way, having nailed it to the cross.*

The Messiah would also "make reconciliation for iniquity." This too was part of our Lord's redemptive work.

*2 Corinthians 5: 18 Now all things are of God, who has **reconciled** us to Himself through Jesus Christ, and has given us the ministry of **reconciliation**, 19 that is, that God was in Christ **reconciling** the world to Himself, not imputing their trespasses to them, and has committed to us the word of **reconciliation**. 20 Now then, we are ambassadors for Christ, as though God were pleading through us: we implore you on Christ's behalf, be **reconciled** to God.*

*Colossians 1: 20 and by Him to **reconcile** all things to Himself, by Him, whether things on earth or things in heaven, having made peace through the blood of His cross. 21 And you, who once were* *alienated and enemies in your mind by wicked works, yet now He has **reconciled** 22 in the body of His flesh through death, to present you holy, and blameless, and above reproach in His sight...*

*Hebrews 2: 17 Therefore, in all things He had to be made like His brethren, that He might be a merciful and faithful High Priest in things pertaining to God, to **make reconciliation** for the sins of the people. (KJV)*

Reconciliation for iniquity was accomplished once and for all by Jesus when He was crucified, because, as Isaiah 53: 6 says, "the Lord hath laid on him the iniquity of us all"

The Messiah also brought "in everlasting righteousness." Again, this too was accomplished by Jesus on the cross.

2 Corinthians 5: 21 For He made Him who knew no sin to be sin for us, that we might become the righteousness of God in Him.

Romans 3: 21 But now the righteousness of God apart from the law is revealed, being witnessed by the Law and the Prophets, 22 even the righteousness of God, through faith in Jesus Christ, to all and on all who believe... 26 to demonstrate at the present time His righteousness, that He might be just and the justifier of the one who has faith in Jesus.

This eternal or everlasting righteousness that was accomplished at Calvary is contrasted to the old sacrifices which, under the law, were only of a temporary nature and value - they had to be offered repeatedly - but Christ, once for all time, offered Himself - thus providing, as the prophecy of Daniel predicted, "everlasting righteousness."

I would think that if Dispensationalists would but read the great redemption passages of Romans, Corinthians, Colossians, Ephesians, and Hebrews, even they would see how an end of transgressions and sins - reconciliation for iniquity, and everlasting righteousness - was all accomplished at Calvary by our Lord Jesus Christ. This is what

Daniel 9 is about. It is what Daniel prayed for and received as his answer.

Certainly there is no logical or Scriptural way these things will be accomplished during a supposed future seventieth week at the end of the age. To teach such is to make the Bible contradictory and take away from the glory of that great redemption of Calvary which so beautifully and completely fulfilled these prophecies.

The Messiah would also "seal up the vision and prophecy." The use of the metaphor "to seal" is taken from the ancient custom of attaching a seal to a document to show that it is genuine (See 1 Kings 21:8; Jeremiah 32:10, 11; John 6:27; 1 Corinthians 9:2). Christ "sealed" Old Testament prophecy by fulfilling what was written of him. He proved that it was genuine, inspired by God. All of the Old Testament prophets wrote concerning Him, as He said in Luke 24. In many passages of Scripture we read concerning Him: "...that it might be fulfilled which was spoken by the prophets." Acts 3:18 says: "Those things which God before had showed by the mouth of all his prophets, that Christ should suffer he hath so fulfilled." Truly Jesus Christ fulfilled what was written in the visions and prophecies of the Old Testament concerning Him, and thus, He "sealed" them - He showed that they were genuine.

But there is also another sense in which Christ's coming sealed up the vision and prophecy in connection with Daniel's people. In rejecting Jesus as the one foretold in the Scriptures, the Bible became a closed book to them, they became spiritually blind - their vision was "sealed up."

Isaiah 29: 10 For the LORD has poured out on you the spirit of deep sleep, and has closed your eyes, namely, the prophets; And He has covered your heads, namely, the seers. 11 The whole vision has become to you like the words of a book that is sealed, which men deliver to one who is literate, saying, "Read this, please." And he says, "I cannot, for it is sealed.

Even today, the Scriptures are still sealed, they are closed to those Jews who still have not received Jesus as their Messiah, their Savior from sin. Indeed, the Word of God is a sealed book to anyone, Jew or

Gentile, who does not receive the Lord Jesus Christ as their Savior, and as a result of that salvation, receive also the indwelling Holy Spirit who reveals to us the message of the Bible and the things of God. But this prophecy deals with the people of Daniel, the Jews.

Romans 11:.. that blindness in part has happened to Israel...

2 Corinthians 3: 14 But their minds were blinded. For until this day the same veil remains unlifted in the reading of the Old Testament, because the veil is taken away in Christ. 15 But even to this day, when Moses is read, a veil lies on their heart.

Every one of the details of this prophecy has been fulfilled in the first coming of Jesus. It is not yet to be fulfilled in some imagined future seventieth week. I sometimes feel like a reformed alcoholic who just cannot tolerate those who will not seek help to gain victory over their drinking, especially when they know the truth of continued alcohol abuse. I am a reformed Pre-Tribulationist/Pre-Millenial/Dispensational abuser of the Word of God. I cannot for the life of me understand why anyone would want to continue in believing a system that is utterly false and a dishonest interpretation of God's Holy Word. It is a matter of believing truth or error.

So, when did the seventieth week end? Let's think about what the prophecy stated again. The prophecy was for Daniel's people, the Jews, and for their city, Jerusalem. Jesus clearly stated in *Matthew 15:24 "I was not sent except to the lost sheep of the house of Israel."*

The Lord's earthly ministry was to Israel. He was anointed at the beginning of the seventieth week and crucified in the middle of the week, or three and a half years after He began His ministry to Israel. According to church historians, the same year in which Jesus was crucified, Stephen was martyred and Saul of Tarsus was converted and became the Apostle Paul. In Galatians chapter one, Paul explains that after his conversion, he went immediately to the Arabian desert and "after three years I went up to Jerusalem to see Peter" (verse 18). In Acts 10 we read that he then was sent by Peter and the other apostles to the Gentiles to preach the gospel. This marked the end of the seventieth week that was determined "for Israel." Israel was no longer the focus of the gospel. It was for the world. This has been the historic interpretation of Daniel's prophecy for centuries prior to the intrusion of Dispensationalism into the church.

As I have previously stated, for those who believe it today, who believe it only because they have been trained in it but have not *honestly* sought the truth of the Scriptures, it is not a belief that condemns the soul. I do, however believe that those who originated this system, who history proves were not men of integrity but who sought to propagate their own doctrines regardless of the rebukes of their contemporaries, who knew exactly what they were doing, may not have been honest interpreters of the Word of God. Not that I have any authority in the matter – I cannot see the heart nor judge the intents of the heart, but I can judge the product that is presented whether it is fit for consumption or not. I leave all other judgment in the hands of the All Knowing, All Wise God.

Chapter 5

Misinterpreted Scriptures

Every Christian believes that Jesus will come again and resurrect the dead. Every Christian believes that the dead in Christ will rise first, then the Christians who are alive at that time will rise together with them to meet Jesus in the air, and we shall forever be with Him. So saith the Scriptures. But, boy, that is where the agreement between so many Christians stops. There are several imagined scenarios that follow this meeting in the air. And much disagreement. Again I ask, does it matter what details we believe concerning the Second Coming of Jesus Christ, does it matter if we if we believe a made up system or if we believe what the Bible truly teaches? It does not affect our eternal life for that is guaranteed by the blood of Jesus shed on the cross – as long our faith is in Him and Him alone for our salvation. Some people, unfortunately, place as much faith in the details of the Second Coming of Jesus as in the atonement. We have discussed this travesty in preceding chapters.

What are some of the Scriptures that Pre-Tribulationists and Dispensationalists misinterpret, that they adamantly declare teaches their point of view? Again, I insist that a Scripture must be crystal clear in what it is saying if we are to base any significant doctrine upon it. It must be unambiguous. There can be no other explicit or implied meaning to it. If it is not clear in its teaching, then the passages of Scripture that are clear *MUST* be used to give proper meaning to the unclear, the prophetic portions of God's Word.

Unfortunately, for the "rapture" advocates, nothing they use to promote their theory – and that is what it is, a theory, and a loosely based one at that – ***CLEARLY*** teaches a "rapture" as defined by them – the first stage of the Second Coming of the Lord Jesus Christ - followed by a seven year tribulation period followed by the second stage of the Second Coming of the Lord Jesus Christ. It is based at least in great proportion if not in its entirety on the misinterpreted seventieth week of Daniel.

1 Thessalonians 4: 13 - 18

The first passage that I remember being used to teach the "rapture" is the most well known one among Christians. When I first heard the Pre-Millennial explanation of this passage back in the mid sixties, I remember thinking, "Wow! I never heard that before. This is neat." Yeah. Neat, but wrong.

1 Thessalonians 4: 13 But I do not want you to be ignorant, brethren, concerning those who have fallen asleep, lest you sorrow as others who have no hope. 14 For if we believe that Jesus died and rose again, even so God will bring with Him those who sleep in Jesus. 15 For this we say to you by the word of the Lord, that we who are alive and remain until the coming of the Lord will by no means precede those who are asleep. 16 For the Lord Himself will descend from heaven with a shout, with the voice of an archangel, and with the trumpet of God. And the dead in Christ will rise first. 17 Then we who are alive and remain shall be caught up together with them in the clouds to meet the Lord in the air. And thus we shall always be with the Lord. 18 Therefore comfort one another with these words.

This passage deals primarily with the resurrection of the dead, not the "rapture." The catching up of the saints is secondary to the primary event, the resurrection. Paul was concerned about the Christians in Thessalonica who had been taught by someone that the resurrection had occurred (see 2 Thessalonians 2). He wanted to set them straight on that...again. They had been taught the truth, then someone had come into the church and taught a false doctrine that had shaken the faith of some of them. So, Paul had to re-teach them the truth. Much in the same way the "rapture" teaching has moved so many people away from Biblical doctrine.

Dispensationalists, Pre-Tribulationists, and Pre-Millennialists have an interpretation of this passage that just does not add up Scripturally. According to this currently held popular view, the "rapture" is when Jesus leaves Heaven, but He does not come all the way to earth. See again *Acts 3: 20 and that He may send Jesus Christ, who was preached to you before, 21* **whom heaven must receive until the times of restoration of all things...** Jesus *cannot* leave Heaven until He comes again and restores all things – the new heavens and new earth.

They teach that only the dead church age saints will be resurrected and the living church age saints will be transformed and together they will be caught up to meet the Lord in the air. This is what they term the first resurrection. They say that this is what this passage deals with. This is Jesus coming "for the saints." If this is Jesus coming "for the saints", why then does this passage say specifically that Jesus is bringing "with" Him those who have fallen asleep in Christ? Sounds to me like He is coming "with His saints" also.

Seven years later, Christ will leave Heaven again and those of us who have been "raptured" will accompany Him all the way to earth, and the Old Testament saints and the saints who have died since the first resurrection seven years earlier will be resurrected. I guess this the second resurrection. This is their explanation of Jesus coming "with the saints."

After that comes the "millennium", a thousand years in which Jesus reigns on earth. During this time, people in resurrection bodies – Old Testament saints only – church age saints will be living in the New Jerusalem which is suspended over the earth - will share the earth with people still in their mortal bodies, those who have lived through the "tribulation period." When the "millennium" is over, the saints who died during that thousand year period will be resurrected and the lost who died in their sins from the beginning of time will resurrected. I guess that resurrection is number three.

See how complicated this scheme is? This is definitely not what Scripture teaches. There are not three resurrections. Or, two resurrections, the second of which is in two phases that are separated by a thousand years – much in the same way they teach the "rapture." Let's hack up the resurrection of the dead like we do the Second Coming. As we have seen before, Jesus explained this very simply. We will glance again at a few passages in which He explains the resurrection.

*John 5: 25 Most assuredly, I say to you, **the hour** is coming, and now is, when the dead will hear the voice of the Son of God; and those who hear will live. 28 Do not marvel at this; for **the hour** is coming in which **all who are in the graves will hear His voice 29 and come forth**—those who have done good, to the resurrection of life, and those who have done evil, to the resurrection of condemnation.*

The hour. **One** hour. **All** who are in the graves, not just those of the "church age", not one select group, but **ALL** who are dead will hear His voice and His command to "come forth" and they will be resurrected.

In the parable of the wheat and the tares, Jesus emphatically states that both the wheat and the tares, the Godly and the ungodly, the saved and the unsaved are to grow together until He sends the angels to separate the wicked from among the just. Again, the wicked are separated from among the righteous on one day. One day of resurrection and separation. One harvest. One gathering of the wicked and casting into the furnace of fire. One. Not a multiplicity of resurrections and judgments.

In Matthew 25, the angels are again seen gathering all nations, all peoples together for the judgment. This is the same angelic activity as is seen in Matthew 13 when they gather the tares for burning. Everyone is placed either on the Lord's right hand or His left hand. They are separated into either "sheep" or "goats." The "goats" are cast into the lake of fire and the "sheep" enter into eternal life with Jesus.

Let's get back to 1 Thessalonians 4. Paul clearly states that he does not want the church there to be in such as state of sorrow that they get to the point that they have no hope. Christianity gives hope, the hope of the resurrection and of eternal life. He then begins to re-explain to them what happens when Jesus returns. In verse 14 he reassures them that their departed loved ones are with Jesus now and that when Jesus returns, they will be reunited with them in bodily form.

*14 For if we believe that Jesus died and rose again, even so God will **bring with Him those who sleep in Jesus.***

The Bible has much to say about Christians who have died. These passages are near and dear to us and give us comfort concerning our loved ones who have preceded us in death. They are with Jesus if they know the Lord.

To the thief on the cross Jesus promised that on that very day, after he died, he would be with Him in Paradise.

Luke 23: 43 And Jesus said to him, *"Assuredly, I say to you, **today** you will be with Me in Paradise."*

Paul teaches clearly that when a Christian dies, he goes to be with the Lord, which is preferable to staying here on earth.

*2 Corinthians 5: 8 We are confident, yes, well pleased rather to be **absent from the body and to be present with the Lord.***

*Philippians 1: 21 For to me, to live is Christ, and to **die is gain**. 22 But if I live on in the flesh, this will mean fruit from my labor; yet what I shall choose I cannot tell. 23 For I am hard-pressed between the two, having a desire to **depart and be with Christ, which is far better.***

The Lord is not unconcerned about our loved ones and our desire to see them again. He knows we want to see Jesus above all, but He knows we also love our family and friends who have gone to be with Him. I had a pastor friend several years ago who was in a denomination that believes in soul sleep, which means that the soul of the one who died "sleeps", or is in an unconscious state, not aware of anything, until the time of the resurrection. I asked him how then is dying gain and far better than living and having a conscious awareness of the presence of the Lord in this life? His answer was, "I don't know." Being with Jesus, in His very presence, seeing Him face to face, is far better than living here on earth. My pastor friend is now experiencing what he had questions about. He knows far better than you or I the truth of these verses.

15 For this we say to you by the word of the Lord, that we who are alive and remain until the coming of the Lord will by no means precede those who are asleep. 16 For the Lord Himself will descend from heaven with a shout, with the voice of an archangel, and with the trumpet of God. And the dead in Christ will rise first. 17 Then we who are alive and remain shall be caught up together with them in the clouds to meet the Lord in the air. And thus we shall always be with the Lord.

When Jesus returns, those who have died "in Christ" will rise from their graves before those who are alive will rise with them to meet Jesus in the air. We will be changed into His likeness as is shown in 1 Corinthians 15.

51 Behold, I tell you a mystery: We shall not all sleep, but we shall all be changed— 52 in a moment, in the twinkling of an eye, at the last trumpet. For the trumpet will sound, and the dead will be raised incorruptible, and we shall be changed. 53 For this corruptible must put on incorruption, and this mortal must put on immortality.

We all agree on this. But, that is where agreement ends. Things get a little twisted and convoluted after that.

A Secret Rapture?

The popular teaching states that this is a "secret rapture", that the world will not see this, that Jesus is like a thief that breaks into a house at night and takes away valuables unseen. No one will know

He has returned and "raptured" His people until after they realize that millions are missing. This is a horribly twisted interpretation of this passage. Nowhere in the context is this found. Nowhere in the Bible is this found. This is another example of protecting the system at all costs. Every passage that mentions the Lord's coming as a "thief" refers to His coming at an *unexpected time*, when people are at ease, not watching or praying. It does not even imply that His coming as a thief is secretive and quiet and unknown. That is a distorted view of our Lord. He is not hiding His coming when He comes. The entire world – living and dead – will hear His return and see it.

Here are the thief passages.

*Matthew 24: 42 Watch therefore, for **you do not know** what hour your Lord is coming. 43 But know this, that if the master of the house had known what hour the thief would come, he would have watched and not allowed his house to be broken into. 44 Therefore you also be ready, for the Son of Man is **coming at an hour you do not expect**. (also Luke 12:39)*

*1 Thessalonians 5: 2 For you yourselves know perfectly that the day of the Lord so comes as a **thief in the night**. 3 For when they say, "Peace and safety!" then **sudden destruction** comes upon them, as labor pains upon a pregnant woman. And they shall not escape. 4 But you, brethren, are not in darkness, so that this Day should overtake you as a thief.*

*Revelation 3: 2 **Be watchful**, and strengthen the things which remain, that are ready to die, for I have not found your works perfect before God. 3 Remember therefore how you have received and heard; hold fast and repent. Therefore **if you will not watch, I will come upon you as a thief, and you will not know** what hour I will come upon you*

*Revelation 16: 15 "Behold, **I am coming as a thief. Blessed is he who watches**, and keeps his garments, lest he walk naked and they see his shame."*

The context of every one of these passages is watchfulness, prayerfulness, being alert to the possibility of His return. Peter refers to the Day of the Lord, His Second Coming. He mentions that the Lord's coming is like "a thief in the night." But, listen to the noisy, boisterous words of that verse.

*2 Peter 3: 10 But the day of the Lord will come as a **thief in the night**, in which the heavens will pass away with a **great noise**, and the elements will melt with **fervent heat; both the earth and the works that are in it will be burned up**. 11 Therefore, since all these things will be dissolved, what manner of persons ought you to be in holy conduct and godliness,*

Does that sound to you like it is a quiet, secretive "rapture" that no one will know about until it is over and millions are missing? Someone just said, "Hold it right there, John. Peter is talking about the Day of the Lord, not the rapture, which is the Day of Christ." Oh really? The Day of the Lord speaks of judgment, which happens at the same time as the resurrection and rapture, or catching up to meet the Lord in the air, which occurs on the last day. Remember? There is no time remaining after He comes as a thief in the night. It is over. Eternity is here.

Listen closely to what Paul says about this translation from earth to the air in our 1 Thessalonians passage.

*16 For the Lord Himself will descend from heaven with a **shout**, with the **voice** of an archangel, and with the **trumpet** of God.*

The Lord Himself will shout – calling forth the dead from their graves, like He did with Lazarus. The archangel will voice His second coming. A trumpet will sound. Not just any trumpet, but God's trumpet – guaranteed to get everyone's attention, even those who are dead. Do you really believe that this is silent and secretive?

How is it possible for anyone to not witness this event and to not know exactly what is happening? How is it possible for this event to escape anyone's attention? How is it possible for anyone to question what is going on? Well, you know the answer. It isn't.

*Revelation 1: 7 Behold, He is **coming with clouds**, and **every eye will see Him**, even they who pierced Him. And **all the tribes of the earth** will mourn because of Him. Even so, Amen.*

Notice, please, in 1 Thessalonians 4 that we will meet the Lord "in the clouds" that are in the air when we are resurrected. In Revelation 1:7 it is stated that He is "coming with clouds" and every eye will see Him. Same clouds. Same event. Not different. How then can it be a "secret rapture" that every eye sees and all the tribes of the earth witness? Well, it isn't, is it? Why do the proponents of Pre-Tribulationism insist that it is a "secret"? That only those who participate in it will experience it and know that it is happening?

Now, the fact that we are "caught up", or if you prefer the word "rapture", is not in doubt. The verse clearly states it. If you wish to use the word "rapture", fine. Use it. But do not redefine the word to include the entire supposed system that is popular today. Use it as it is. Do not add anything to it. We will simply be caught up to meet the Lord in the air. Nothing at all is implied that there is a seven year "tribulation period" to follow this catching up.

Meeting the Lord in the Air

What happens after we meet the Lord in the air? Do we go back to Heaven with Him while the wicked are left behind as has been serialized by popular books and movies? The verse does not say so nor is it implied. Yet, I have heard countless preachers adamantly declare that "this is the 'rapture' and the wicked will be left behind to go through the 'tribulation period.'"

Let's look at the word "meet" to get the Biblical and historical meaning of it. This word "is to be understood as a technical term for a civic custom of antiquity whereby a public welcome was accorded by a city to important visitors" (Theological Dictionary of the New

Testament, I.380). This word was "the ancient expression for the civic welcome of an important visitor or the triumphal entry of a new ruler into the capital city and thus to his reign" (The New International Dictionary of New Testament Theology, I.325).

In other words, when a king of antiquity approached his capital city to begin his reign from that location, citizens of the city went out to meet him and to escort him into the city. It was the ancient equivalent of rolling out the red carpet. This word is found two other places in the New Testament. It occurs in Matthew 25: 1-10 in the parable of the foolish virgins.

*Matthew 25: 6 "And at midnight a cry was heard: 'Behold, the bridegroom is coming; go out to **meet him!**' 7 "Then all those virgins arose and trimmed their lamps. 10 "... the bridegroom came, and those who were ready went in with him to the wedding; and the door was shut.*

The bridegroom was going to the city to claim his bride and the bridesmaids went out to meet him, to give him a welcome in order to escort him to the city and into the house of the bride. He continued on his journey until he reached his destination. He did not reverse his direction and go back the way he came when the virgins met him. He had a goal in mind and he was going to continue to that destination.

This word also occurs in Acts 28 in the account of Paul's arrival at Rome:

*Acts 28: 15 And from there, when the brethren heard about us, they came to **meet** us as far as Appii Forum and Three Inns. When Paul saw them, he thanked God and took courage. 16 Now when we came to Rome, the centurion delivered the prisoners to the captain of the guard; but Paul was permitted to dwell by himself with the soldier who guarded him.*

Friends of Paul heard that he was on his way to Rome, so they left their cities and met him and escorted him to Rome. They were his welcoming committee. Paul was an important visitor and they accorded him the welcome he was due. Paul did not change his direction and go back the way he came from, but he continued to his destination, the city of Rome, and the others followed him there.

A closely associated word is used in John 12: 13 when the crowd went out to meet Jesus as He entered into Jerusalem. They provided an escort for Him in His triumphal entry. In each example, the dignitary had a welcoming committee that escorted him to his final destination. Just like the word is defined in the theological dictionaries we referenced.

The same will happen when Jesus returns to resurrect the dead and we rise to meet him in the clouds in the air. The word does not change its meaning in 1 Thessalonians 4 regardless of who tries to make it mean that Jesus now will reverse His direction and go back to Heaven and take us with Him. It is a distorted interpretation that has no precedent in Scripture or in a historical setting.

This is just another example of protecting the system and forcing a meaning into a passage. The meaning and intent are the same here as in other passages. A Dignitary is coming to earth, and we who are His people will go out and meet Him to welcome Him as He returns and escort Him back to earth; we will "roll out the red carpet" so to speak when He comes again to renew the earth and to rule over it for eternity.

There is absolutely no indication in any of these accounts where the word "meet" is used that there is any delay at all. No gap of any time in the continuation of the dignitary to his desired destination, let alone one of seven years. There will be no delay, no gap between the time He calls forth the dead, leaves Heaven and comes down to the earth. The "rapture" occurs simultaneously with the Second Coming. We rise up to meet Jesus in the clouds in the air, then we descend with Him as His royal escort to the earth. No missing millions. No airplanes crashing. No out of control cars. No being "left behind." No worldwide rule of an "anti-christ." It is all over except for eternity.

Resurrection and Second Coming at the Same Time

There are no less than three other passages that show us that the resurrection of the saints, the "rapture", or catching up of the saints and the Second Coming of Jesus occur at the identical time.

1 Thessalonians 5: 1 But concerning the times and the seasons, brethren, you have no need that I should write to you. 2 For you yourselves know perfectly that the day of the Lord so comes as a thief in the night. 3 For when they say, "Peace and safety!" then sudden destruction comes upon them, as labor pains upon a pregnant woman. And they shall not escape. 4 But you, brethren, are not in darkness, so that this Day should overtake you as a thief. 5 You are all sons of light and sons of the day. We are not of the night nor of darkness. 6 Therefore let us not sleep, as others do, but let us watch and be sober.

The final verses of chapter 4 deal with the resurrection and the rapture *(notice I did not put the word rapture in quotes this time because I am using it correctly to mean the catching up of the saints to meet Jesus and escort Him back to earth)* and the beginning of chapter 5 deals with "Day of the Lord", the judgment that is coming on all workers of iniquity. There is no separation of time between the two, because there is no separation of thought in Paul's discourse. He is writing to the Thessalonians about the Second Coming of the Lord. The word "but" that begins chapter 5 is showing the contrast between what Christians will experience in the resurrection and rapture and what the wicked will experience as they face eternal judgment. We experience eternity with the Lord and they experience His eternal wrath. Both the resurrection and the judgment on the wicked are part of the same event. They both happen on the same day. Again, the parable of the wheat and the tares explains this. Both grow together until the time of final separation on the last day.

Another passage that deals with the rapture and the Second Coming of Jesus as being the same event is found in 2 Thessalonians 1.

6 since it is a righteous thing with God to repay with tribulation those who trouble you, 7 and to give you who are troubled rest with us when the Lord Jesus is revealed from heaven with His mighty angels, 8 in flaming fire taking vengeance on those who do not know God, and on those who do not obey the gospel of our Lord Jesus Christ. 9 These shall be punished with everlasting destruction from the presence of the Lord and from the glory of His power, 10 when He comes, in that Day, to be glorified in His saints and to be admired among all those who believe, because our testimony among you was believed.

Paul clearly shows that when Jesus returns, Christians experience rest. This rest happens at the time we are resurrected and meet the Lord in the air and are in His presence forever. At that same time, the wicked experience the wrath of God, His vengeance manifested in flaming fire and everlasting destruction from His presence. It is the same event that accomplishes both rest for the people of God and punishment for the ungodly. God's wrath is not, as some suppose, the beginning of the seven year "tribulation period", but it is eternal in nature and far more terrifying than any earthly punishment could envision. One event on one day.

A third passage that Paul shows that the resurrection and Second Coming are identical is found in Titus 2.

11 For the grace of God that brings salvation has appeared to all men, 12 teaching us that, denying ungodliness and worldly lusts, we should live soberly, righteously, and godly in the present age, 13 looking for the blessed hope and glorious appearing of our great God and Savior Jesus Christ,

These verses speak of the appearing of the great God and Savior Jesus Christ. Some people say that this means that God and the Savior Jesus are two distinct Persons. But, this phrase "God and Savior" is a compound reference to Jesus alone. In the Greek, there is only one definite article before both words and not a separate definite article before "great God" and a separate definite article before "Savior Jesus Christ." Therefore, Jesus is our "great God and Savior."

The same rule of grammar tells us that "the blessed hope" and the "glorious appearing" is a reference to one and the same event. If "the blessed hope" and "the glorious appearing" were two separate events – as is taught by Dispensationalists and Pre-Tribulationists – there would be a separate definite article before both expressions. But, it is not there. There is only one definite article before them both, thus making it one event.

So then, "the blessed hope," which is a term that refers to the resurrection - which is the hope our Lord Jesus secured for us by His resurrection – will occur at the same time as "the glorious appearing," which refers to the Second Coming of Jesus. The English Standard Version (ESV) has translated this verse "our blessed hope, the appearing of the glory." The NIV has "the blessed hope – the glorious appearing." These translations make clear that "the blessed hope" and "the glorious appearing" are two descriptions of the same event, just as "great God" and "Savior" are two descriptions of the same person, Jesus.

John tells us that our change that Paul so eloquently describes in 1 Corinthians 15 occurs when Jesus appears. It is His appearing that is the catalyst for our "being like Him." We are changed into His likeness because "we shall see Him as He is." It is this hope of seeing Him and being like Him that mandates our purity in this life, our Christlikeness. So, our "blessed hope" – our resurrection and change – will occur at "the glorious appearing" of our Lord Jesus Christ.

*1 John 3: Beloved, now we are children of God; and it has not yet been revealed what we shall be, but we know that **when He is revealed, we shall be like Him, for we shall see Him as He is.** 3 And everyone who has this hope in Him purifies himself, just as He is pure.*

There is one more passage in 1 Thessalonians we need to examine briefly. It, too, is a passage shown by the Dispensationalists and Pre-Tribulationists to prove that the "rapture" will happen as they espouse.

1 Thessalonians 5:9

9 For God did not appoint us to wrath, but to obtain salvation through our Lord Jesus Christ,

This is one of the favorite passages of Dispensationalists and Pre-Tribulationists. It proves, they say, that the church will be "raptured" so God can pour out His wrath on the unbelieving world. Their mistake is in thinking that the wrath of God in this passage has anything at all to do with what they term "the great tribulation." As with all of their interpretations, they must force the passage to fit their system. This wrath is the outpouring of "everlasting destruction from the presence of the Lord and from the glory of His power" as shown in 2 Thessalonians 1: 5-10.

No, God has not appointed His children, those who know God and who obey the gospel, to wrath, but He has appointed us to salvation, to eternity in His presence. His wrath is poured out unmixed, undiluted, upon all workers of iniquity – eternally - not merely for seven years.

Another thought to consider is this. Since when does God have to remove His people from the presence of harm in order to keep them safe from it? He kept Israel safe from the plagues of Egypt before He led them out of Egypt. He protected them as they passed through the Red Sea which He used to punish the Egyptians. He kept the three Hebrew children, Shadrack, Meshach and Abednego safe in the middle of the fiery furnace while He destroyed the soldiers who would harm them. David boasts in the Lord's protection in the middle of tribulation in that God "prepares a table for me in the presence of my enemies." (Psalm 23: 5) God did not remove David from Saul's hatred, but He protected him from it.

He certainly has not removed present day Christians from the earth, yet He maintains His wall of protection around them. Many have been the times of blessed safety from the attacks and snares of the evil one. Many times He has protected us from physical harm and has provided food and basic necessities for us in the presence of our enemies. God keeps us safely and securely in the midst of adversity and earthly tribulation. He has not failed us yet. Nor has He removed us from earth.

Revelation Passages

I will deal briefly with the book of Revelation in a later chapter, but we will look at a couple of passages in Revelation used by Dispensationalists and Pre-Tribulationalists to "prove" their "rapture" theory.

The first one is *3:10 Because you have kept My command to persevere, I also will keep you from the hour of trial which shall come upon the whole world, to test those who dwell on the earth.*

The Dispensationalist and Pre-Tribulationists argue that "the hour of trial which shall come upon the whole world" is referring to "the great tribulation" which they define as the "seventieth week of Daniel" or the "seven year period between the 'rapture' and the 'second coming.'" They teach that the church is promised a removal from the earth, and that is what protects them from "the hour of trial."

Again, these advocates of the "rapture" totally disregard the context of the passage. Revelation in general and this letter – one out of seven specifically addressed letters – was written and addressed to a specific church, the one in Philadelphia, a city in Asia Minor that existed in the first century. How can this possibly not apply to them, but instead apply to the universal church 2000+ years in their future? Application of context and common sense are not in play here with that interpretation. In fact, what Jesus promised them did not apply to all of the churches in Asia Minor who received a letter addressed to them.

The church at Smyrna was told that they "**would** have tribulation for ten days." They were told to be "faithful unto death." They were to take comfort from the promise that they would not be hurt by the second death. They were not promised a removal from the tribulation that was coming. But Philadelphia was. Their protection from the tribulation that was coming – in their time, the first century – was based on their obedience to Christ in the past – "you did keep My word" – therefore "I will keep you from." The promise is based on the behavior of the church in Philadelphia in the first century, therefore it cannot be made to include all Christians in the distant future. If we do that, then the commendation to Philadelphia means nothing. It is negated.

The passage itself says that the time of testing was about to happen then, not some 2000 years in the future. I will use four different translations to show this.

*10 'Because you have kept the word of My perseverance, I also will keep you from the hour of testing, **that hour which is about to come** upon the whole world, to test those who dwell on the earth. (NASV)*

*10'Because thou didst keep the word of my endurance, I also will keep thee from the hour of the trial that is **about to come** upon all the world, to try those dwelling upon the earth. (Young's Literal Translation)*

*10"Because you kept my Word in passionate patience, I'll keep you safe in the time of **testing that will be here soon**, and all over the earth, every man, woman, and child put to the test. (The Message)*

Now, the surprise translation.

*10 Because thou hast kept the word of my patience, I also will keep thee out of the hour of trial, **which is about to come** upon the whole habitable world, to try them that dwell upon the earth. (Darby Translation)*

Yes. Mr. Dispensationalism himself says that the trial, the time of tribulation was about to come. Then. First century. Not 2000 years in the future. I guess he didn't believe his own translation. Me thinks he writes with forked pen.

The tribulation that was about to come upon the whole earth was imminent. It was about to occur. David Chilton, author of "The Days of Vengeance", a commentary of Revelation, writes: "Does it make sense that Christ would promise the church in Philadelphia protection from something that would happen thousands of years later? 'Be of good cheer, you faithful, suffering Christians of first century Asia Minor: I won't let those Soviet missiles and killer bees of the 20th century get you!' When the Philadelphian Christians were worried about more practical, immediate concerns - official persecution, religious discrimination, social ostracism, and economic boycotts - what did they care about Hal Lindsey's lucrative horror stories?"

They make another mistake in interpretation in that they apply the word "from" (Greek word "ek") in verse 10 to mean a spatial removal, separated from the earth to heaven. This word is never used in that sense. In fact, no theological commentary prior to the mid 1800's ever thought of such a usage. If indeed "ek" meant to remove physically, why was not the Philadelphian church so removed or "raptured" to Heaven? After all, the letter was written to them and the promise made to them.

So, what does the word "ek" mean? How does Scripture use it? Let's look at another passage to get a reasonable understanding of it. Jesus used it in John 17 during His High Priestly prayer.

15 I do not pray that You should take them out of the world, but that You should keep them from the evil one.

Was Jesus praying that His disciples would be physically removed from the earth, that Scottie would "beam them up", or that they would be protected from the attacks and deceptions of the devil? I think you know the answer. The answer is right there in the passage. "I do not pray that You should take them out of the world." "Do not 'rapture' them out." In the same manner, the Philadelphian church was going to be protected as they endured the coming trials that were coming through the auspices of the Roman Empire and godless antagonists who were bent on destroying them.

Furthermore, according to the Dispensational understanding of the great tribulation, Gentile Christians will be "raptured" at the beginning of the tribulation while the Jews must stay on earth and go through the tribulation. As was previously stated, they say they are friends of the Jews, but they insist that the Jews go through the "tribulation period" while the Gentiles escape it. Gee, isn't that nice and friendly of them?

One of the problems with this interpretation is that it abandons the literal principle of interpretation – that they proudly assert that they maintain - and alleges an arbitrary interpretation of the word "from" (ek). In other words when "ek" is used of Christians it means they will be "raptured", taken away to heaven where they will be safe from "the great tribulation", but when it is used of Jews it means they will remain on earth to endure "the great tribulation", but they will receive protection from God. How do they do this? Twist meanings of words to suit their system? I should say "why do they do this?" Is the system more important to them than the revealed Word of God? Are these passages so hard to understand that they have to make up their own interpretation? The word means the same no matter what group of people, Jews or Gentiles, is the subject.

There are many verses in which God promises that He will protect His people through trials and earthly tribulation. That is the meaning of Revelation 3:10 also. Protection for the church of Philadelphia as they went through the "hour of testing."

One other point to make here. The interpretation given by Dispensationalists to this passage completely disproves their claim of giving a literal interpretation to all Scripture whenever possible. What they really do is force all Scripture to fit into their scheme of interpretation. In the Dispensational scheme of things, the seven churches represent seven different church ages, chronologically ordered by the letters as they are given in chapters 2 and 3. This method is much like they divide time into seven "dispensations."

According to the Dispensational order of events, the church of Philadelphia, the sixth church listed in these chapters represents the period of time between 1750 and 1925, the time in which the church experienced revival and great missionary activity. Laodicea, the seventh church represents, according to them, the final period of church history, one in which there is compromise and apostasy, the one that makes Jesus sick to His stomach.

Now, if this interpretation is true, then somebody put the "rapture" in the wrong place. Why is the rapture passage in the sixth period of church history (according to them), the time of revival and not the seventh and last period, the time of apostasy? Here is the truth of the matter. There is not one word within the text or context of this passage that indicates that the seven letters are somehow prophetic of seven long periods of church history. Not one word. Just because it is a popular interpretation, in no way makes it a truthful one. Don't believe it just because someone taught it to you.

There is another Revelation passage we want to examine, that is claimed to be another "proof" of the "rapture." In fact, it is supposed to be a picture of "the rapture" itself, a portrayal of "the rapture", which, according to them, occurs at the end of the church age, the conclusion of chapter 3 of Revelation. In Chapter 4, verse 1.

1 After these things I looked, and behold, a door standing open in heaven. And the first voice which I heard was like a trumpet speaking with me, saying, "Come up here, and I will show you things which must take place after this."

Pre-Tribulationists love this verse. This is, to them, the "rapture." How do they get that out of this verse? Well, they say, the church is not seen on earth again until Revelation 19 when believers return to earth for the millennial reign of Christ. Since the church is not mentioned as being on earth during the "great tribulation" which begins after Revelation 4:1, then John's removal to heaven must be the "rapture" itself.

Hal Lindsey writes: "It's important to note that the Church has been the main theme of Revelation until Chapter 4. Starting with this chapter, the Church isn't seen on earth again until Chapter 19, where we suddenly find it returning to earth with Christ as He comes to reign as King of kings and Lord of lords.... Although Revelation 4:1 does not specifically refer to Christ's reappearance at the Rapture, I believe that the Apostle John's departure for heaven after the church era closes in Chapter 3 and before the tribulation chronicle begins in Chapter 6 strongly suggests a similar catching away for the Church."

How does he get that out of those passages? Does the fact that the church is not portrayed to their satisfaction until chapter 19 prove that what John experienced in verse 1 of chapter 4 pictured the "rapture" as defined by them? This is an "argumentum ex silentio", an argument from silence, which, in logic, is recognized as a fallacy.

A fallacy in any logical argument renders the whole of the argument invalid. Just because the church is not mentioned by name in these chapters holds no proof that the church is absent from earth and in Heaven.

But, if you want the grammatical truth of the matter, the word "ekklesia" is not used again in Revelation until 22:16. How do they explain that? If they want to be grammatically precise, as they claim, then the church is not seen from chapter 3 until chapter 22. Using their argument from silence, that removes the church from the Second Coming of Jesus entirely, which, according to their system, is shown in chapter 19. It removes the church from the "millennium" of chapter 20, and the new heavens and new earth of chapter 21. The whole thought is ridiculous. God's people always have and always will have a part in the outworking of His plans.

The immediate context says that the Apostle John – alone – no one else - is transported – via a vision, not literally - to the throne room of Heaven. There is not one word that even remotely suggests that John represents the church and that the people of God as a whole are taken to heaven. Also, if this indeed represented the "rapture", where is any mention or any indication in this passage of the resurrection of the saints or that Christ was leaving Heaven and bringing the dead in Christ with Him? Don't see it? Not there? No "rapture" in this passage.

In Revelation 4:1 there is mention of a trumpet sound, but this is not the trumpet blast announcing the "rapture." It is a voice that has a sound like that of a trumpet - just like the voice that John heard in Revelation 1:10, "I was in the Spirit on the Lord's Day, and I heard behind me a loud voice, as of a trumpet." What occurred in Revelation 4:1 with John was no different than what Old Testament prophets experienced when God was showing them what could not be explained in words. (Ezekiel 1:1, 22-28; 8:3-4; Isaiah 6:1) The Apostle Paul was shown a vision of Heaven that was unlawful for him to explain in 2 Corinthians 12:1-4. There were no words suitable to explain to humans what he saw. He and he alone was the recipient of that vision.

An argument from silence, which is what the Dispensationalists and Pre-Tribulationists use to prove the church has been "raptured" in Revelation 4:1 can also be used to prove that the saints are *not* in Heaven, either. Where is it stated that the church (ekklesia) is in Heaven in chapters 4-18? Perhaps the church has been sent to Limbo or Purgatory for a season? I'll leave you to research that.

It is just as valid an argument from silence to say that the church is not in Heaven as it is to say that it is not on earth. Arguments from silence are used when there is not enough evidence to prove your point otherwise. Dispensationalists and Pre-Tribulationists have no Biblical evidence to prove their assumption, so they invent evidence from the silence of Scripture.

So, where is the church during this time of tribulation that 3:10 speaks of that was to come upon the whole earth? Right where it always has been during other times of testing. On earth. If we examine Revelation 4 - 19 carefully, we will see that the church is still on earth during this period. Just because John does not use the word "ekklesia" - church - in these chapters does not mean she is not there. We need to remember that Revelation constantly uses prophetic language from the Old Testament in order to express coming events.

For example, in chapter 6 after the opening of the fifth seal the martyred saints ask God to avenge their deaths on those who had persecuted and martyred them who were still dwelling on the earth. These martyred Christians are told wait "until both the number of their fellow servants and their brethren, who would be killed as they were, was completed" (v. 11). The phrase "fellow servants" and "brethren" is used in Revelation to describe Christians in chapters 6:11, 19:10 and 22:9. Paul uses the identical words in Colossians 1:7; 4:7. There is not a shred of evidence to support the idea that those martyred during the tribulation are Jews, which untruth is taught by Dispensationalists and Pre-Tribulationists. These are Christians of every nation (Revelation 7:9, 14) who die because the church of Christ is persecuted on earth.

The idea that the 144,000 are Jews is found in 7:4 "One hundred and forty-four thousand of all the tribes of the children of Israel were sealed." Well, there you go. 144,000 Jews. It says so there. Being literal in interpretation is good except where a symbolic interpretation is required. This passage is literally symbolic. There are many problems with making this literal. First of all, it is obviously not meant to be interpreted literally. In Revelation chapter 7 God uses the image of Israel's military camp divisions which is found in 1 Chronicles 4 - 7. He uses it to symbolize the church as a conquering army of God.

How do you mean that? First, the book of Revelation often employs descriptions of Old Testament Israel directly to the new covenant church. These descriptions of the church that are identical to Old Testament Israel are numerous, and show in no uncertain terms that there is no distinction between Israel and the church, that all believers are one body. All are saved by grace through faith. There are many more comparisons than what I am showing here. But a few will suffice.

The church is called a kingdom of priests which is an allusion to the Old Testament identification of Israel in Exodus 19:6 (found in Revelation 1:6; 5:10; 20:6). The church of Jesus Christ is identified as the New Jerusalem - the gates of which bear the names of the twelve tribes of Israel. The foundation of the city bears the names of the twelve apostles. One city, one body, one way of salvation, one eternal destination for all the redeemed, Jews and Gentiles alike.

If we assign a literal interpretation to Revelation 7:4, then we must ignore the fact that ten of the twelve tribes had disappeared into Assyria and virtually all the ten tribes had inter-married with pagans and had lost their ethnic identity. If racial or national Jews were meant by the 144,000, why would Ephraim and Dan be excluded from the list? Also, why is Judah mentioned first rather than Rueben, the firstborn? Judah is mentioned first because our Lord Jesus Christ was born of the tribe of Judah. He is the Preeminent One, not any ethnic tribe or person or nation.

Another reason this passage is not referring to Jews according to the flesh is that in the New Testament the church is made up of both Jews and Gentiles. Both Jews and Gentiles are the true Israel of God (Rom. 2:28-29; 9:6; Gal. 6:16; 1 Pet. 1:1; 2:9-10). Paul taught that all who believe in Christ are the true sons of Abraham (Rom. 4:11-17; Gal. 3:7); that the middle wall of partition has been removed by Christ; the believing Jews and Gentiles are one body (Eph. 2:14).

The church of Christ is one building (Eph. 2:20-22) and one bride (Eph. 5: Rev 21:9).

Revelation 4:1 has nothing at all to do with a "rapture" but is merely describing the experience of John as he envisioned Heaven and the events that were about to unfold on earth.

We have looked at several passages, not all of them, that Dispensationalists and Pre-Tribulationaists use to prove their "rapture" theory. I have not spent a lot of time in refuting them, but what I have shown should suffice in demonstrating the fallacies of their arguments for the "rapture." Nothing they show proves beyond a doubt that the "rapture" is true. Every one of their arguments are "full of holes" as Dr. Ironside said. Yet, instead of believing the Biblical truth, they insist on maintaining their system. They, like Dr. Ironside, have too much time and effort into the system to reverse their beliefs now, even if they did see the errors of their ways.

I honestly do not understand why anyone would keep to the system when shown it is wrong. Why argue with truth? It is nothing but pride that prevents a change of mind. It is fear of rejection by others. It is also "I have never heard this before. If I've never heard it before, it can't be true. What I have been taught is true." Yes, I know that chances are you have never heard these arguments presented before, but read the Bible for yourself, allowing the words of Scripture to speak to you without any preconceived notions of interpretation, and you will see that what I have presented is the truth and the popular belief system is wrong.

Chapter Six

The Great Tribulation

"The Great Tribulation" is defined by Dispensationalist and Pre-Tribulationists as the seven year period between the "rapture" and the Second Coming of Jesus. It is also called "Daniel's Seventieth Week" or "The Time of Jacob's Trouble." As we have seen, this seven year period is something that neither Jesus nor the apostles taught, the early church knew nothing about, and the church through the centuries up until the early to mid 1800's did not even suspect existed. It is something that was born amid the influx of cults in both Britain and the United States. "The Great Tribulation." What is it? What is it all about?

In it, so it is supposed, God deals directly with the Jews as a nation. With the "rapture" of the church, Israel again becomes the focal point of God's actions. God has merely allowed the church to exist as a "parenthetical" group until they are taken out of the way so the anti-christ can be revealed and he can be the world dictator and have complete control of the world's economy and cause everyone to worship him. He will cause everyone to receive his mark on either their forehead or right hand. He will allow the Jews to begin worship and animal sacrifice again in the rebuilt temple. The enemies of the anti-christ will be 144,000 Jews who will preach the gospel and have greater success than the church ever did through the years from the ascension of Jesus until the "rapture." Many of them will be martyred by beheading.

There will be plagues that affect all of nature, the land, sea, rivers, and the air. There will be pestilences and diseases the affect the body and soul of men who do not have the seal of God upon their foreheads. There will be upheavals in nature and the heavenly bodies that are beyond the scope of scientific understanding – sun turning black, moon turning red, stars falling, mountains being cast into the seas.

The anti-christ will receive a mortal head wound, but he will recover. There will be two witnesses of God – most likely Moses and Elijah – who will cause plagues to come upon the earth, but who will be overcome by the beast and killed in Jerusalem where their bodies will lie for three and a half days before coming back to life and ascending to Heaven.

There will be intense war that kills much of the population of the world. Missiles, bombs, helicopters, planes, killer bees, locusts, and I'm not sure what else will wreak havoc on the world. Two beasts will be in power, the second of which will cause the world to worship the first.

The texts used to prove this is the book of Revelation and the Olivet Discourse that is found in Matthew 24, Mark 13 and Luke 21. There are a few other passages that are used to promote this scenario. But how realistic, how Biblical is this interpretation? If this is indeed the interpretation the Holy Spirit intended for us to believe, why, oh why, was it not known prior to the teaching of Ribera and the writing of Lacunza and the sick bed "visions" of Margaret MacDonald and the "new revelations" of Irving and Darby and the new interpretive methods of Schofield? Why did it take a prophetic "tongues" utterance for it to gain popularity? Why did it take so long to surface in the teachings of the church? If it is true, then why did God withhold from His saints this truth for over 1800 years?

As has been pointed out in previous chapters, this scheme of interpretation was foisted upon the church by men who admitted that they were standing alone in their theological foibles, but who continued with their new and strange doctrines in the attempt to draw disciples unto themselves. They were obviously successful in doing so and now in the year 2008 have countless thousands who have bought into their schemes. But the fact that it is popular and well received today does not make their interpretation the correct one. The fact of the matter is that God did not withhold truth from His church for 2000 years. Men have interjected their thoughts into sound theology, and many Christians have unwittingly accepted a deception in the place of truth.

What is "The Great Tribulation" about then if it is not what has been taught by Dispensationalists and Pre-Tribulationists? We must start somewhere in the explanation, so we might as well start with the Olivet Discourse, which is presumed by Dispensationalists and Pre-Tribulationists to refer to this period of time they have termed as "The Great Tribulation."

It is important to say – again - that there are many Godly men and women who disagree on this subject. When I write of deceptive theology and misleading schemes I refer to the originators of the system, not to the rank and file Christians who believe it today. Most teachers, perhaps not all, of Dispensationalism and Pre-Tribulationism do so honestly and with integrity. To repeat, they have been taught that system and nothing else, so they take it as truth. But no matter how sincere one may be in their doctrine, an untruth is still an untruth.

There are many different views on the Olivet Discourse. I shall merely mention them with few if any explanatory comments. One interpretation of this passage is that it deals strictly with the time prior to the Second Coming of Jesus and says nothing at all of the destruction of the temple. Hello? What is the question the disciples asked?

A second view is that Jesus was speaking of both the destruction of the temple and of His Second Coming, but He did not separate the two events. He intertwined His predictions of both, thereby causing confusion. This is called prophetic foreshortening. The signs He gave apply to both events because some of the same details apply to both the destruction of the temple and Jerusalem and the events that precede the Second Coming. Since both events were in the future when the Jesus gave the Olivet Discourse, they were seen in the same way as mountain tops are seen from a distance. They appear to be close together, but when viewed from the air, you can see that there are miles and miles between the two mountain tops. It is similar to the destruction of Jerusalem and the Second Coming of Jesus. From a distance of time, they appear to be close, but when one event occurs, then the separation in time is seen as it is. Hence, the intertwining of the predictive signs.

A third view is an unbiblical view that the destruction of the temple, the end of the age, and the Second Coming all three occurred in the life span of "this generation." Of necessity, this view must include the resurrection, judgment and the eternal state having taken place in the first century. No further comment is needed to disprove this view.

What I see the three passages teaching is that they do indeed teach both the destruction of the temple and the Second Coming, but the signs of each are distinct and separate from the other. There is no confusion of details that pertain to each event. The point of separation is found in the following verses.

*Matthew 24: 34 Assuredly, I say to you, **this generation** will by no means pass away till **all these things take place**.*

*Mark 13: 30 Assuredly, I say to you, **this generation** will by no means pass away till **all these things take place**.*

*Luke 21: 32 Assuredly, I say to you, **this generation** will by no means pass away till **all things take place**.*

In each of the accounts Jesus states with certainty that the generation then alive would not pass away – not everyone then alive would die – prior to the fulfillment of the words He had just spoken. For anyone to say that the words that precede these verses apply to the Second Coming and not to the destruction of the temple and Jerusalem do not believe the words of Jesus. He said that all things He had just spoken would be fulfilled within the current generation's lifetime. Period. Nothing to discuss. He said what He meant and meant what He said.

"No, no, no. It's not that simple. 'This generation' refers to the Jews as a people." I can hear the objections now. Where in the Word of God do the words "this generation" refer to a nation of people rather than contemporaries of those hearing the words? I know. The word "genea" does carry that meaning, but the context of its usage establishes the meaning.

Here is a list of all the references where our Lord Jesus said the words "this generation" in the gospel accounts. After reading these verses, tell me where the words "this generation" means anything other than what it appears to mean.

*Matthew 11: 16 "But to what shall I liken **this generation**? It is like children sitting in the marketplaces and calling to their companions,*

*12: 41 The men of Nineveh will rise up in the judgment with **this generation** and condemn it, because they repented at the preaching of Jonah; and indeed a greater than Jonah is here. 42 The queen of the South will rise up in the judgment with **this generation** and condemn it, for she came from the ends of the earth to hear the wisdom of Solomon; and indeed a greater than Solomon is here*

*45 Then he goes and takes with him seven other spirits more wicked than himself, and they enter and dwell there; and the last state of that man is worse than the first. So shall it also be with **this wicked generation**."*

*23: 36 Assuredly, I say to you, all these things will come upon **this generation**.*

*24: 34 Assuredly, I say to you, **this generation** will by no means pass away till all these things take place.*

*Mark 8: 12 But He sighed deeply in His spirit, and said, "Why does **this generation** seek a sign? Assuredly, I say to you, no sign shall be given to **this generation**."*

*8: 38 For whoever is ashamed of Me and My words in **this adulterous and sinful generation**, of him the Son of Man also will be* *ashamed when He comes in the glory of His Father with the holy angels."*

*13: 30 Assuredly, I say to you, **this generation** will by no means pass away till all these things take place.*

*Luke 7: 31 And the Lord said, "To what then shall I liken the men of **this generation**, and what are they like?*

*11: 29 And while the crowds were thickly gathered together, He began to say, **"This is an evil generation.** It seeks a sign, and no sign will be given to it except the sign of Jonah the prophet. 30 For as Jonah became a sign to the Ninevites, so also the Son of Man will be to **this generation**. 31 The queen of the South will rise up in the judgment with the men of **this generation** and condemn them, for she came from the ends of the earth to hear the wisdom of Solomon; and indeed a greater than Solomon is here. 32 The men of Nineveh will rise up in the judgment with **this generation** and condemn it, for they repented at the preaching of Jonah; and indeed a greater than Jonah is here.*

*50 that the blood of all the prophets which was shed from the foundation of the world may be required of **this generation**, 51 from the blood of Abel to the blood of Zechariah who perished between the altar and the temple. Yes, I say to you, it shall be required of **this generation**.*

Anyone reading these verses can easily see that in each and every one of these eleven passages that the words "this generation" means exactly what it appears to mean. This generation. Not a generation of people 2000 years in the future, not a race of people, but this generation that is now alive. So, if words have any meaning at all, then everything the Lord says prior to saying the words "this generation" must have applied to them and not to some people 2000 or more years in His future.

Even if we want the words "this generation" to apply to the Jewish nation, it would still carry the same meaning and outcome.

The destruction of Jerusalem and the temple meant the destruction of the Jewish nation. Not of every single Jew, but of the nation of Israel and the community of worship it embodied. When the temple and the city that housed it were destroyed in 70 AD, the nation as an entity was also destroyed.

In the three accounts of the Olivet Discourse – Matthew 24, Mark 13, and Luke 21 – the disciples were looking at the temple and admiring its beauty and grandeur and magnificence. Jesus, in response to their wonder, told them in no uncertain terms that the temple would be destroyed to the point that there would not be one stone left upon another. What follows next in our Lord's discourse is His explanation of the events that were about to unfold upon Jerusalem and the Jews as a people. It is His commentary on Daniel's prophecy.

There is a strict correlation between Daniel's seventy week prophecy and the destruction of Jerusalem and the temple. The "finishing of the transgression" would bring about the unparalleled destruction of Jerusalem and slaughter of the Jews. Daniel's people, the Jews, were to be the ones who brought about the final transgression and Daniel's holy city, Jerusalem, was to be the place where the transgression would be completed and the seventieth week would be the time when it would occur.

The Lord had previously taught that terrible consequences and retribution was coming upon Jerusalem because of their sin in denying Him and crucifying Him and their killing of the prophets in Matthew 23. He declared that, in putting Him to death they were proving themselves to be the children of those who killed the prophets; and they were also about to "fill up the measure of their fathers."

But, their wickedness would not end there. He further stated that when the ministers of the gospel should come to them teaching them of God's love and grace, they would scourge, persecute, kill and crucify them. Thus would they bring upon themselves a punishment of such terrible severity, that it would seem as if their punishment was God's retribution for all the righteous blood that had ever been shed upon the earth. He emphasized this truth by declaring "Verily I say unto you, All these things shall come upon this generation."

Jesus further states in verses 37 and 38 a clear affirmation of that part of the prophecy of the seventy weeks which foretold the destruction of Jerusalem.

Mt 23: 37 "O Jerusalem, Jerusalem, the one who kills the prophets and stones those who are sent to her! How often I wanted to gather your children together, as a hen gathers her chicks under her wings, but you were not willing! 38 See! Your house is left to you desolate;

This is the Lord's commentary on the prophecy of the finishing of the transgression in Daniel 9: 24. Truly, the Jews "finished the transgression", they sinned to the uttermost, there was no sin that could possibly be committed again that would approximate the sin of the crucifixion of the Son of God, the Messiah, the Lamb of God. Punishment in the most extreme would be the only possible one due for their transgression of killing God in the flesh. The Olivet Discourse further amplifies what the finishing of the transgression would involve for the Jews and for Jerusalem.

What I fear has happened is that many people have underemphasized the importance of the destruction of Jerusalem and the temple. The failure to recognize the significance of that event and the vast amount of prophecy which it fulfilled has been the cause of great confusion for so many. If we fail to recognize the past fulfillment of prophecy, there is a consequence to pay. We are left with a boatload of prophecies for which we are forced to scheme fulfillments in the future.

By not recognizing fulfilled prophecy, we miss the opportunity to point out to others that God's Word is true, that it is absolutely reliable and faithful in what it says, that it can be trusted in all that it says, that it is truly the Word of the Living God. Also, it makes the Bible student confused by forcing him to transfer to the future something that has already been fulfilled and for which there are historical records. These are harmful consequences. It is obvious, is it not, that we cannot study and interpret with any degree of certainty any unfulfilled prophecy until we have been assured of the fulfillment of the prophecy of things which have already come to pass?

This is the case with the Olivet Discourse. Many students of the Word of God have not realized or they have neglected or rejected the truth of the fulfillment of this prophecy of our Lord's. They have placed the "great tribulation" of Matthew 24: 21 in the future as yet unfulfilled. Yet, the Bible makes clear by our Lord's unmistakable words that all these things would happen to "this generation", that this "great tribulation" is in the past, never to be repeated.

*21 For then there will be **great tribulation**, such as has not been since the beginning of the world until this time, **no, nor ever shall be**.*

This "great tribulation" was something that would occur in the middle of history, not at the end of it. It was something whose likes had never been seen before nor ever again would be seen. It was specifically designed by God for the punishment of the generation who was responsible for "crucifying the Lord of Glory" (1 Corinthians 2:8). This was the time prophesied in Daniel 12: 1 as "a time of trouble, such as never was since there was a nation" and in Jeremiah 30: 7 as "the time of Jacob's trouble."

These prophecies and our Lord's own words concerning "this generation" make it clear that the destruction of Jerusalem by Titus in 70 AD was the event in mind when Jesus gave the Olivet Discourse. Jesus even specified the very sins for which that generation was to be punished beyond anything known before or that could possible come after it, making it impossible that the tribulation and vengeance which He predicted could possibly occur in any subsequent generation.

Even so, there are those today who insist that this "great tribulation" is yet in our future. It is a strange interpretation that says that God will again deal with the Jews as a nation when the church has been removed from earth via the "rapture", that He will demonstrate His mercy to the Jews by drawing them back to Israel and allowing them construct a new temple and reinstituting animal sacrifice and then dealing so harshly with them through these events which, according to the Dispensational and Pre-Tribulational scheme of things, are far worse than what occurred in 70 AD.

What the Lord said to the scribes and Pharisees in Matthew 23 described a punishment of such magnitude that there could not possibly be a national punishment of a more severe nature in the distant future. Within the next few minutes after excoriating the scribes and Pharisees in the temple, and prophesying of the punishment that was coming on them for their rejection of truth and of killing the prophets and their Messiah, Jesus is teaching His disciples about the destruction of the temple and of the "great tribulation" that would accompany that destruction. There is no room for any other interpretation than that He was referring to this event rather than some far distant one.

The enormity of the catastrophe that was about to fall upon the Jews and their city and the reason for it can be better understood when compared to the first destruction of Jerusalem by Nebuchadnezzar. As we have seen in a previous chapter, the captivity in Babylon was a result of the rejection of God's commandments and the mocking and the despising of the preaching of the prophets, of God's words, and the killing of the prophets.

2 Chronicles 23:15 And the LORD God of their fathers sent warnings to them by His messengers, rising up early and sending them, because He had compassion on His people and on His dwelling place. 16 But they mocked the messengers of God, despised His words, and scoffed at His prophets, until the wrath of the LORD arose against His people, till there was no remedy. 17 Therefore He brought against them the king of the Chaldeans...

But now they despised the words of the very Son of God and they mocked Him. Jesus said that "this generation" was to fill up the measure of the guilt of their fathers who killed the prophets by killing Him. The culmination of the sin of these Jews would be fulfilled in the crucifixion of Jesus. Who can measure the enormity of this crime? Is there or can there be a greater sin than to kill the Lord? If so, who would commit it and what could it possibly be?

And if that were not enough for them, then they would then kill, crucify, scourge and persecute the messengers that would be sent to preach to them forgiveness of sins and the salvation of the

Lord through the death of Jesus. Because of that, the punishment for "all the righteous blood shed on the earth, from the blood of righteous Abel to the blood of Zechariah, son of Berechiah, whom you murdered between the temple and the altar" would come upon them. That single generation of Jews would have to pay the penalty for the death of every prophet, of every righteous man that had ever been murdered by unrighteous men beginning with Abel through their present time. They refused to acknowledge Jesus as the Messiah, they refused to believe that He was sent from God, they attacked Him verbally at every opportunity, they plotted His death from the beginning of His ministry, they refused to believe the works He performed that could only have been done by God, and eventually they murdered Him. They chose their own destruction.

The Apostle Paul confirms this in 1 Thessalonians 2.

14 ...For you also suffered the same things from your own countrymen, just as they did from the Judeans, 15 who killed both the Lord Jesus and their own prophets, and have persecuted us; and they do not please God and are contrary to all men, 16 forbidding us to speak to the Gentiles that they may be saved, so as always to **fill up the measure of their sins; but wrath has come upon them to the uttermost.**

There is no doubt whatsoever that the sin and iniquity of that generation of Jews went far beyond the wickedness of their fathers; and that the "wrath" which was then about to be poured out upon them was to be "to the uttermost." There is no doubt that that generation was to "finish the transgression." There was no transgression to follow. It was complete. Nothing they could do, or nothing any subsequent generation could possibly do, would approximate the despicableness of killing Jesus.

Now, considering these historical facts, if there is to be a future generation of people upon which is to fall a yet greater tribulation, what could they possibly do that would be the cause of it? What greater sin or crime could they commit which would cause greater punishment? What sin or crime can they commit which would be in any way greater than that of betraying and crucifying the Son of God?

No. No. You got it all wrong again. The "great tribulation" is punishment against the wicked who will not repent, who receive the "mark of the beast." It punishes the generation who are still alive who have rejected Jesus prior to when He "raptures" the church. Oh? If the Olivet Discourse is used as a description of what will occur during this future "great tribulation" when the "anti-christ" is ruling and deceiving the nations – except for the Jews - then why are so many distinctly Jewish scenes depicted? "The Christ", "false prophets", "lawlessness", "the kingdom", "abomination of desolation", "Daniel the prophet", "holy place", "Judea", "Sabbath"; these are all words that are associated with Jews, not Gentiles. This discourse of our Lord's deals with the generation of Jews that were then alive who were about to be guilty of killing their Messiah. It does not deal with a future generation of any people, at least up until verse 34. And even after that I'm not positive that it does.

*34 Assuredly, I say to you, **this generation will by no means pass away till ALL these things take place.** 35 Heaven and earth will pass away, but My words will by no means pass away.*

What did Jesus mean by His words in verse 34 if He did not mean what He said? Just because Bible commentators and teachers today may have difficulty in placing all of the signs and events He mentioned in the proper context – which is the first century – and that difficulty comes from the faulty teaching that they have been subject to - that by no means implies that they are misplaced or misspoken by our Lord as referring to the generation then alive. It merely means that we must work harder in our studying and pray harder for the Holy Spirit's guidance and understanding of passages that are hard for us to grasp.

There is something else to consider. Israel is promised blessing through believing the gospel. In Romans 11 Paul argues that God has not cast off Israel completely. Israel was a branch of the holy root, but God has broken off that branch of the olive tree because of unbelief and has grafted into the olive tree branches that were not native, but a wild olive tree, namely the Gentiles. When anyone, Jew or Gentile, repents of their sins and believes the gospel, they are grafted into the olive tree. They become members of the Body of Christ.

15 For if their being cast away is the reconciling of the world, what will their acceptance be but life from the dead? 26 And so all Israel will be saved, as it is written: "The Deliverer will come out of Zion, And He will turn away ungodliness from Jacob; 27 For this is My covenant with them, When I take away their sins."

There is a prophecy in Isaiah 51 that deals with the destruction of Jerusalem and the desolation that she would suffer. Because of the wording of this prophecy, it is clear that it deals with the destruction of Jerusalem by Titus in 70 AD and not the destruction associated with the Babylonians. That it deals with the destruction of Jerusalem under Titus rather than the Babylonians is evident from the final phrase of verse 22.

17 Awake, awake! Stand up, O Jerusalem, you who have drunk at the hand of the LORD the cup of His fury; You have drunk the dregs of the cup of trembling, and drained it out. 18 There is no one to guide her among all the sons she has brought forth; Nor is there any who takes her by the hand among all the sons she has brought up. 19 These two things have come to you; Who will be sorry for you? — Desolation and destruction, famine and sword— By whom will I comfort you? 20 Your sons have fainted, they lie at the head of all the streets, like an antelope in a net; They are full of the fury of the LORD, the rebuke of your God. 21 Therefore please hear this, you afflicted, and drunk but not with wine. 22 Thus says your Lord, the LORD and your God, Who pleads the cause of His people: "See, I have taken out of your hand the cup of trembling, the dregs of the cup of My fury; **You shall no longer drink it.**

It is clear from this passage that Jerusalem would never again suffer like it suffered under Titus. It could not refer to the Babylonians because Jerusalem did indeed suffer even more severely under

Titus. So, if the Word of the Lord through Isaiah has any credence, this "great tribulation" cannot be yet in the future, but is an accomplished event in the first century - the events of 70 AD.

So, if we are to arrive at the proper interpretation of the Olivet Discourse, then there are certain rules of interpretation that we must follow. First of all, the passage of Scripture must be interpreted as the original audience would understand it. For example, how would a first century Jewish audience regard a phrase such as "blood, fire, vapor and smoke" as used in Acts 2:19, Revelation 6:12, Joel 2:28-32? Would they see it as referring to nuclear war or as old covenant prophetic imagery for God's impending judgment on Israel?

Secondly, as I have mentioned previously, Scripture must be used to interpret Scripture. In Matthew 24 Jesus uses terminology that comes directly from the Old Testament prophetic books. What makes more sense to you, using the Bible to give us the meaning of such prophetic images or using modern day images and vivid speculations and wild imaginations of "prophecy experts" founded upon newspapers, magazine articles and TV commentary based on world events?

Thirdly, we must interpret the passages under consideration according to their literary type. Many prophetic passages use metaphors, figures of speech and apocalyptic imagery in order to portray a truth much in the same way Jesus used parables to portray a Spiritual truth to His listeners. Does it make sense to interpret apocalyptic or poetic imagery in the same manner as we interpret a straight-forward historical account? I think not. Neither do you.

The key then to understanding prophetic imagery such as stars falling from heaven, the sun becoming dark, the sky rolled up like a scroll, etc. is to see how such imagery is used in the Bible, rather than use current events and modern scientific discoveries to speculate as to their meaning and proper interpretation. Did the ancient Hebrew writers and the apostles really foresee nuclear war, bar codes, computer chips in the hand and forehead, attack helicopters, tanks, etc.? Or did they have another meaning in view? Most books written on prophecy today are so far disconnected from the biblical text that they are nothing more than the clever fantasies of the different authors.

The fourth rule of interpretation is the time indicators within the discourse and the immediate context that relates to the discourse. As I have mentioned before, the words "this generation" have a significant bearing on the meaning of the Olivet Discourse. These words - if taken at face value - prove that Jesus' discourse at least up to verse 34 must be applied directly and solely to the destruction of Jerusalem in 70 AD and the complete end of the Jewish age by the destruction of the temple.

Fifthly, whenever we are interpreting a section of Scripture in the synoptic gospels, Matthew, Mark and Luke, parallel accounts should be carefully compared and analyzed. Matthew wrote to a predominately Jewish audience while Mark and Luke wrote to a predominately Gentile audience. Therefore, if Matthew uses a phrase from Old Testament history or poetical prophetic imagery that would be obscure or difficult for a Gentile audience, the other gospels should be checked for clarification. This rule is seen most clearly in the disciple's question in Matthew 24:3, Mark 13:4 and Luke 21:7. It is also seen in the definition of the abomination desolation, which very clearly places it in the first century, not in some future setting. Compare Matthew 24:15 and Luke 21:20.

Let's go back to the beginning of the Olivet Discourse and examine the question the disciples asked the Lord.

Matthew 24: 3 Now as He sat on the Mount of Olives, the disciples came to Him privately, saying, "Tell us, when will these things be? And what will be the sign of Your coming, and of the end of the age?"

Mark 13: 4 "Tell us, when will these things be? And what will be the sign when all these things will be fulfilled?"

Luke 21: 7 So they asked Him, saying, "Teacher, but when will these things be? And what sign will there be when these things are about to take place?"

Matthew's account differs from Mark's and Luke's in that he adds questions regarding the Lord's coming again and the end of the age. Mark and Luke omit these questions. Why? Why does Matthew include them and Mark and Luke omit them? If indeed the disciples were asking about two different events, the destruction of the temple and the Lord's coming again at the end of the age, would not Mark and Luke also have included them? There is no doubt that they would have. It seems apparent that that the questions refer to the one event under consideration, the coming destruction of the temple and Jerusalem.

We must bear in mind to whom Matthew was primarily writing. His audience was mostly Jewish. To the Jewish mind, the world must end if there was no temple. The disciples, being Jewish, were of the same mind set. How could there be a continuance of time if there was no temple? They were equating the destruction of Jerusalem and the temple with the end of time and the Lord's Second Coming. To them, and the Jews, the temple represented their entire existence. It was their life, their worship, the center of their being. Their failure to understand this is not surprising since on many occasions they did not grasp the simple teaching of the Lord about His crucifixion and resurrection. It was not until after the resurrection that they began to comprehend many of the Lord's teachings. So, for them to not understand that the temple would be destroyed, but it's destruction did not mean the end of time and His coming in judgment, is not the least bit surprising.

Mark and Luke wrote primarily to Gentiles, so they did not include the Lord's coming and the end of the age questions. Mark and Luke understood that the questions the disciples asked referred to the destruction of the temple and of Jerusalem, not to the end of the age and the Lord's second coming. Gentiles would not equate the destruction of the temple and the city with the end of the age, but of punishment for the crucifixion of Jesus.

All three accounts are, of course, inspired by the Holy Spirit. They are not in contradiction to one another. They all state the same thing, but from different perspectives. One is from the Jewish point of view, and the other two from the Gentile point of view. The three passages mean the same thing.

The Lord's answers to the questions posed give us insight into what is important and what is not. The disciples asked pointed questions as to when the destruction would occur, but the Lord does not answer them in the way that they anticipated. "When will these things occur?" The disciples wanted a direct answer as to the time the destruction would happen – the day and the hour, but instead, Jesus gave them warnings to heed. They were focused on what He had already condemned and appointed to destruction, the temple and the city, so He directed them away from them and focused their attention on Himself.

We will use Mark 13 as our "home passage" and will go to the other Olivet passages for additional comments. Many of the comments to follow are taken from the author's commentary on Mark entitled, "The Beginning of the Gospel: A Devotional Commentary on Mark".

The questions posed to Jesus were quite natural questions for the disciples to ask. Jesus had just told them of the destruction of their most holy place and their system of worship. It seems like Jesus kind of skirts the question and instead of answering it, He gives them a warning against deception. He turns their focus from the temple to Himself. "Take heed – beware – that no one deceives you. Many will come in My name saying, "I am He" and will deceive many."

The Lord's warning to His disciples was to guard against focusing their attention on what was temporary – what was going to be destroyed – the temple – thereby being deceived and susceptible to further deception. The further deception would manifest itself in accepting false christs – false teachers – as true. Many people, Jesus warned, would believe the liars and false messiahs and be led into a false sense of security and a false belief system – one that rejected Him as the true Messiah. By focusing their attention on the temple – rather than Jesus – they could be led astray.

Many people today worship at the temple of gold and silver, of pleasure, of industry, of power, and therefore are deceived and led from Jesus. All of the world's idols will be destroyed by fire – they are temporary at best – and are not to consume the attention of God's people. We need to focus our attention and desire on what and who is eternal. Desiring the temporary over the eternal is deception.

This warning against deception is critical. Jesus spoke this warning directly to the disciples, and by extension, to us today who are Christians. "Take heed – beware – be careful – be on guard – that no one deceives you." The personal pronoun "you" emphasizes the Lord's point that His people would be the target of deception. Other people who are not believers will attempt to deceive those who have trusted in Christ. "Take heed that NO MAN deceive you." Jesus lists many ways that people will try to deceive the Lord's people into believing a lie.

Verse 6 "I am He." Many people have claimed to be the Christ – it seems incredible – unbelievable – but many have deceived others into thinking that they are the messiah. The power of Satan to deceive people is not to be taken lightly. Jesus warns His people not to be smug and think they are above deception. Verse 22 says "if possible to deceive even the elect." No one – in and of themselves – has the ability to resist all of the devil's temptations and snares. Only the Holy Spirit indwelling us can give us the strength to resist and deny his attacks against our faith.

The apostle John in his epistles - 2 John and 3 John especially – warns against departing from the truth and believing the deceivers and anti-christs who were at work against the gospel. Jude exhorts us to "earnestly content for the faith which was once for all delivered to the saints." Why? Deceivers were at work fighting against the truth. If anyone adds to or subtracts from the faith that was delivered to the saints once and for all, they are deceivers and are to be rejected as heretics.

Another way people will deceive God's people is when wars occur. "God cannot be in control if there are wars and nations rising up against other nations." "How can you believe in a God of love who allows that?" Jesus tells us not to be troubled over war, for war must happen. Why must war happen? Why must there be such slaughter of human life? What is God's purpose in mandating war? I believe the main reason is to allow sin to play itself out to its logical conclusion. It is to show all people the consequences of rejecting God and His Divine authority over mankind. Instead of blaming God for allowing war, man should be asking themselves, "Why are we choosing war and sin over the peace that God offers us through Jesus Christ?"

People do not realize that they have been deceived because the gospel – the truth of the matter – has been hidden from them. Their minds – their ability to discern truth from error – has been blinded by Satan.

2 Corinthians 4:4 whose minds the god of this age has blinded, who do not believe, lest the light of the gospel of the glory of Christ, who is the image of God, should shine on them.

They are unable to believe truth; therefore we who do believe the truth should intercede to God in their behalf so they will come to the same knowledge of the truth that we have and accept it.

In the same manner as war, people will be deceived by earthquakes, famines, and other natural disasters. These, like war, are the result of sin and is its consequence. Romans 8:19-22

19 For the earnest expectation of the creation eagerly waits for the revealing of the sons of God. 20 For the creation was subjected to futility, not willingly, but because of Him who subjected it in hope; 21 because the creation itself also will be delivered from the bondage of corruption into the glorious liberty of the children of God. 22 For we know that the whole creation groans and labors with birth pangs together until now.

This Romans passage tells us vividly that creation itself has suffered because of sin. Creation is groaning with expectation of deliverance from the "bondage of corruption." Let no one deceive you into thinking that God does not care about people because He allows earthquakes, famines, hurricanes, tornadoes, tsunamis, and other natural disasters to occur. They are the result of man's sin and disregard for God and rebellion against Him. What does man expect God to do in response to our sin? Jesus again reiterates that these things must occur, that they are only the beginning of sorrows.

Another deception that men would attempt to foist on the disciples was persecution. Jesus warned them, and He warns believers today, that persecution will occur, that they would be dragged before the authorities. But instead of seeing persecution as God not loving them or caring for them, they – and we – should view it as an opportunity to preach the gospel to those who need to hear it. The gospel may never be preached to some people outside of the fact that they are persecuting a Christian and demanding them to renounce their faith in Jesus. It is far more important to God that the gospel is preached to all nations than it is that Christians not be persecuted for their faith. Persecution has been one of God's methods of having the gospel preached through the years.

In Acts 8:1, a great persecution arose against the church that scattered believers throughout the region, and the result was, in verse 4, that they went everywhere preaching the gospel. Persecution is not pleasant to think about, but it does accomplish God's purpose of preaching the message of salvation to those who have never heard it. It forces believers to take a stand for the Lord. Those who are instrumental in persecution may be saved just as was Saul of Tarsus.

One way we can know that persecution and arrest for our faith in Christ is not a sign of God's displeasure with us, but is instead God's blessing (that's hard to say, isn't it?) to us, is that the Holy Spirit will fill our mouths with words when called upon to give a defense for our faith. We are not to plan in advance what to say, but to trust the Lord to give us words that will honor Him.

Another attempted deception against Christians is betrayal by family. Jesus had previously spoken to this betrayal in Matthew 10:34-39.

34 "Do not think that I came to bring peace on earth. I did not come to bring peace but a sword. 35 For I have come to 'set a man against his father, a daughter against her mother, and a daughter-in-law against her mother-in-law'; 36 and 'a man's enemies will be those of his own household.' 37 He who loves father or mother more than Me is not worthy of Me. And he who loves son or daughter more than Me is not worthy of Me. 38 And he who does not take his cross and follow after Me is not worthy of Me. 39 He who finds his life will lose it, and he who loses his life for My sake will find it.

He plainly tells His disciples that His purpose in coming to earth was not to unite, but to divide, and that division would many times be within a family. Father against son, daughter against mother. Our enemies many times will be our family members. Jesus warns that He is to be loved pre-eminently, and if family comes before Him, then we are not worthy of Him. If family tries to keep us from Him, they are to be rejected and Jesus embraced. If we seek to maintain our familial relationships over our relationship and dedication to Christ, we will be the loser.

But, if we honor Him over all else – including family – then we will find our life – it will be more satisfying than we can imagine. We are not to be deceived into focusing on another temporary relationship – family – over the eternal relationship – with Jesus. We are to love our family and do all we can to win them to Christ, but if they demand we reject Christ in favor of them, they are to be refused and Christ chosen. Earthly relationships are temporary, but spiritual ones are eternal.

These are hard decisions to make, and can be deceptive, so the Lord warns us to choose carefully, but His promise is that we will find real life in Him to be more satisfying than any sense of fulfillment that we might have with an unsaved family member who desires to drag us away from Christ.

Another deception that the elect would be susceptible to is being hated by everyone because of their love for the Lord. The Lord speaks to this hatred in other passages, most notably, John 15:18-25.

18 "If the world hates you, you know that it hated Me before it hated you. 19 If you were of the world, the world would love its own. Yet because you are not of the world, but I chose you out of the world, therefore the world hates you. 20 Remember the word that I said to you, 'A servant is not greater than his master.' If they persecuted Me, they will also persecute you. If they kept My word, they will keep yours also. 21 But all these things they will do to you for My name's sake, because they do not know Him who sent Me. 22 If I had not come and spoken to them, they would have no sin, but now they have no excuse for their sin. 23 He who hates Me hates My Father also. 24 If I had not done among them the works which no one else did, they would have no sin; but now they have seen and also hated both Me and My Father. 25 But this happened that the word might be fulfilled which is written in their law, 'They hated Me without a cause.'

In exacting detail Jesus explains that the world's hatred of His disciples is predicated upon their hatred of Him. Because He spoke plainly of people's sin and their need to repent and trust Him for their deliverance from sin rather than trusting in their own works to save them, they rejected Him and hated Him unto death. It is not bad news to hear that you are a sinner in need of a Savior. It is good news – great news – because the rest of the story about needing is Savior is that God has provided salvation for us in His Son.

As stated before, how can it possibly be bad news – news to be rejected – that God has pronounced every man a sinner worthy of death, and then sent His Son to serve our sentence of death in our place? God is saying, in effect, "You are guilty. You deserve death, but here is Jesus, My only Son, to die for you. You do not have to pay the penalty of death that you owe Me – Jesus will pay it for you." How is that bad news?

Yet, people hate God for pronouncing them sinners and hate Jesus for coming to be the sacrifice for sin, for exposing their sin, and they hate Christians for proclaiming God's message to them. Their pride makes them reject it. This hatred is to be expected because of their hatred against Jesus and His Father.

10 And the gospel must first be preached to all the nations.

Jesus was insistent that they not be bogged down in what was not important, what was temporary, but to be occupied with what was eternal, the preaching of the gospel. After His resurrection, just before His ascension into Heaven, the disciples brought up the same question again concerning when the kingdom would be restored to Israel. Again Jesus turned their minds from what they – and we – should not be concerned with – the time of His Second Coming - and said, But...ye shall be witnesses unto Me, both in Jerusalem, and in all Judea, and in Samaria, and unto the uttermost part of the earth (Acts 1:6–8). The end of the age will come when, and only when, the work of the Gospel shall have been finished.

The Second Coming of Jesus

The preaching of the Gospel is the matter of supreme importance. All the things mentioned – wars, earthquakes, famines, troubles of every sort, false christs, etc, are not signs of His second coming. He clearly states that; yet, through the ages, even to this present day, there are those who take these events as signs that His coming is near, especially when they happen in connection with the appearance of some supposed "antichrist." Many Christians have been deceived into thinking that the second coming of Jesus is at the door.

It is really surprising that the Lord's people continue to believe that these things are signs of His coming when He so clearly stated that they were not to be regarded as such.

Yes, everything mentioned through verse 15 occurred during the time between the resurrection of Jesus and the destruction of the temple. All of these things have also occurred in the time since the destruction of the temple to this present day and will continue to occur until the Lord returns. The Lord's people are to always be on guard against these deceptions by the devil through other people.

In Matthew 24: 6 the disciples were told that just because they saw all of these things occur, it did not mean that the end was in sight. And it certainly did not imply that He was ready to return. These occurrences are **_not_** signs of His Second Coming or even of the destruction of Jerusalem.

*Matthew 24: 6 ...See that you are not troubled; for all these things must come to pass, but the **end** is not yet.*

What end was Jesus referring to? What was the question that precipitated this discourse? The question regarding the destruction of the temple and the city. There was one sign of the immediate destruction of the temple and city, and that was the Roman army encircling Jerusalem. The other deceptions that Jesus warned of were **_not signs of anything_** but were given by the Lord to prepare His disciples for the coming trials and tribulations. Here is the sign of when these things would occur; here is the answer to their question.

14 "So when you see the 'abomination of desolation,' spoken of by Daniel the prophet, standing where it ought not" (let the reader understand...

These verses are the same words as is recorded in Matthew 24: 15.

15 "Therefore when you see the 'abomination of desolation,' spoken of by Daniel the prophet, standing in the holy place" (whoever reads, let him understand),

What is the "abomination of desolation"? Luke 21: 20 tells us precisely what it is.

20 "But when you see Jerusalem surrounded by armies, then know that its desolation is near.

As far as I know, everyone agrees that the words recorded by Luke refer to the then approaching destruction of Jerusalem by Titus. So do the words recorded in Matthew. If we look at them carefully, we will see that refer to the same destruction of Jerusalem. We will also see that our Lord was speaking of an event then close at hand.

These next verses also apply directly to the destruction of Jerusalem and the temple. They have a distinctly Jewish flavor that had a fulfillment in the destruction of Jerusalem in 70 AD. Jesus directly calls to remembrance Daniel's prophecy concerning the abomination of desolation. The abomination of desolation prophesied by Daniel was not fulfilled in 168 BC when Antiochus Epiphanes, the Syrian ruler, desecrated the temple and sacrificed a pig on the altar. Although the Jews saw that desecration of the temple – and it most certainly was a desecration of the holy temple – as the abomination that makes desolate, Jesus says that Daniel's prophecy was yet future. If Daniel's prophecy dealt with Antiochus Epiphanes, Jesus would have said so. He did not. He said **when you see** – still in their future - the abomination of desolation that Daniel the prophet spoke of standing where it ought not to stand, then you are to flee. Jesus said it was still future – for them – that generation - not for us. What was going to happen to Jerusalem and the temple would completely destroy both. Jesus clearly and unambiguously stated that this destruction of Jerusalem and the temple is the great tribulation. It is not yet to come. It is passed. It occurred in 70 AD.

Let's think about the abomination of desolation. The word "abomination" means any hateful or detestable thing. In our Lord's discourse to His disciples it applies to the Roman armies as they surrounded Jerusalem in order to destroy it. The modifying words "of desolation" gives the meaning a sure definition. Yet, according to the widely held interpretation today, it means the setting up of an idol for worship – or the "anti-christ" himself sitting in the holy of holies - in a Jewish temple which (it is supposed) will be built at Jerusalem in the days of "the antichrist." But, if that were the true interpretation, the words "of desolation" would be quite out of place. Does the Bible teach anywhere that Jerusalem is to be again made a desolation? Another insurmountable objection to that view is that God would not regard any part of such a temple as the "holy place."

Dispensational and Pre-Millennial expositors have been misunderstood the expression "the holy place" that Matthew uses. They have assumed that it meant the holy of holies in the temple. But it does not mean that at all. Anyone who can use a Strong's or Young's concordance can readily determine that the word used for "place" in Matthew 24:15 is *"topos"*, which means simply a "locality." It is used in expressions like a desert place, dry places. The holy land, Judea, is therefore the "holy place", where the heathen armies, with their idolatrous standards and pagan sacrifices, were to stand. Mark puts it simply as standing where it ought not. On the other hand, the term *"topos"* is never used of the holy of holies of the temple.

Another consideration that the abomination of desolation has nothing at all to do with an idol – or the "anti-christ" himself - being set up in a future temple is this. When the disciples would see this abomination, they were to know it was time for them to flee. Think about it. The setting up of an idol in the inner sanctuary could not be a sign to the Lord's people to flee. That would be a thing which only the priests could see. And it could not possibly be a sign to them that were in Judea. But, the invading armies would be a sight which all could see, and when they saw them, they could flee.

Furthermore, an idol could not be set up in the sanctuary until the city and temple had already been taken by the enemy, which would be at the end of the siege. Therefore, it could not possibly serve as a sign to the disciples to save themselves from the horrors of the siege by fleeing.

Matthew 24: 21 **For then there will be <u>great tribulation</u>, such as has not been since the beginning of the world until this time, no, nor ever shall be.**

14... "then let those who are in Judea flee to the mountains. 15 Let him who is on the housetop not go down into the house, nor enter to take anything out of his house. 16 And let him who is in the field not go back to get his clothes. 17 But woe to those who are pregnant and to those who are nursing babies in those days! 18 And pray that your flight may not be in winter. 19 For **in those days there will be tribulation, such as has not been since the beginning of the creation which God created until this time, nor ever shall be***. 20 And unless the Lord had shortened those days, no flesh would be saved; but for the elect's sake, whom He chose, He shortened the days. 21 "Then if anyone says to you, 'Look, here is the Christ!' or, 'Look, He is there!' do not believe it. 22 For false christs and false prophets will rise and show signs and wonders to deceive, if possible, even the elect. 23 But take heed; see, I have told you all things beforehand.*

In verses 14-23, Jesus further elaborates what He said as recorded in Luke 19:41-44.

41 Now as He drew near, He saw the city and wept over it, 42 saying, "If you had known, even you, especially in this your day, the things that make for your peace! But now they are hidden from your eyes. 43 For days will come upon you when your enemies will build an embankment around you, surround you and close you in on every side, 44 and level you, and your children within you, to the ground; and they will not leave in you one stone upon another, because you did not know the time of your visitation."

As Jesus is entering Jerusalem during His triumphal entry, He pauses to view the city. As He looks over the city, He is overcome with grief and He weeps. He is foreseeing the total destruction of Jerusalem, and He weeps with compassion for the unsuspecting citizens. They had not recognized Jesus for who He really was. They defined Him their own way as teacher, rabbi, good man, healer, miracle worker, but not as God incarnate. If they only would have understood Him and who He was, they would have enjoyed the peace they sought, but they were seeking peace as they defined it, not as God was providing it.

This is a realistic commentary on human nature – sin nature. All through the Bible we see man doing things his own way – defining life and circumstances his own way – defining God as suits himself rather than seeing life as God defines it and following His commandments. Man continues to rebel against God and do things his own way. Jesus tells us why in this passage in Luke. "They are hidden from your eyes." You have rejected God for so long that you are unable to see the truth. The Jews of Jerusalem could not see the truth of their situation. They could not see they were in peril of utter destruction because they had not seen Jesus for who He really was.

"You did not know the time of your visitation." You did not pay attention to what was happening around you – you continued on your merry old way doing things just as you always had done them, even though you saw the miracles I did and you heard My words. You knew I spoke truth, you enjoyed the food I provided for you, you were happy when I healed you, but you did not change your lifestyle. You continued doing things your own way. Because you chose to do things your own way, you will be destroyed, and that breaks My heart. It did not have to be this way, but you chose it."

This is the same message He gives to men today. You have been visited by God, you have heard the gospel, you know that you are sinners in need of a Savior, you know that I died for your sins and if you will but confess your sins and receive the forgiveness I offer, you will be saved. But, you are rejecting the truth. You are rejecting Me. You are choosing your own way – the way that leads to utter destruction – and that breaks My heart and I weep for you because your eyes are blinded to the truth because you are deliberately choosing to be blind.

The destruction of Jerusalem is but a shadow of the destruction of the soul in hell. The warning is there. Jesus gave very clear instructions on how to flee Jerusalem when the attack comes. Flee to the mountains – do not go back to your house for anything, not even clothes. Be prepared. Pray that the attack does not occur during the winter and that you are not pregnant or have a young baby at the time. It will be a time of great tribulation such as has not been since time began nor will such a time ever occur again. It will be so horrendous that God will shorten the time that it could occur for the sake of the elect. If God does not shorten the time of tribulation – no one – not even the elect of God would survive. All would be killed.

During this time there would be many false messiahs and prophets arise. They would work signs and wonders to the degree that – if it were possible – they would deceive even the elect. Satan can manifest himself as an angel of light.

2 Corinthians 11:14 And no wonder! For Satan himself transforms himself into an angel of light.

His entire purpose is to deceive as many people as he can so that their souls will be destroyed in hell. God protects His elect from total deception by Satan by sealing them on their foreheads, Revelation 7:3 saying, "Do not harm the earth, the sea, or the trees till we have sealed the servants of our God on their foreheads."

The seal of God on believers is the Holy Spirit. Ephesians 4:30 And do not grieve the Holy Spirit of God, by whom you were sealed for the day of redemption. God Himself is our protection against the devises and wiles of the devil.

In the same way that Jesus warned the disciples to flee when they saw the sign of the abomination of desolation encircling Jerusalem – the Roman army – we are also warned to flee when we see the enemies of our souls encamping around us, ready to attack and destroy.

What are some of the enemies of our souls that the Bible gives specific warnings to flee?

1 Corinthians 6:18 Flee sexual immorality. Every sin that a man does is outside the body, but he who commits sexual immorality sins against his own body.

1 Corinthians 10:14 Therefore, my beloved, flee from idolatry.

1 Timothy 6:9-11 But those who desire to be rich fall into temptation and a snare, and into many foolish and harmful lusts which drown men in destruction and perdition. 10 For the love of money is a root of all kinds of evil, for which some have strayed from the faith in their greediness, and pierced themselves through with many sorrows. 11 But you, O man of God, flee these things and pursue righteousness, godliness, faith, love, patience, gentleness.

2 Timothy 2:22 Flee also youthful lusts; but pursue righteousness, faith, love, peace with those who call on the Lord out of a pure heart.

We have been warned to flee sexual immorality, idolatry, youthful lusts, false teachings, pride, disputes, envy, strife, revilings, evil suspicions, useless wranglings, greed, lack of contentment. If we do not heed the warnings to flee these things, but think either that they do not apply to us or that we can handle them, we are setting ourselves up for absolute misery as Satan defeats us and causes destruction in our lives. The Lord lovingly warns us – will we take heed and listen and obey?

The disciples were warned to flee from the coming destruction of Jerusalem and the temple because this destruction was the "… days of vengeance, that all things which are written may be fulfilled." The expression "the days of vengeance" indicates a definite period of judgment; and this is emphasized by the words, "that all things which are written" - which means, of course, all the threats of judgment, recorded in the law and the prophets – "might be fulfilled." Again, if words have any meanings, then all things of that nature were fulfilled at the destruction of Jerusalem in AD 70. There cannot be after that another tribulation, especially one that is worse than this one.

I am fully aware that the next verses we will discuss, Matthew 24: 29-31, are hard to bring into the time frame of the first century. Yet, if we believe the words of the Lord that "this generation will by no means pass away till all these things take place", then we must do so. We cannot place them outside of the Lord's direct reference to "this generation" which is in verse 34. So we must rely upon the Holy Spirit for interpretive wisdom. We will look at Matthew 24: 29-31.

29 "Immediately after the tribulation of those days the sun will be darkened, and the moon will not give its light; the stars will fall from heaven, and the powers of the heavens will be shaken. 30 Then the sign of the Son of Man will appear in heaven, and then all the tribes of the earth will mourn, and they will see the Son of Man coming on the clouds of heaven with power and great glory. 31 And He will send His angels with a great sound of a trumpet, and they will gather together His elect from the four winds, from one end of heaven to the other.

In the immediate days following the destruction of Jerusalem and the temple, there would be a shaking of the heavens and a darkening of the sun and the moon. Is this a literal event or a symbolic one? Well, I think you know the answer, although many will not accept it because of faulty teaching.

As we have seen in previously, God uses hyperbolic symbolism to emphasize His judgment upon nations. Jesus did the same. The sun, the moon and the stars refer to the rulers of Israel and the political powers thereof. They would collapse entirely. There would be no more Israel. It's political and religious infrastructure would no longer exist. The Romans would destroy it completely.

The symbolism of sun, moon and stars referring to rulers goes back to Joseph and his dream of the sun, moon and stars bowing before him in Genesis 37.

9 Then he dreamed still another dream and told it to his brothers, and said, "Look, I have dreamed another dream. And this time, the sun, the moon, and the eleven stars bowed down to me." 10 So he told it to his father and his brothers; and his father rebuked him and said to him, "What is this dream that you have dreamed? Shall your mother and I and your brothers indeed come to bow down to the earth before you?"

Jacob acknowledges that the sun symbolized him as the leader of the family, the moon symbolized Joseph's mother, Rachel, and the stars symbolized the brothers. There is a rule to be used in interpretation of Scripture, and it is called the law of first mention. The first mention of a word or a figure of speech or a symbol in Scripture sets its meaning for the rest of Scripture. Especially when used in hyperbole as Jesus used it here. The powers of Israel would collapse.

Verse 30 has caused a lot of confusion. The better translation of it is: "And then shall appear the sign of the Son of Man in heaven: and then shall all the tribes of the earth mourn; and they shall see the Son of Man coming in the clouds of heaven with power and great glory."

What is it that appears in heaven, the sign or the Son of Man? A sign will appear to the tribes of the earth, to Israel, that the Son of Man is in heaven. In contrast to the sun, moon and stars of Israel losing their power and authority, Jesus, the Son of Man, has now assumed that power that was, is and always will be His. He is the Sovereign Ruler of the universe and He will grant a sign to all that He is in heaven ruling with all authority.

Israel would mourn when they see the power of Jesus displayed. The words "tribes of the earth" refers to Israel, not every other nation on earth (Strong's Concordance # G5444 **1)** a tribe **a)** in the NT all the persons descending from one of the twelve sons of the patriarch, Jacob). Israel would see that the destruction of their beloved city and temple was because of their rejection of Jesus. They would mourn, but would not repent.

The authority that the Lord displays would be because of His "coming on the clouds of heaven with power and great glory." "But", I can hear many saying, "He has not done that yet. He has not come on the clouds of heaven with power and great glory yet." Oh yes He has. This verse refers absolutely to His ascension, not His second coming. This is a quote taken from Daniel 7: 13, 14.

13 "I was watching in the night visions, And behold, One like the Son of Man, coming with the clouds of heaven! He came to the Ancient of Days, and they brought Him near before Him. 14 Then to Him was given dominion and glory and a kingdom, that all peoples, nations, and languages should serve Him. His dominion is an everlasting dominion, which shall not pass away, and His kingdom the one which shall not be destroyed.

Daniel clearly says that "One like the Son of Man", which is the same title used by Jesus to describe Himself in Matthew 24, was "coming with the clouds of heaven", which is the identical activity that Jesus describes in the Olivet Discourse. Daniel further states that "to Him was given dominion and glory and a kingdom, that all peoples, nations, and languages should serve Him." Jesus says that when He comes with the clouds of heaven, it would be with "power and great glory", and that He would send forth His angels – His messengers - who would "gather together His elect from the four winds, from one end of heaven to the other." Again, both Daniel and Jesus describe the same result which is the One who is like the Son of Man coming with the clouds is to be worshiped by people from every nation. The sign that of the Son of Man is in heaven is that the gospel is being preached to all peoples from every nation and they are responding to the gospel and are serving Him. Can there be any doubt that Jesus was referring to His ascension rather than His second coming? Only those with a predisposed tendency toward Dispensational and Pre-Millennial doctrine would think otherwise.

Jesus then gives the illustration of the fig tree. He said that when the tender branch of the fig tree puts forth is leaves, it means that summer is near, not that it had actually come. The distinction is important. When "all these things" began to take place, it indicated to them that "it" was "near, even at the doors." The fact that "all these things" were to be fulfilled before "this generation" had passed away simply could not have referred to the second coming of Christ, but must apply to the prophecy of the destruction of Jerusalem and of the Jewish nation.

This is a very simple answer to the question the disciples asked as to when the temple and city were to be destroyed. "When you see these things begin to happen", then know that it will be soon. But, if you attempt to make them apply to the second coming of Jesus, then you are faced with many problems of interpretation.

Alfred Edersheim points out in this connection that the bursting of the fig tree into leaf is not the sign of harvest, which is the end of the age, but of summer, which precedes the harvest. This too, is significant.

So many people read into the Lord's words in Matthew 24: 4-8 that these are signs of His second coming. But, these words merely describe what would occur during the course of the ages between His ascension and His second coming. In describing the deceptions and wars and other commotions which were to characterize this age from the very start, the Lord used an expression that we need to take notice of. All these, He said, are the beginning of "sorrow" (Matthew 24:8). This word is a feminine noun that describes the pain of child birth (Strong Concordance #G3601). But there is hope in the labor pains of child birth, for they give way to joy in the birth of a child.

The age in which we live is the period of the birth pangs which will end at the last trumpet sound that ushers in eternity. It will be the day of the "revealing of the sons of God" (Romans 8:19). The word "birth pangs" connects this part of our Lord's prophecy with that of Paul in (Romans 8:22, where the same word occurs in its verb form, "For we know that the whole creation groans and labors with birth pangs together until now." But the verses which precede tell what the joyful outcome will be, namely, the manifestation of the sons of God, also called the adoption, at which time the creation itself also shall be delivered from the bondage of corruption into the glorious liberty of the children of God.

The words used to describe birth pains are found again in a similar connection in 1 Thessalonians 5:3, where, speaking of the coming of the day of the Lord, Paul says: 3 For when they say, 'Peace and safety!' then sudden destruction comes upon them, as labor pains upon a pregnant woman. And they shall not escape.

These and other passages of Scripture indicate that woes and pains of the sort specified by the Lord in Matthew 24:6–8 will visit the earth with intensified force at the very time of the end. But, it is important to understand that the frequency of such occurrences throughout the age in no way means that they are signs of the nearness of the second coming. They have always occurred, and always will until the Lord returns. At times wars, famines, and earthquakes have been more frequent than at other times. The wars and other woes are the beginning of birth pangs, not the birth itself. We must remember that birth pangs, after the first intense ones, are intermittent until, at the very end, they become the most severe of all. Then comes the joy of a new life. For us, it is a new life in eternity.

The division of the two events in the Olivet Discourse, the destruction of Jerusalem and the second coming of Jesus appear to occur after the illustration of the fig tree. In Mark and Matthew, Jesus then says that "of that day and hour no one knows, not even the angels of Heaven, but My Father only." This statement must refer to His second coming because in verse 23 of Mark 13, Jesus says, "23 But take heed; see, I have told you all things beforehand."

Jesus very clearly tells His disciples the events that would transpire prior to the siege of Jerusalem. He told them exactly what to look for so they could escape the city and the destruction. These were the things that would happen to that generation then alive. But of His second coming, there were no signs that would precede it. In Matthew's account, Jesus gives the example of the days of Noah. Life was going on as it always had. Nothing special was happening to warn the people then of impending disaster except for the preaching of Noah, which was totally ignored by the people then alive.

Faithful ministers of the gospel are preaching that there is a day of judgment coming for all the world, but most people ignore them and their words of warning. That is all the warning that anyone will receive. There are no special signs that will precede His second coming. Jesus strictly spoke of an "evil and adulterous generation" that seeks after signs. He owes no one a sign of His coming. We are to be prepared through faith in Him and being alert to the possibility that He could return today. We are to live holy lives and expect that He could return at any time.

Those who expect signs and wonders to precede His return are looking for the wrong things. Nothing will announce His return except for the shout, the trumpet, and the voice of the archangel.

Why do so many people attempt to set times for the Lord's return? Why cannot people be content to take the Lord at His word that "no one knows the day or the hour...but My Father only"? But, someone says, Jesus says the "day and the hour", not the year. Through the years, there have been multitudes of "Bible students" (I put that in quotes because a real Bible student would understand the force of the Lord's words to mean that no one was to try to compute even the general time of His return) who have attempted to set a year of His return. Guess what? They are all wrong. They have deliberately refused to heed the words of Jesus that "no one knows the day or the hour...but My Father only." Somehow they think that they are excluded from that meaning, that because they have "studied" the Scriptures, that they are specially chosen by God to announce to the world when Jesus will return. How foolish of them. If they really believe the Bible, they will cease from their nonsense of date setting – and trying to impress others with their "special knowledge" - and simply live the lives that God has called all of His people to live.

Jesus gives a parable to illustrate His words. He tells of a man who takes a journey into a far country and leaves his servants with the authority to do what was needed in order to maintain his household. He tells them to watch for his return, because they did not know when he would come home. Jesus emphasizes the need to "watch" in these verses. He says it four times. Why watch? Because, NO ONE knows when He will return. No one can even guess the time period He will return. So why try? Because not even those who deem themselves to be fine Christians and Bible students will believe every word of the Lord. They must think that Jesus did not mean them when He spoke these words. I can't think of any other reason why they persist.

I am reminded of a well known "prophecy expert" who was speaking in a large church in Virginia many years ago. If memory serves my correctly, it was in the early seventies. He was speaking of the wars and rumors of wars, earthquakes, famines, etc. as occurring at a rate that the Lords' return MUST happen at any time. He was getting excited and jumping around the pulpit area. He turned to the host pastor and said (I still remember these words), "Brother Jerry, if these are the signs of His second coming, and the rapture must happen seven years before Jesus returns, that means that the rapture must happen any day now." Then he and the host pastor started whooping it up.

Well, quite obviously, Jesus did not return in the seventies, nor did the "rapture" occur then to usher in the "great tribulation" that supposedly precedes the second coming. Over thirty years later, this "prophecy expert" is still at it. I have no doubt as to His salvation or his sincerity in his belief system, but it is a wrong system. Time has proven – and Jesus has declared - that what this "expert" deems to be signs of the Lord's return are not signs at all, but are merely normal occurrences that will continue until Jesus does return.

For the first event under consideration in the Olivet Discourse, the destruction of Jerusalem, there was a specific sign, the Roman armies surrounding the city. For the second event, the second coming of Jesus, there are no signs. Period. Nor is there a coming "great tribulation period" of Bible prophecy. It is past history. Never to be repeated again.

Now, having said all of this, it very well may be that in our future God has a period of distress that will come upon the earth. There have been such periods in the past – times of plagues and extreme hardship and war and the devastating results of it - and the Bible declares that they will continue until the end. From studying history, it appears that these events are cyclic in nature and intensity. Again, as Jesus said, "this is the beginning of sorrows." Only the beginning. Which means a continuation of the same.

Man, believing that he knows what is best, and desiring to be the lord and master of his own life, continues to ignore God and to live according to the "dictates of his evil heart." God is under no obligation to withhold any form of discipline or judgment that He may deem necessary to get the attention of mankind. Yet, as we read in Revelation 9: 20, 21; 16; 9, 11, that even with God sending judgment upon the arrogance and sin of humanity, man refuses to repent and to worship God.

There is no doubt that we are nearer the second coming of Jesus than the disciples of the first century were. Time marches onward. Each passing hour, day, week, month and year closes in on the culmination of mankind's earthly existence. Until that day, man will go merrily on his way, living life as if there is no accountability for his actions or any judgment. Then the Lord will come when least expected and time will end and man will face His Maker.

The time of preparation is now. There will be no warnings or signs. Be watchful and alert, praying with anticipation and hope, living with the sure knowledge that Jesus is coming again, and it could be today.

Chapter Seven

The Millennium

The idea of a literal one thousand year reign of Jesus upon the earth, ruling from a literal throne in Jerusalem, is another misunderstanding of Scripture that the Dispensationalists and Pre-Millennial brethren have. Again, this is something that they have been taught as an important part of their systematic theology and that they have received as truth, but in all likelihood, have never considered from any other point of view. If they have considered another interpretation, it most likely would be from the Pre-Millennial writers who discredit it. To consider anything other than what they have received would, to their minds, be tantamount to the vilest of heresy.

As with the other Scriptures we have examined in this discourse, there is another, more reasonable explanation of the ONLY Scripture that mentions this "thousand years". The only passage that mentions the "thousand years" is in Revelation 20, where it is mentioned six times in the first seven verses.

Since God has left us His Word to read, study, explore, interpret, and proclaim, and since we all are human, and as humans, have limited intelligence, we are therefore not to approach Scripture from a preconceived and predetermined system into which all Scripture must fit, but we are to allow the passage under consideration to manifest itself to us through the leading of the Holy Spirit. We are to allow the passage to speak for itself, reading nothing more into it than is there. We are to use other Scripture to interpret it. Again, as has been stated, it is the clear teaching of Scripture that must be used to interpret the more obscure passages, the ones harder to understand. The passage before us is clear in what it does not teach and in what it does teach.

The Views of the Millennium

The "millennial" passage has caused much confusion among Christians. This is another passage that has many views. There are three main ones. The first and predominant one today is the Pre-Millennial view. This view states that this is the time between the second coming of Jesus – which occurs seven years after the "rapture" – and the great white throne judgment. During this time, Jesus rules from His (David's) throne in Jerusalem. He rules over the earth with a rod of iron, putting down all insurrection and rebellion immediately. The prefix "pre" means that Jesus returns before the millennium.

The second view is what is called Post-Millennialism. There are many offshoots of this view, but the general view is that the gospel has effectively converted much of the world and has ushered in the "millennium", a one thousand year period of relative peace and prosperity for the world. Jesus returns after this period. "Post" means after.

The third view is A-Millennialism. The prefix "A" means no. No millennium. It holds that there is no literal one thousand year reign of Jesus upon the earth either before or after the second coming of Jesus. It sees the thousand years as symbolic in nature rather than literal. It sees the ruling and reigning that is mentioned in Revelation 20 as occurring in Heaven rather than on earth. It understands that during this time the power of Satan is limited in its ability to hinder the work of the gospel as it is preached throughout the world. It sees the "thousand years" as symbolizing the entire period between the first and second comings of Jesus, the gospel age.

In each of these views, there are many variations that very well may include parts of other interpretations. Not all millennial views strictly adhere to the definitions given above as to what the thousand years are about. What I believe is important to keep in mind is that we all are fallible and are not perfect in our understanding of Scripture. We should be convinced in our hearts that we have reached the truth as revealed by the Holy Spirit as we study before Him. We must all give account of ourselves to God, not to others, as to what we believe and why we believe it. We should, however, be ready to give an explanation as to why we believe what we believe. As I have stated before, no one should believe anything simply and only because they were taught it, but should reach conclusions based upon their own study and prayerful consideration of God's Word.

It has already been established in another chapter using passages of Scripture that cannot be misunderstood unless done so intentionally that there is nothing that can occur on this present earth after the second coming of Jesus. The second coming of Jesus occurs on the last day when the last trumpet sounds that defeats the last enemy, which is death. Death is defeated by the resurrection. Then comes the end. Eternity. So, what the Pre-Millennialists teach as to the millennium cannot be. Scripture will not allow it. There are no people left in flesh and blood bodies to inhabit the earth. Everyone has faced the judgment and been either given new bodies or cast into hell. The new heavens and new earth are in existence then when the Lord restores all things to their original creation or better. We are then in eternity, not a period of time that the Jews have a renewed kingdom of David.

What Does Revelation 20 Teach?

So, what does Revelation 20 teach if it does not teach a literal one thousand year reign of Jesus on the earth? Let's look at the passage and see what we can determine.

1 Then I saw an angel coming down from heaven, having the key to the bottomless pit and a great chain in his hand. 2 He laid hold of the dragon, that serpent of old, who is the Devil and Satan, and bound him for a thousand years; 3 and he cast him into the bottomless pit, and shut him up, and set a seal on him, so that he should deceive the nations no more till the thousand years were finished. But after these things he must be released for a little while. 4 And I saw thrones, and they sat on them, and judgment was committed to them. Then I saw the souls of those who had been beheaded for their witness to Jesus and for the word of God, who had not worshiped the beast or his image, and had not received his mark on their foreheads or on their hands. And they lived and reigned with Christ for a thousand years. 5 But the rest of the dead did not live again until the thousand years were finished. This is the first resurrection. 6 Blessed and holy is he who has part in the first resurrection. Over such the second death has no power, but they shall be priests of God and of Christ, and shall reign with Him a thousand years. 7 Now when the thousand years have expired, Satan will be released from his prison 8 and will go out to deceive the nations which are in the four corners of the earth, Gog and Magog, to gather them together to battle, whose number is as the sand of the sea.

Let's begin our study of this passage by asking a few pertinent questions that will aid us in our study. We will use the predominant teaching of the day, the Pre-Millennial position, as the basis of our questions. Since Pre-Millennialists declare adamantly that they have the correct interpretation of eschatology and of the millennium – which they specifically base upon this passage - then we will ask all of these questions in regard to their interpretation.

1. Where in this passage is the second coming mentioned as preceding this thousand years? Answer: it is not.
2. Where in this passage is it stated that people are ruling on the earth during this time? Answer: it is not. It is the "souls of them" who had been beheaded for the sake of Jesus who are ruling and reigning with Christ in Heaven. Not one mention is made of the bodies of people on the earth.
3. Where in this passage is it said that anyone is ruling on earth, even Christ? Answer: nowhere.
4. Where in this passage is the throne of David, Jerusalem, a restored temple or kingdom or Israel mentioned? Answer: nowhere.
5. Where in this passage is peace and prosperity mentioned as prevailing upon the earth? Answer: nowhere.

I think it is important at this point to ask what Jesus Himself taught concerning this important aspect of Pre-Millennial eschatology. He taught absolutely nothing. Every student of Scripture knows this, even those who adhere to Pre-Millennialism and Dispensationalism. He said not a word. Jesus taught only what He had heard from His Father.

John 8: 28 Then Jesus said to them, "When you lift up the Son of Man, then you will know that I am He, and that I do nothing of Myself; but as My Father taught Me, I speak these things... 38 I speak what I have seen with My Father.

If Jesus did not teach a word concerning a literal millennium, and He taught only what His Father taught Him, why do so many cling tenaciously to this teaching? If it were true, Jesus would have taught it. Everything the Lord taught in His direct teachings and His parables forbid the literal thousand year reign. Jesus told His disciples in John 14:2 "if it were not so, I would have told you." I think we can safely say – without being guilty of going beyond the intent of Scripture - that if the millennium were so, He would have told us because His Father would have told Him.

The Jews of our Lord's day were seeking relief from Roman domination. And who can blame them? It was a quite natural desire. As a result of their desire to be free from Roman tyranny, they misinterpreted the prophets as foretelling a day that their enemies would be defeated and they would rule over the nations of the world. They greatly desired their Messiah to be the One who would reestablish their dominance in the world. What the prophets actually foretold was a Messiah who would defeat their greatest enemy, sin, and give them victory over it and its dominion. He would do so through His sacrificial death, burial, and resurrection.

Jesus clearly stated in *John 18: 36 ... "My kingdom is **not** of this world. If My kingdom were of this world, My servants would fight, so that I should not be delivered to the Jews; but now **My kingdom is not from here.**"*

Why is it that after this unmistakable statement from Jesus so many Christians today are still looking for the same kind of Messiah that the Jews were seeking, one who would set up an earthly kingdom for the Jews? How much clearer of a statement can Jesus make about His kingdom not being earthly in nature than what He has said? That statement was true then, is true now, and will be true in the future. Jesus is **not** setting up an earthly kingdom. His is an eternal kingdom, not merely one thousand years, and it is spiritual in nature, not earthly, political, or material.

If you do believe in a literal millennium of one thousand years with all the goodies that the Dispensationalists and Pre-Millennialists accrue to it, let me give you a challenge. Find one word in the Scriptures that the Lord speaks of it and I will believe it. Find one word that the apostles speak of it - as defined by Dispensationalists and Pre-Millennialists - and I will believe it. Find the passage that clearly and unambiguously defines the thousand years as such and you will convert my thinking. As one leading Pre-Millennialist said when confronted with that challenge, "You know I can't do that." If it can't be done, then why believe it? "Because I was taught it. It fits my preference of systematic theology." Or, "I don't know enough about the Bible to dispute it."

Is holding to what you prefer to believe because you were taught it more important to you than receiving the truth of Scripture? Is being on the popular bandwagon more important to you than believing the simple truth of the Word of God? Is believing what is not clearly and unambiguously taught in the Bible - because it is more spectacular and sensational - more important to you than believing what is clearly taught?

If this passage does not refer to a literal one thousand years on earth, then what does it refer to? The "one thousand years" are symbolic. In fact, most of Revelation is symbolic in nature. If we do not understand that, then most of Revelation will be misinterpreted, as it has been by many. The first verse of Revelation sets the paradigm for interpreting the entire book.

*1 The Revelation of Jesus Christ, which God gave Him to show His servants—things which must shortly take place. And He sent and **signified** it by His angel to His servant John,*

Revelation is primarily a book that uses symbols (signified – signs) to make known God's truth. Numbers are an important part of the signifying or making known of truth in Revelation. Revelation uses numbers extensively to reveal what God is teaching. I am not going to attempt to give the meanings of other numbers as used in Revelation. We will only look at the number 1000. In the Bible, the number 10 is the number of fullness in quantity, while the number 7 is the number of fullness in quality, or perfection. The number 1000 is ten times ten times ten. "A thousand years" is symbolic for a vast, undefined period of time which is the complete quantity, or fullness of an age. It means "the sum total" or a fulfilled period of time, a long period of time. It has a similar meaning in other Scriptures.

Let's look at another passage that uses "a thousand" in a symbolic way.

Psalm 50: 10 For every beast of the forest is Mine, and the cattle on a thousand hills.

Using the Pre-Millennial method of interpretation – the literalism that they claim is the proper method of interpretation - this verse must mean that the cattle on hills number 1001 and higher do not belong to the Lord. As has been forcefully told to me by Pre-Millennialists - "a thousand" always means "a thousand." It always equals the "numerical value." Well, there you go. That settles it, doesn't it? I wonder if God is worried about or concerned with the cattle on the other hills in excess of the first thousand that do not belong to Him?

It is obvious, is it not, that "a thousand hills" is symbolic of every hill? If God owns "every beast of the forest", as He so states in the verse, does He not also own all the cattle on every hill? Even if it is so stated as Him owning the cattle on "a thousand hills"? Does not "a thousand hills" mean "every hill"? An innumerable amount of hills? Of course it does. No one would – at least I don't think anyone would – dispute this and make it mean exactly one thousand hills, no more, no less, the numerical value of one thousand.

The verses that follow, 11 and 12 amplifies the fact that it is every hill that is in view in the Psalmist's phrase "a thousand hills."

*11 I know **all** the birds of the mountains, and the wild beasts of the field are Mine. 12 "If I were hungry, I would not tell you; For the **world is Mine, and all its fullness**.*

Another example of the Bible usage of "a thousand" is that God promised His blessings on those who keep His covenant to "a thousand generations."

*Deuteronomy 7: 9 "Therefore know that the LORD your God, He is God, the faithful God who keeps covenant and mercy for **a thousand generations** with those who love Him and keep His commandments;*

*1 Chronicles 16: 15 Remember His covenant forever, the word which He commanded, for **a thousand generations**,*

*Psalm 105: 8 He remembers His covenant forever, the word which He commanded, for **a thousand generations**,*

To insist that "a thousand generations" means exactly that, to limit God's covenantal promises to a mere thousand generations, would do great disservice to the Lord. His promises to His people are forever. "A thousand generations" have the obvious meaning of forever. If we put a literal meaning to these thousand generations, then we are obliged to give each generation a Biblical length of forty years, which then translates to God's covenantal promises lasting a mere forty thousand years, 40 years times 1000 generations. Does not make any sense at all, does it? But, there are those of the literal hermeneutic who maintain that "a thousand" always means "a thousand." OKAY.

I hope we all can see the symbolism of "a thousand" as used in the Bible. Now, when the context demands the numerical value be used, there is no argument as to that. In the context before us, it does not demand a literal numerical value, but it does demand a symbolic meaning. In Revelation 20 "a thousand years" represents the entire period of time between the first and second comings of our Lord Jesus Christ. This is the time frame that the saints rule and reign with Christ. This is the time of the gospel age, the "golden age" of which the prophets spoke. The definition of the "golden age" in the context of my usage is the time between the first and second coming of the Lord Jesus Christ in which His glorious gospel is being proclaimed to all nations, peoples, and tongues.

The Scene on Earth or the Binding of Satan (verses 1 – 3)

This gospel age is the time of the binding of Satan. It has absolutely nothing to do with a literal chain that is wrapped around a spiritual being (not possible anyway) in order to keep him in the abyss for a thousand years. Satan's binding is for the specific purpose that he not be able to "deceive the nations." The "binding" means that he is limited in his ability to deceive nations as he was able to do in the past, prior to the incarnation of Jesus. God has bound him so he can no longer have entire nations under his dominion. Today, all nations have heard and have responded to the gospel. In ages past, entire nations were deceived and led into idolatry. The gospel has put an end to that. On the day of Pentecost, Acts 2: 6 declares with certainty, every nation under heaven heard the gospel. Those present on the day of Pentecost took the gospel message back to their respective countries. In addition, the apostles preached the gospel to the nations they visited.

*Acts 2: 6 And there were dwelling in Jerusalem Jews, devout men, from **every nation under heaven**.*

*Romans 1: 5 Through Him we have received grace and apostleship for obedience to the **faith among all nations**...*

Romans 16: 26 but now made manifest, and by the prophetic **Scriptures made known to all nations**, *according to the commandment of the everlasting God, for* **obedience to the faith**

Colossians 1: 5... the word of the truth of the gospel, 6 which has come to you, as it has also **in all the world**...

These verses declare in language that cannot be misunderstood that the gospel, the Word of Truth, had already gone into all nations during the first century. *(I know that there are those who will argue this point, and usually they are of the "literal hermeneutic." They will assign a symbolic meaning to this in order to fit into their system. Well, if "every nation under heaven" does not mean exactly what it says, what does it mean? If "all nations" does not mean "all nations", who is to say what it does mean? Isn't it just a whole lot easier to just believe the simple Word of God? There may be some who will find fault with this statement thinking, "if 'a thousand' does not mean 'a thousand', why does 'all nations' mean 'all nations'? Again, context and prior usage determines the meaning. Nowhere does Scripture use the phrase "all nations" in a symbolic way. So therefore, "all nations" or "every nation" means exactly what is appears to mean.)*

Satan, in the first century, was already bound in his ability to deceive entire nations. He has been since the first coming of our Lord, His crucifixion, and subsequent ascension into Heaven and still is today. This is not at all to say that most individuals within nations would accept the truth of the gospel, but that there would be those in every nation who would respond positively to the gospel of Jesus Christ. We are still commanded to "preach the gospel to every creature", and to "make disciples of every nation." We are still commanded to send missionaries to do just that. Satan is bound. People will respond to the good news of salvation through Jesus Christ. Satan cannot prevent it.

This is exactly what the Lord Jesus Christ said would happen in Matthew 12.

28 But if I cast out demons by the Spirit of God, surely the kingdom of God has come upon you. 29 Or how can one enter a strong man's house and plunder his goods, unless he first binds the strong man? And then he will plunder his house.

The Pharisees had accused Jesus of casting out demons by the power of Beelzebub, or Satan. Jesus responded by saying that a house divided against itself could not stand. If He were casting out demons by the power of Satan, that would mean that Satan was fighting against himself, which would mean that he was trying to destroy himself. That argument by the Pharisees was ludicrous. Jesus then said that if anyone would want to plunder the house of a strong man, he must first bind the strong man so he could not resist the taking of his goods. The meaning is obvious. If Jesus wanted to take back what Satan had taken by the force of deceit, He must first bind him. Satan must first be limited in his ability to hold on to the goods he had taken for himself. Jesus was saying then and there that Satan had already been bound and could not hold on to all that he had stolen through deceit, but that through the power of Jesus, many people would be redeemed. Many would be taken from Satan, from the kingdom of darkness and translated into the kingdom of light. Satan can no longer deceive everyone. He is bound by Jesus, the stronger man. If Satan were still able to deceive entire nations, it would, of necessity, mean that he was stronger than Jesus and had in fact bound Him so He could not enter into his house and take back the stolen goods, the souls of men.

There are other passages that teach this same doctrine, the defeat of Satan through the gospel. These verses make manifest the ultimate objective of the binding of Satan – his utter destruction.

John 12: 31 Now is the judgment of this world; **now** *the ruler of this world will be* **cast out***. 32 And I, if I am lifted up from the earth, will draw* **all peoples** *to Myself.*

Colossians 2: 15 Having **disarmed** *principalities and powers, He made a public spectacle of them, triumphing over them in it.*

*Hebrews 2: 14 Inasmuch then as the children have partaken of flesh and blood, He Himself likewise shared in the same, that through death He might **destroy** (render inoperative, to nullify, or to render ineffective) him who had the power of death, that is, the devil*

*1 John 3:...for this purpose the Son of God was manifested, that He might **destroy** the works of the devil.*

But it says that the devil is cast into a bottomless pit. Again, the symbolism is of restraint. He is bound and thrown into a bottomless pit. It is a double symbol of being restrained in his access to people and ability to deceive them. This double symbol is the Holy Spirit's way of reinforcing His intent so there will be no misunderstanding of the meaning – Satan is restrained from being able to act at will against the gospel, those who preach it and those who hear it. The gospel is the power of God unto salvation to everyone who believes, and it is the gospel that Satan is intent on hindering and destroying, but, thank God, that he is the one who is hindered and bound in that endeavor.

Well now, if Satan is bound, why is the world in such a mess? Why is there so much evil in the world? Our text does not say that Satan is bound in everything he does but he is only bound in his ability to deceive entire nations. Revelation 20 does not say that Satan cannot still work his deception on individuals within nations. Satan still deceives many people - it is only entire nations that will not be deceived.

Jude verse 6 gives further explanation as to the fact that being bound in chains does not bring to an end all Satanic activities. Jude 6 very clearly declares that the angels who rebelled with Satan are bound in chains: "And the angels who did not keep their proper domain, but left their own abode, He has reserved in everlasting chains under darkness for the judgment of the great day." Jude describes these angels as locked up in chains, yet we know that demonic activity occurred throughout Christ's ministry and continues today. So, we can say with confidence that to be chained does not mean all evil activity will cease. In spite of being bound, Satan continues his evil work. What is the chain that binds the activities of Satan and his hoard of demons? The decree of God. God has spoken, His command has gone forth, and Satan is restricted by God's word in the same way as God limited Satan's ability to attack Job. Satan is only allowed to act in the manner prescribed by God. He cannot deceive entire nations as he did previous to the first coming of Christ. Because God has bound Satan by His sovereign decree, people are being saved out of every tribe, tongue and nation.

Those who insist that this binding in Revelation 20 is a physical binding for a literal thousand years rather than a spiritual binding for the duration of the gospel age forget that the message of the Word of God – from beginning to end – is the gospel, the redemption of man from sin through the death, burial, and resurrection of Jesus. The message of the Bible is not a message of an earthly kingdom for the Jews.

At the end of the "thousand years" the devil is loosed from his prison for a brief period of time in order that he may "go out to deceive the nations which are in the four corners of the earth." After this extended period of restraint, this binding, Satan is given authority once again to deceive nations. He goes out with great fury because he knows his time is short, and with great authority, he deceives the nations. After being under the influence of the gospel and its saving power, people will choose to rebel against the power of God (the gospel) and believe "the lie." It all ends when Jesus returns "in flaming fire taking vengeance on those who do not know God, and on those who do not obey the gospel of our Lord Jesus Christ" (2 Thessalonians 1:8). They shall be "punished with everlasting destruction from the presence of the Lord and from the glory of His power" (verse 9).

This brief period of the loosing of Satan from his restraining decree of God is described, I believe, in 2 Thessalonians 2.

1 Now, brethren, concerning the coming of our Lord Jesus Christ and our gathering together to Him, we ask you, 2 not to be soon shaken in mind or troubled, either by spirit or by word or by letter, as if from us, as though the day of Christ had come. 3 Let no one deceive you by any means; for that Day will not come unless the falling away comes first, and the man of sin is revealed, the son of perdition, 4 who opposes and exalts himself above all that is called God or that is worshiped, so that he sits as God in the temple of God, showing himself that he is God.

5 Do you not remember that when I was still with you I told you these things? 6 And now you know what is restraining, that he may be revealed in his own time. 7 For the mystery of lawlessness is already at work; only He who now restrains will do so until He is taken out of the way. 8 And then the lawless one will be revealed, whom the Lord will consume with the breath of His mouth and destroy with the brightness of His coming. 9 The coming of the lawless one is according to the working of Satan, with all power, signs, and lying wonders, 10 and with all unrighteous deception among those who perish, because they did not receive the love of the truth, that they might be saved. 11 And for this reason God will send them strong delusion, that they should believe the lie, 12 that they all may be condemned who did not believe the truth but had pleasure in unrighteousness.

It very well may be that Satan incarnates himself in human flesh – the "man of sin" and "son of perdition" - and becomes a leader who holds sway over the entire world during this time of delusion. At the time just prior to the Lord's return, there will be period of extreme apostasy, of declension of faith, of a hatred of God, of a worship of Satan, whether a spiritual or fleshly manifestation. God has lifted His restraining decree, has taken it out of the way, and has given the devil free reign again in his ability to deceive the nations. How is it possible that nations can be deceived after being under the influence of the gospel for so long? Because, verse 10 states, "they did not receive the love of the truth that they may be saved." Because, verse 12 says, "they did not believe the truth, but had pleasure in unrighteousness." But this deception will only be for a short amount of time, the exact limit not known. Then, the Lord returns and destroys the destroyer with "the breath of His mouth and the brightness of His coming". The eternal punishment of the deceiver begins.

The Scene in Heaven (verses 4 – 6)

These verses portray thrones and those who sit upon them have power to judge. Who are these who are sitting on the thrones and judging? Verse 4 does not say who they are, but the following verses give us a clue as to who they are. Those who are portrayed as sitting on the thrones are "the souls of those who had been beheaded for their witness to Jesus and for the word of God, who had not worshiped the beast or his image, and had not received *his* mark on their foreheads or on their hands. And they lived and reigned with Christ for a thousand years."

This is a heavenly scene, not an earthly one. John saw "the souls" of those who had been beheaded for their witness to Jesus. He saw "the souls" of those who had not worshiped the beast or his image and had not received his mark on their foreheads or their hands. "The souls" of them. The invisible to human eyes spiritual and immaterial part of every human being that lives on forever. The part of our being that is made in the image of God. The very real part of our personage that is eternal in nature. The real us that goes to be with the Lord when we die. They are the ones who are reigning with Christ on the thrones.

Yet, are we all who are saved not a part of this scene? Ephesians 2 teaches that when we are saved, we become a part of this heavenly scene.

4 But God, who is rich in mercy, because of His great love with which He loved us, 5 even when we were dead in trespasses, made us alive together with Christ (by grace you have been saved), 6 and raised us up together, and made us sit together in the heavenly places in Christ Jesus,

The apostle Paul declares that when we were made alive by the grace of God, we were raised up and made to sit together in the heavenly places in Christ Jesus. Spiritually, we are already in the heavenly places according to this verse. Colossians 1 teaches the same truth.

13 He has delivered us from the power of darkness and conveyed us into the kingdom of the Son of His love,

He "has delivered us from" and has "conveyed us into". It is past tense. It has occurred. We are in the kingdom of the Son of God now. It is not to occur later, but it has occurred already. We are reigning with Jesus in His kingdom right this very minute.

Revelation 1:5-6 states that Jesus Christ *"has made us kings and priests to His God and Father, to Him be glory and dominion forever and ever. Amen."*

Revelation 5: 9 says *"...You were slain, and have redeemed us to God by Your blood out of every tribe and tongue and people and nation, 10 And have made us kings and priests to our God; And we shall reign on the earth."*

The moment we are saved we are translated into His kingdom and begin reigning with Him. We become "kings and priests" through faith in Jesus Christ. The saints who have died are currently with the Lord in Heaven ruling with Him. We who are still on earth are ruling with Him also. We are reigning with Him right now. We have all of His power and authority available to us right now.

Matthew 28: 18 And Jesus came and spoke to them, saying, "All authority has been given to Me in heaven and on earth.

Jesus has all power and authority in heaven and on earth right now and He has delegated to His disciples that authority so they can preach the gospel to every nation. We hold down a royal position of representing Jesus on earth. He promises that He is able to do far greater things than we can even imagine. His power surpasses our wildest imaginations.

Ephesians 1: 19 and what is the exceeding greatness of His power toward us who believe, according to the working of His mighty power 20 which He worked in Christ when He raised Him from the dead and seated Him at His right hand in the heavenly places,

Ephesians 3: 20 Now to Him who is able to do exceedingly abundantly above all that we ask or think, according to the power that works in us

We have all the power of the risen Lord at our disposal. Why would we even need it? To overcome temptation. To stand firm when oppressed by others. To minister the grace of God to those who oppose us. To demonstrate mercy to those who attack us. To faithfully preach the gospel to those who will not hear. To allow the life of Jesus to be lived in us. We are reigning with Jesus when we rule over our sinful nature and lusts. When we are faithful to Him in the face of opposition.

Reigning with Jesus is a current position, and it will continue throughout eternity. We will be in His presence forever, enjoying the position in His eternal kingdom. Wait a minute! Revelation says it is those who did not receive the mark of the beast in their foreheads or their hands. How do you explain that? That happens in the tribulation period. Everybody knows that.

We have already established that the "tribulation period" as defined by Dispensationalists and Pre-Tribulationalists is a misnomer and an invention of man. So this "mark of the beast" is not what they say it is. It has no bearing on computer chips under the skin or tattoos or any such like. It, like almost everything in Revelation is symbolic, not literal. Or, if you prefer to say, it is literally symbolic.

The mark of the beast is said to be in either the forehead or the right hand. Using this symbolism, Jesus is saying that those who have this "mark" are serving Satan through their thoughts – the mark on the forehead – and serving him through their deeds – the mark on the hands. Anyone who has received Jesus as Lord and Savior cannot receive such a mark because they have the Holy Spirit indwelling them. Those who choose to rebel against the gospel and live life their own way serve Satan both in their thoughts and deeds. They have received his "mark" on themselves, and because of that, have no part in the "first resurrection." They do not live again until the "thousand years" are finished. They are not resurrected until the judgment day when Jesus returns. They are resurrected in order to face judgment and sentencing.

The First Resurrection

Our passage in Revelation 20 puts the first resurrection in opposition to those who "lived not again until the thousand years were finished." Doesn't that mean that the first resurrection is at the rapture when the "dead in Christ shall rise first"? No. Not at all. There is no "rapture" that precedes the second coming by seven years. *(Pre-Millennialists tout three resurrections. One at "the rapture" which are the church age saints; another at the end of the "tribulation period" which are the "tribulation saints", which I suppose is the "second stage of the first resurrection" if their theology is to be consistent; the third at the end of the "millennium" which is everyone else. The Word of God knows of only two resurrections. Explanation follows.)*

Revelation 20: 5...This is the first resurrection. 6 Blessed and holy is he who has part in the first resurrection. Over such the second death has no power, but they shall be priests of God and of Christ, and shall reign with Him a thousand years.

What is the "first resurrection" and when does it occur if it has nothing to do with the "rapture"? Well, looking at our passage, who is in view here as having taken part in the first resurrection? It is those who have not received the mark of the beast, nor worshiped him. It is the ones who are seated on the thrones, who are reigning with Jesus. It is the ones who have placed their faith in the crucified and risen Lord Jesus Christ and have trusted in Him for salvation. The first resurrection is the spiritual resurrection that has made us alive unto God. Anyone who has been made alive spiritually will never see "the second death".

The Bible clearly, repeat, clearly teaches that the first resurrection is a spiritual one, not a physical one. Just because the popular system does not recognize that does not negate its truth. Let's examine some verses that teach this first resurrection as being a spiritual one.

We will start with what the Lord Himself taught.

*John 5: 24 "Most assuredly, I say to you, he who hears My word and believes in Him who sent Me has everlasting life, and shall not come into judgment, but has passed from death into life. 25 Most assuredly, I say to you, the hour is coming, and **now is**, when the dead will hear the voice of the Son of God; and those who hear will live.*

Jesus clearly said that the hour for resurrection is NOW. He was raising those who heard His voice. The dead – spiritually dead – heard the voice of Jesus, believed what He said, obeyed His words, and were raised from the dead to life, spiritual, eternal life.

In verses 28 and 29 He speaks of the second resurrection, which is the physical one.

28 Do not marvel at this; for the hour is coming in which all who are in the graves will hear His voice 29 and come forth—those who have done good, to the resurrection of life, and those who have done evil, to the resurrection of condemnation.

This is the general resurrection, the physical one, in which all who have ever lived will participate. Some will be resurrected to life, others to condemnation, but all will be resurrected in "the hour" designated by the Father.

Ephesians 2: 5 even when we were dead in trespasses, made us alive together with Christ (by grace you have been saved), 6 and raised us up together, and made us sit together in the heavenly places in Christ Jesus

We were "dead in trespasses" and He "made us alive". That is a resurrection. He "raised us up" and made us to "sit in the heavenly places". How can we be raised up and be seated in the heavenly places if we have not been "raised up, made alive" spiritually? If we are positionally in "the heavenlies", then we have been put there by Someone, somehow. Spiritual resurrection by Jesus is how.

Colossians 2: 12 buried with Him in baptism, in which you also were raised with Him through faith in the working of God, who raised Him from the dead. 13 And you, being dead in your trespasses and the uncircumcision of your flesh, He has made alive together with Him, having forgiven you all trespasses

When Paul discusses baptism, which is a sign and seal of regeneration, he also connects the resurrection of the soul with the resurrection of Jesus Christ. What Jesus experienced physically, death, burial, and resurrection, we experience spiritually through faith in Him. We have died to self, been buried through baptism with Him, and resurrected with Him so we now walk in "newness of life."

Romans 6: 4 Therefore we were buried with Him through baptism into death, that just as Christ was raised from the dead by the glory of the Father, even so we also should walk in newness of life.

The first resurrection is a spiritual one, not a physical one. It is the being "born again" of John 3. It is the giving of life, of the abundant life of John 10. The physical resurrection follows when the Lord Jesus Christ is revealed from Heaven when He comes again. There are no resurrections to follow. Period.

Those who have been resurrected through faith in Jesus Christ rule and reign with Him throughout the "thousand years" and the second death will never have power over them. They shall live with Christ eternally.

But, if we carefully analyze all the Pre-Millennial doctrines associated with "the millennium", we will find a multitude of serious discrepancies. These discrepancies, although deserving of in depth study, will only be mentioned with a few explanatory notes. Serious study and consideration of these discrepancies will serve the reader well and give a great benefit in further understanding of these issues.

Millennial Discrepancies

Pre-Millennialists claim that the Old Testament gives weight to their arguments. But, where in the Old Testament do we read anything at all that the Millennium is as they define it? Nowhere is anything of the like mentioned even vaguely. The prophets do not give any prediction at all that approximates the teachings of Dispensationalists and Pre-Millennialists. The prophets do not prophesy of a limited reign of the Messiah that ends in a fierce battle after He comes back to earth. They do not teach anything other than destruction and eternal punishment for the unsaved at the second coming of Jesus. They do, however, speak of a spiritual kingdom that lasts forever for those who trust in the Lord (Psalm 37:39; 110:13; Isaiah 45:17; 46:13; 53: 6; and many others). The prophets were spiritual men who preached repentance to Israel. They wanted spiritual renewal, not earthly kingdoms.

The prophets taught an everlasting kingdom over which Messiah would reign forever and ever. Nowhere is a limited one thousand year reign of Messiah mentioned in the prophets. Nowhere is it mentioned that at the end of the thousand years there would be a rebellion against Him that would result in a fierce battle. The fulfillment of their prophecies is to be in "the last days", "those days", "latter days." Nothing at all is said that there is to be a millennial kingdom of a thousand years that culminates earthly time. We are told that since the first coming of Jesus that we are "in the last days."

Acts 2:16 But this is what was spoken by the prophet Joel: 17 ' And it shall come to pass in the last days, says God, that I will pour out of My Spirit on all flesh; Your sons and your daughters shall prophesy, your young men shall see visions, your old men shall dream dreams. 18 And on My menservants and on My maidservants I will pour out My Spirit in those days; And they shall prophesy. 19 I will show wonders in heaven above and signs in the earth beneath: Blood and fire and vapor of smoke. 20 The sun shall be turned into darkness, and the moon into blood, before the coming of the great and awesome day of the LORD. 21 And it shall come to pass that whoever calls on the name of the LORD shall be saved.'

Peter specifically states that what occurred on the Day of Pentecost was what the prophet Joel had prophesied would occur in the "last days." "This is what was spoken. This is the fulfillment of Joel's prophecy. These are the last days." The prophesying, the visions, the dreams, the pouring out of the Holy Spirit, the wonders in Heaven and signs on earth, the blood, fire, vapor of smoke, the sun turning dark and moon turning into blood; all of these signs occurred on the Day of Pentecost and was indicative of the power of the gospel to save all who call upon the name of the Lord. The power of the gospel message to save all who call upon the Lord is the sign of the "last days."

Hebrews 1: 1 is another verse that declares with certainty that the "last days" began with the earthly ministry of Jesus.

1 God, who at various times and in various ways spoke in time past to the fathers by the prophets, 2 has in these last days spoken to us by His Son,

The last days will endure until Jesus returns. Then comes the end. Eternity.

The prophets predicted judgment, not a second chance in the "millennium." Many are the passages in the Old Testament that speak of judgment. I will quote but one. It is in the New Testament, quoting an Old Testament saint.

Jude 14 Now Enoch, the seventh from Adam, prophesied about these men also, saying, "Behold, the Lord comes with ten thousands of His saints, 15 to execute judgment on all, to convict all who are ungodly among them of all their ungodly deeds which they have committed in an ungodly way, and of all the harsh things which ungodly sinners have spoken against Him."

Enoch, the seventh generation from Adam, prophesied that the Lord would come with His saints (holy ones, angels) in order to execute judgment upon the ungodly. Judgment, not entrance into a "millennium" is what occurs at the second coming of Jesus. Both testaments concur with this analysis.

In the New Testament, the apostles gave witness to Biblical truth as contained in the Old Testament concerning the second coming. Peter, in Acts 3 states, *24 Yes, and all the prophets, from Samuel and those who follow, as many as have spoken, have also foretold these days. 25 You are sons of the prophets, and of the covenant which God made with our fathers, saying to Abraham, 'And in your seed all the families of the earth shall be blessed.' 26 To you first, God, having raised up His Servant Jesus, sent Him to bless you, in turning away every one of you from your iniquities."*

All of the prophets, every one of them, spoke of the days of the gospel going forth into all the world according to the covenant God made with Abraham. The covenant was not of an earthly nature, not of a "millennial kingdom", but of salvation from sin through Jesus Christ and His sacrifice. Is that too hard to grasp? Why then do so many insist upon their imagined "millennial kingdom" upon the earth?

Jesus Himself had nothing at all to say of this millennial doctrine. Listen to the words in Mark 1: *14 Now after John was put in prison, Jesus came to Galilee, preaching the gospel of the kingdom of God, 15 and saying, "The time is fulfilled, and the kingdom of God is at hand. Repent, and believe in the gospel."*

The kingdom of God is directly related to repentance and believing the gospel. The time of the kingdom of God was right then and there when Jesus was preaching it. He was preaching it because it was present then. Ah hah! someone says. That was the "kingdom of God" that Jesus was preaching, but the millennial kingdom is the "kingdom of heaven." There is a difference. So teach all good Dispensationalists and Pre-Millennialists. Oh? Is that so? *(Another butchering of the Word of God - or should we say it is a surgically precise operation?)*

Matthew 4: 17 From that time Jesus began to preach and to say, "Repent, for the kingdom of heaven is at hand."

From His baptism onward, Jesus preached the "kingdom of heaven" according to Matthew. Mark says the "kingdom of God." Was Jesus confused? Or were the gospel writers confused?

According to Schofield and company, somebody must have gotten it wrong. Dispensationalists make a distinction between the "kingdom of God", which they admit is a spiritual kingdom and the "kingdom of heaven", which they assign as an earthly kingdom. Yet, the gospel writers refer to the same event when they say that Jesus was preaching the "kingdom of God" and the "kingdom of heaven." So, which kingdom did Jesus preach? Wasn't He aware that they are two separate kingdoms – according to Dispensationalists - or did He intend to deceive His listeners so they would be confused? Well, sarcasm aside, common sense dictates that they are not two separate kingdoms. They are identical, regardless of the popular teaching.

Again, we must bear in mind the audiences to which each were writing. The "kingdom of heaven" was something the Jews would understand and the "kingdom of God" was designed to make more sense to Gentiles. They both refer to the one and only kingdom into which those who trust Jesus as Lord enter – the kingdom of the Son of God. It is a kingdom ruled by Christ, and it is "within" us.

Luke 17: 20 Now when He was asked by the Pharisees when the kingdom of God would come, He answered them and said, "The kingdom of God does not come with observation; 21 nor will they say, 'See here!' or 'See there!' For indeed, the kingdom of God is within you."

The Pharisees questioned Jesus as to when the kingdom of God would come. They, like many today, were looking for something to be observed, something that would come in a physical, material, earthly way. But Jesus instructs them that the kingdom of God was a spiritual kingdom that was within the person receiving it. Nothing is said that even intimates an earthly kingdom.

Everything that the Lord spoke during His earthly ministry dealt with His mission of redemption. There is no clue that He insinuated a "millennial kingdom". There was no offer of an earthly kingdom to the Jews which was refused, thereby resulting in the cross. The cross was always God plan. It was never an unforeseen interruption in His dealings with the Jews. It is a despicable doctrine that subjugates the cross to the whims of the Jews who rejected the kingdom when it was offered.

Have Dispensationalists repented of this horrid doctrine? No. They still maintain that aberration of the gospel. Paul warns of preaching "another gospel", which in reality, is no gospel at all. It is precisely this twisted doctrine of an earthly kingdom for the Jews that is the basis for all millennial teachings. It is not to be excused as simply an alternative interpretation of Scripture. It is a deliberate distortion of truth and not to be tolerated among God's people. The cross is the gospel. The cross is the power of God unto salvation to everyone who believes, both Jew and Gentile. No other means of salvation exists for anyone, Jew or Gentile.

Another aberrant doctrine of millennialism is that it shreds the Bible into pieces. It places certain portions of Scripture into this imagined period of time and takes it out of the hands of God's people today. I have heard it said from pulpits and read it in books that the Sermon on the Mount, which includes the Lord's prayer, is a "kingdom passage." It does not apply to the church but is for the Jews of the millennium. They also divide Revelation into sections, some of which apply to "the church", other portions apply to "tribulation saints", and other portions to those who enter the "millennium." Others determine through their superior wisdom and intellect that the Old Testament has no bearing on "the church", but it is strictly Jewish in nature. What? Who gave anyone the right to make such a determination? Would the average Christian be able to figure this out for themselves? You know the answer to that. It is only those who have a "special revelation" from God who can decipher these "hidden truths" that are not truths at all but a lie. The entire Word of God is for all people of all times.

God's people have been given the treasure of His Word to live by. The Old Testament, the New Testament, the Law, the Prophets, the Poetry, the books of Wisdom, the Apocalyptic books – all are given to us as the revelation of the mind and heart of God and is meant to instruct us and conform us to the image of Jesus.

*2 Timothy 3: 16 **All Scripture** is given by inspiration of God, and is profitable for doctrine, for reproof, for correction, for instruction in* *righteousness, 17 that the man of God may be complete, thoroughly equipped for every good work.*

What other verse is necessary to prove this point? Do not let anyone rob you of your heritage. Do not allow anyone to mutilate God's Word in order to protect their "theological system." What they are doing – wittingly or unwittingly – is adding to and taking away from Scripture. Let the Bible be the Bible. Let it speak for itself.

All of Scripture speaks of Jesus. For anyone to refuse another person of the blessings of any portion of Scripture is a travesty. Jesus told the disciples on the road to Emmaus that all Scripture taught truths concerning Himself.

*Luke 24: 27 And beginning at Moses and all the Prophets, He expounded to them in **all the Scriptures** the things concerning Himself.*

No one has the right to dissect the Word of God and to deprive others of its truths.

Another problem with the millennial teachings of Dispensationalists and Pre-Millennialists is that it is racist at its core. It makes the Jews to be superior to the church. As I have pointed out in a previous chapter, the apostle Paul clearly states in Ephesians 2 that the enmity between the Jews and Gentiles has been abolished in the cross, that there is no distinction between them, that they are now one body.

*14 For He Himself is our peace, who has made both one, and has broken down the middle wall of separation, 15 having abolished in His flesh the enmity, that is, the law of commandments contained in ordinances, so as to create in Himself **one new man from the two**, thus making peace, 16 and that He might reconcile them both to God in **one body through the cross**, thereby putting to death the enmity. 17 And He came and preached peace to you who were afar off and to those who were near. 18 For through Him we both have access by one Spirit to the Father.*

Peter, at the Jerusalem council, made the firm declaration that there is no distinction between Jews and Gentiles, that God gave the Gentiles the Holy Spirit just as they had received and that both are saved through faith.

*Acts 15:8 So God, who knows the heart, acknowledged them by giving them the Holy Spirit, just as He did to us, 9 and made **no distinction** between us and them, purifying their hearts by faith.*

So, where does anyone get off saying that there is coming a time of special dispensation for Jews? Galatians 2:6 states emphatically that "God shows personal favoritism to no man." How, then, does God show personal favoritism to "millennial kingdom Jews" if He has previously stated that He does not do so? Is God guilty of double speak? Do you see the serious interpretive problems with this entire system of theology? I should say with this mis-theology. This system, as I have previously stated - but bears repeating here - is not a friend to the Jews, although they claim it to be. It is entirely anti-Semitic because it promises national salvation through another means than the cross, this after Jesus has returned. Their "salvation" comes through recognizing Jesus as their Messiah and receiving Him as such. This system also promises peace and prosperity to unsaved Gentile nations – as long as they treat the Jews properly.

The Bible clearly states that after Jesus returns, after the resurrection, "then comes the end" (1 Corinthians 15: 24). So, there is no "millennium" as promised by Pre-Millennialists and Dispensationalists. Yet, they continue to make outlandish claims of salvation for the Jews during this period. Peter declared the day and means of salvation for the Jews in Acts 2 on the Day of Pentecost.

*36 "Therefore let **all the house of Israel** know assuredly that God has made this Jesus, whom you crucified, both Lord and Christ." 37 Now when they heard this, they were cut to the heart, and said to Peter and the rest of the apostles, "Men and brethren, what shall we do?" 38 Then Peter said to them, "**Repent**, and let every one of you **be baptized in the name of Jesus Christ** for the remission of sins; and you shall receive the gift of the Holy Spirit. 39 **For the promise*** *is to you and to your children, and to all who are afar off, as many as the Lord our God will call."*

The preaching of the gospel convicted the Jews who heard it. The day of salvation for Israel was right then and the means was repentance and faith in Jesus Christ; and the promise was not only for those alive then, but for "all who are afar off". It was for anyone, Jew or Gentile, in any period of time, who would respond to the gospel call and call upon the name of Jesus. No other means of salvation is promised or offered to anyone. Ever. Period.

Well, isn't the "millennium" the "hope of Israel"? Isn't that what the prophets foretold? Isn't that what Paul preached in Acts 28?

*20 For this reason therefore I have called for you, to see you and speak with you, because for the **hope of Israel** I am bound with this chain."*

It must be said the "hope of Israel" was not an exclusive for the Jews. It was not something that the nation even desired. In fact, Paul clearly states that the reason he was in chains was because he was preaching this hope. The Jews hated him and the message of this hope. So, the Jewish nation as such was not at all interested in what Paul describes as "the hope of Israel." Further, what Paul preached as "the hope of Israel" was not theirs exclusively no more than "the God of Israel" was theirs exclusively. God is the God of the whole earth. Jesus was not only the Messiah but He was also the "Desire of all nations."

The "hope of Israel", the Messiah, the God of Israel; these appellations do not imply that the "hope", the Messiah, and God belonged strictly to Israel. It simply means that these truths were revealed to the world through Israel. Israel had the advantage Paul says in Romans 3: 1, 2 because they were the recipients of the Word of God through the prophets and, of course, through the birth of Jesus through Jewish stock.

Now, the Jews did have a hope – a desire - for an earthly kingdom, but it was not the kingdom that God had promised them. They, like many through the ages and up to this day, hope for riches and earthly honor. It is a human desire to be comfortable and to be free from oppression and being downtrodden by despots. But, when we use a Biblical term, we must use it in the manner that the Holy Spirit defines. The Biblical usage of the word "hope" does not mean a human desire, but it means a "confident expectation" that is based upon the promise of God. God nowhere promised Israel a "thousand year" kingdom in which they reigned over the Gentile nations.

The "hope" that Paul speaks of is defined by him as "the hope and resurrection of the dead" (Acts 23:6). It was his preaching about the resurrection of Jesus Christ from the dead and the hope of resurrection (Acts 24: 21 *"Concerning the resurrection of the dead I am being judged by you this day")* and eternal life with Jesus *("the hope which is laid up for you in heaven"* Colossians 1:5) that landed him in so much hot water with the Jewish leaders. If he had been preaching and teaching an earthly kingdom over which Jews would rule, they would have loved him and exalted him to a high office.

Paul again clearly defines exactly what the "hope of Israel" is as specified in the Law and the Prophets; it is the resurrection of the dead. That is the hope that God gave to Israel, and that hope is based upon His promise to them through His Word. The "hope" is not a "millennial" kingdom.

Acts 24: 14 But this I confess to you, that according to the Way which they call a sect, so I worship the God of my fathers, believing **all things which are written in the Law and in the Prophets.** *15 I have* **hope in God**, *which they themselves also accept, that there will be a* **resurrection of the dead**, *both of the just and the unjust.*

Acts 26: 6 And now I stand and am judged for the hope of the **promise made by God to our fathers**. *7 To this promise our twelve tribes, earnestly serving God night and day, hope to attain. For this hope's sake, King Agrippa, I am accused by the Jews. 8 Why should it be thought incredible by you that* **God raises the dead?**

Paul is insistent that the Law and the Prophets declare the resurrection of the dead. That is the hope of all peoples, Jew and Gentile - that we will live forever in the presence of God. There are those, however, who have no hope. Paul tells the Ephesians in Ephesians 2 says that at one time they were without hope and God in the world, but because of the blood of Jesus, they now do have hope.

*12 that at that time you were without Christ, being aliens from the commonwealth of Israel and strangers from the covenants of promise, having no hope and without God in the world. 13 But **now** in Christ Jesus you who once were far off have been brought near by the blood of Christ.*

It is only through the blood of Jesus Christ that anyone has hope and any promise of eternal life or of ever entering God's kingdom. Paul says that it is NOW – within his time - that hope has been bestowed to those who have trusted in Christ. It was not a future hope of being a partaker in the "covenant of promise", but NOW. There is no hope of entering any kingdom outside of trusting in the shed blood of Christ on Calvary – for anyone. Anyone who teaches an earthly kingdom for the Jews, ruled by their Messiah, is not being Scriptural and their teachings must be rejected as false.

The concept of a one thousand year kingdom in which the Lord Jesus Christ rules from David's throne in the city of Jerusalem while the Jews are sitting in judgment on the rest of the nations of earth, some of which have responded to their kingdom message and others have not – and as a result of their refusal to obey are being severely disciplined, and the "raptured" saints are dwelling in the New Jerusalem suspended between Heaven and Earth, is a stretch for even the most active imagination.

God's "millennium" is the time between the first coming of our Lord in flesh and humility - during which the gospel is preached and believers enter His kingdom - and His second coming in power and great glory. There is one bodily resurrection at His second advent then the judgment, then eternity. Isn't that a much more reasonable and easier to understand explanation than the one which is popular today?

Chapter Eight

What About Revelation?

Many people avoid reading Revelation because they have difficulty understanding it. It is a sad situation that so many ignore Revelation because of the interpretive difficulties it has. Indeed, many of the problems with Revelation are because it has been so distorted in what it is truly teaching. It may appear to be easier to avoid problems than to discover the truth of the matter, but that is not so. Revelation is still the Word of God, and it is profitable for doctrine, reproof and instruction in righteousness. Let's see if we can discover what Revelation is really teaching. And no, I do not think for one moment that I alone have a lock on truth, but I do see some very important truths in this final book of the Bible.

Somehow the book of Revelation, which was written to first century Christians undergoing extreme persecution, who were in need of great comfort and reassurance of the presence and power of Jesus in their lives, has become a chronological treatise – a prerecorded history if you will - of "the great tribulation" which, according to Dispensationalists and Pre-Millennialists, occurs after the "rapture" of the church to Heaven. How did the unveiling of Jesus Christ to His suffering first century church, given to them to comfort them in their time of need, the manifestation of His dealings with them and the unregenerate world, become a detailed description of "end times" and of "anti-christ" and 666 and beasts and bar-codes and implanted computer chips and missiles and war and cataclysmic natural disasters and Jewish evangelists?

The basic Biblical truth – which is the entire basis of this book that you are reading - that nothing can occur in this world after the Lord Jesus returns to earth because His return is on the "last day" at the "last trumpet" that conquers the "last enemy" and ushers in eternity, forces us to renounce the current popular interpretation of Revelation as error. It is a misinterpretation regardless of how many people write commentaries or novels and make movies and charts and adamantly declare the veracity of their system.

Every day you can turn on your television to Christian channels and see "prophecy experts" staring you right in the eye, making all kinds of gesticulations with their hands, raising their voice to emphasize what they are teaching - all in the effort to teach their system of eschatology in such a manner that you will not question what they say. I have heard them state that "this is the rapture" and "this is the anti-christ" and "this is the mark of the beast" and many other such declarations without adequately explaining how they arrived at such a conclusion. They just simply state it as a fact and expect their listeners to believe them because they said it. I have yet to hear any of them – not that I faithfully listen to any of them – tell their audience what "the last day", "the last trumpet" and "the last enemy" means and how their system fits into these "lasts", the "eschatos", the final end of the subject under discussion. Why have they not explained these clear Scriptural teachings? Because these clear verses destroy once and for all their system. That is all it is - a system devised by man. Should they explain them, I sense that they would twist their obvious meaning to fit their scheme of interpretation.

Revelation is another example of clear passages of Scripture – "last day" – "last trumpet" – "last enemy" – "then comes the end" – and others - being pushed aside in favor of giving a symbolic book – with many passages that are difficult to understand because of lack of historic perspective – preference over them. The "prophecy experts" assign a meaning to Revelation that accords with their systematic theology, and they ignore the obvious meaning of the crystal clear passages that we have previously examined. Their analysis of Revelation is not the interpretation that the church through the ages has accepted because it was not known or even suspected prior to our friends of chapter three, Ribera and Lacunza. Were there early church fathers who saw a degree of futurism in Revelation? Absolutely. But not two thousand years worth of future. They taught that the things of Revelation had already begun and would carry into their immediate future.

Futurism, the system taught today, gained much popularity with the doctrinal idiosyncrasies of Irving, Darby and Schofield. It has been even more popularized through the systematic theology of Chafer and the seminary instruction of Dallas and others. There are countless pastors and teachers who attended seminaries that disseminated Dispensationalism or less hard core Pre-Millennialism who have in turn taught their congregations the same. Strength in numbers, however, does not make right. Large numbers of adherents simply means that many people have been deceived into believing a wrong doctrine. Again, to make it clear, being wrong on this subject in no way implies being wrong on other fundamental doctrines – unless, as has been previously explained – they teach a two-fold soteriology, one for the church and another for Jews. Many Godly Christians believe this system of the second coming because they have been taught it and they have not taken the time to examine it against clear Biblical teachings.

If Revelation does not mean what these teachers say it means, then what does it mean? What is the message of Revelation if it is not a roadmap of end times? Simply put, the purpose of Revelation was to give comfort to the Christians who were undergoing persecution and were struggling against the evil forces that were against them. Of what possible comfort would it have been for the first century Christians – to whom Revelation is addressed - who were undergoing extreme persecution – who were being tortured and martyred for their faith in Jesus - to have a letter written to them telling them that in the twenty first century - or beyond – that after the "rapture" of the church (these Christians will escape the very tribulation and persecution you must endure), there would be an "anti-christ" who would be a world dictator who would allow the Jews to begin animal sacrifice in the temple (rebuilt) again, who will force everyone to take his mark of 666, that there will be world-wide natural cataclysms and political and religious beasts, and 144,000 Jews who will preach to the world and have great success. For those saints who were being persecuted and beheaded for their witness to Jesus, it would be no comfort at all to know these things. They would scratch their heads and rightly wonder what in the world John was thinking by writing these things to them. Maybe the persecution John had endured had injured his mental capacity.

But, the first three verses set the tone for the time frame in which these events would begin to take place.

1:1 The Revelation of Jesus Christ, which God gave Him to show His servants—things which must **shortly take place**. *And He sent and signified it by His angel to His servant John, 2 who bore witness to the word of God, and to the testimony of Jesus Christ, to all things that he saw. 3 Blessed is he who reads and those who hear the words of this prophecy, and keep those things which are written in it; for* **the time is near.**

"Things that must shortly take place"; "for the time is near." There was no delay in the inauguration of these events. These Christians needed to know the truth of the presence and the power of the resurrected Jesus in their lives right now. They needed to know that whatever they endured was not going unnoticed by Jesus. He was ruling and reigning over their affairs and the affairs of the world. If we are to understand this book, we must take into account the situation of the first century and those to whom it was sent. Without doing that, you can make the book mean whatever you want it to mean. And many have done precisely that.

Revelation is also meant to give comfort and help to every generation of God's people who face opposition and face both physical and spiritual warfare for the sake of Jesus. Revelation assures us that God knows what we go through, that there is nothing that occurs in our lives that He is not aware of and that He will not use for our ultimate good and His eternal glory. He hears our prayers and answers them. He is aware of our struggles and gives us comfort and aid. Our final victory is already written in the pages of the Book of Life. Revelation is a book of victory and of hope.

Wait a minute, John. How can you even imply that Revelation is saying that? All I've ever heard about Revelation is the doom and gloom of the world without any Christians in it and the antichrist ruling and killing everyone who doesn't take his mark. At a cursory reading it does seem like the enemies of Christ – the beast, false prophet, the serpent and Babylon are victorious, but in the end, they all are defeated and Jesus reigns supreme. Look at the words of Revelation 17:14 and then you tell me who is victorious and who is defeated.

14 These will make war with the Lamb, and the Lamb will overcome them, for He is Lord of lords and King of kings; and those who are with Him are called, chosen, and faithful."

Sounds like a glorious victory to me, not defeatism and pessimism. All throughout Revelation, Jesus is shown as victorious. He is victorious over those who would destroy His church, the beast, false prophet, death, the grave, the dragon, anyone who worships a false god or demons. The underlying theme of the book teaches that no matter what we as God's people must endure in this life, we are to remain faithful to Him, for He will grant us not only the final victory, but victory over these enemies as we remain faithful to Him. We have His presence to guide us through all the trials and tribulations we face in this life. It may appear at times that Satan and his minions have gained the upper hand, but it is temporary at best. Satan's apparent defeat of us may be likened to a football game in which the lead fluctuates slightly between the underdog team and the heavily favored home team for the first half. In the second half, the home team rallies and overwhelmingly crushes the opposition in a humiliating defeat. He is a defeated foe, and he knows it. And so should we.

We learn a lot by recognizing who is writing the book, to whom the book is addressed, and the theme of the book, its purpose, and the manner of the writing. It was written by John the apostle to seven literal first century churches in Asia. It is not only the first three chapters that were sent to the seven churches, but the entire letter. That fact in itself tells us that the entire letter was meant for them to read and to understand and to apply to their current situation. How could they apply a truth that was meant for over two thousand years in the future to what they were enduring? Well, obviously, they couldn't. They were promised blessings if they heard and kept the words of the Lord that the letter contained. How could they keep these words if they did not apply to them but to a generation that was at least two thousand years in the future? Again, they couldn't.

Revelation is called a prophecy, and it is. One function of prophecy is to strengthen the faith of those who hear it. Peter tells us in *2 Peter 1:16 For we did not follow cunningly devised fables when we made known to you the power and coming of our Lord Jesus Christ, but were eyewitnesses of His majesty. 17 For He received from God the Father honor and glory when such a voice came to Him from the Excellent Glory: "This is My beloved Son, in whom I am well pleased." 18 And we heard this voice which came from heaven when we were with Him on the holy mountain. 19 And so we have the prophetic word confirmed...*

Peter says that believers should not just take his word for what he was saying, but to believe the fulfillment of prophecies. Read the Old Testament prophecies he tells them, and see the fulfillment in Jesus Christ and His death, burial and resurrection. Fulfilled prophecy confirms our faith. If these first century Christians received a prophecy – and they did – Revelation – but they did not see its fulfillment, how could their faith be confirmed and strengthened? But, they did see the fulfillment of much of Revelation in their lifetimes. A small part is yet to be fulfilled. Their faith was indeed strengthened by reading and keeping the prophecy of Revelation. If, as is purported by Pre-Millennialists, that Revelation is for the "tribulation period" when no Christians are on earth because they have been "raptured", according to their doctrine, how would the faith of Christians be strengthened by the prophecy of Revelation? Well, faith would not be strengthened, would it?

The theme is the unveiling of Jesus Christ, and the manner of writing is symbolism. It can be likened to a parable. Jesus used parables and word pictures to teach spiritual truths to His hearers during

His earthly ministry. He states without apology that He taught in parables for two reasons. To hide the truth from those who refused to believe in Him and to reveal the truth to His people.

Matthew 13: 10 And the disciples came and said to Him, "Why do You speak to them in parables?" 11 He answered and said to them, "Because it has been given to you to know the mysteries of the kingdom of heaven, but to them it has not been given. 12 For whoever has, to him more will be given, and he will have abundance; but whoever does not have, even what he has will be taken away from him. 13 Therefore I speak to them in parables, because seeing they do not see, and hearing they do not hear, nor do they understand.

He uses the same method in Revelation to reveal Himself and His purposes to His people and to hide it from those who do not believe. In the first century that was the Romans, those who followed emperor worship and were trying to destroy Christianity. The purpose of Revelation is to bless those who read it and those who hear it read because they have had the Lord Jesus revealed to them. They have gained understanding of His ways and methods in the world through the word pictures that are portrayed to them through the symbols. In order to understand the Lord more fully, they must have a better understanding of themselves and of their current circumstances. Their current circumstances did not manifest the entire truth. There were things going on behind the scenes – like in Job's situation - that they were totally unaware of, and it is precisely these behind the scenes goings on that the word pictures made known to them. As in the spoken parables of our Lord in the gospel accounts, there is one main thought. Every detail contained in each parable does not have a specific spiritual meaning, but is meant to add color and vividness to the parable.

For instance, in the parable of the Good Samaritan, the details such as the robbers, the priest, the Levite, the inn, the innkeeper, the money, the oil, the wine, and the Samaritan do not hold any "deeper spiritual" meaning. They are meant to add to the picture which has one meaning, namely, "who is my neighbor." To try to spiritualize each detail detracts from the parable and its meaning rather than add to it. Doing so will destroy the overall picture rather than explain it.

The same is true in Revelation. The vivid portrayals are meant to intensify the picture, make it more real, and add to the one main thought. I have heard many people attempt to make every little detail in Revelation have a significant spiritual meaning. Not so. Doing so takes away from the one main thought of the picture. For instance, in chapters 21 and 22 we read of the New Jerusalem. There are many details included in this word picture such as the precious stones, the foundations, the gates, the names of the apostles, the streets of gold, the Lamb as the temple, the brilliant light of it, the river of life flowing down its main street, and the tree of life. Does each of these details of the picture have a separate and distinct spiritual application? No. They contribute to the overall theme of perfect fellowship with God as His eternal chosen people.

There are many symbols in Revelation such as the lamp stands, the seals, the trumpets, the bowls, the beasts, the harlot, the locusts, and others. Through the years there have been certain events and people assigned to these symbols, and every time they have been wrong. I have personally heard in my lifetime that the beast, or "anti-christ" (not so called anywhere in Revelation, but named as such by Dispensationalists and Pre-Millennialists) as indentified by "prophesy experts", as Hitler, John F. Kennedy and Henry Kissinger. There have been other names associated with this "anti-christ", but they escape my memory. Others have identified "anti-christ" as a yet to be revealed person from Europe who, in the 1960's as I recall it being taught, was yet a child. To associate any of these symbols with any particular person or event only – to say that this is this person or this event that Revelation is referring to - is absolutely in error. It causes great confusion.

It seems that each successive generation somehow thinks of itself as more important than preceding generations were in the outworking of God's redemptive plan. Each generation has the propensity to think of itself as the focal point of history and of Biblical prophecy, or as "The Terminal Generation" as was popularized in a false interpretation of world events and Bible prophecy several years ago. These symbols represent principles that operate throughout the history of the world; they are not merely the details of one generation or of specific events or persons.

Portraits of Jesus

All throughout Revelation we see Jesus portrayed as King of Kings and Lord of Lords, as the One who rules and reigns over the affairs of men and angels. Truly, Revelation is the revelation of Jesus Christ in all of His offices. Let's look at how He is described in several verses.

In 1: 5 Jesus is called "The Faithful Witness." This title refers to our Savior's prophetic office while He was here on earth. He is the Prophet Moses spoke of in Deuteronomy 18:15. After the feeding of the 5,000, He was recognized in John 6:14 as that Prophet Moses spoke of. He is the faithful witness of God to his people. He reveals all that we need to know about God, ourselves, and eternity. Nothing that is necessary for our understanding and salvation has been omitted. He has faithfully revealed all that the Father has shown Him (For I have given to them the words which You have given Me...John 17:8). He is also our faithful witness before God the Father as our Advocate in 1 John 2:12.

He is also called in 1:5 "The Firstborn from the dead." This refers to our Redeemer's priestly office. If he is "the firstborn from the dead," then he must have once died. He died for the sins of his people and rose again for their justification. "Firstborn" also refers to His position as being rightful and legal heir of His Father, worthy of receiving a double portion in the inheritance.

Because He is the "Firstborn", He is "The Ruler of the Kings of the Earth." (Rev. 1:5). Because He was obedient to His Father unto death...

Therefore God also has highly exalted Him and given Him the name which is above every name, 10 that at the name of Jesus every knee should bow, of those in heaven, and of those on earth, and of those under the earth, 11 and *that* every tongue should confess that Jesus Christ *is* Lord, to the glory of God the Father. Philippians 2: 9-11

Jesus is Lord and King - even over those who reject Him and His authority. There is no earthly king or ruler who rules by any other authority than by His. It is only by His decree that they have any power at all. They may think they have the right to do whatever they desire, but He is in control of all they do. They can do only what He permits. They may not realize that truth now, but one day they will bow the knee before Him and confess with their mouth that He is Lord. It has been eternally decreed by the Almighty God that every knee will bow – even the knees of those who spitefully reject Him now, will bow before Him, and that every tongue will confess – even the tongue that blasphemes Him now – that He is Lord. There is no option in this. It will happen.

Jesus is the One, according to Revelation 1: 5, who "loved us and washed us from our sins in His own blood, 6 and has made us kings and priests to His God and Father".

Because He loved us with an everlasting, immutable love, He chose us through election and we became partakers of the covenant of grace and predestined to become like Him. He "washed us from our sins in his own blood." By the shedding of his blood, the Lord Jesus Christ effectually washed away the sins of those whom God elected to become His children. Our sins have been expunged from the record of heaven, from the memory of God making us holy and righteous in the sight of God.

That is the work of Christ in redemption. All whom He loved, He washed, and in the fullness of time, He makes them "kings and priests unto God." That speaks of regeneration and conversion. Christ, sending His Spirit to redeem sinners, gives us a new, holy nature by which we are made to reign over the lusts of our flesh, so that we are no longer under the dominion of sin. And as priests, consecrated to God, we have direct access to God through his blood.

In 1:18 the Son of God says, "I am He that lives." The implication of that statement is that He lives forever because He is Life. Apart from Him there is no life - ever. He is in complete control of all life everywhere. Further, He lives forever because He is the living God. But here He is talking about Himself as the God-man, our Savior, who died as our Substitute for our sins in order to satisfy God's Divine justice. But now He is alive forevermore, never to die again. His sacrifice is complete. Christ Jesus now lives to make intercession for us according to Hebrews 7:25. His life gives eternal life to all who call upon His name. Because He lives we live also.

1: 18 again states that Jesus Christ holds "the keys of Hades and death." Hades simply refers to the grave. The Lord Jesus Christ, by the virtue of his resurrection, has power, authority, and dominion over death and the grave (I Corinthians 15:51-58). When He died for us and rose again, He gained the eternal victory over death and the grave. For those of us who have trusted in Him, death and the grave have no power over us, and should cause us no fear (Hebrews 2:14-15). Christ has delivered us from spiritual death in the first resurrection (John 5:25), and shall deliver us from death and the grave in the resurrection of our bodies on the last day, when the last trumpet sounds, at the second resurrection, which defeats the last enemy, death. Revelation 20: 6 "Blessed and holy is he that hath part in the first resurrection: on such the second death hath no power."

In 2: 1, Jesus is the One "who holds the seven stars in His right hand, who walks in the midst of the seven golden lamp stands.

The seven golden candlesticks are representative of all the churches of Jesus Christ throughout the ages. We who gather with God's people in public worship are blessed beyond measure. Why? Because the Lord Jesus Christ, the Son of God, walks in the midst of His churches. The ministers of the gospel who faithfully proclaim the message of salvation through faith in Jesus are the seven stars, the angels, messengers of God, to his churches. The Lord Jesus Christ holds them in His right hand, puts them where He wants them, gives them the messages they are responsible to deliver, uses them as He sees fit, and protects them as they go about His business. They are to be honored and esteemed ("worthy of double honor" 1 Timothy 5:17) by Christians as God's messengers sent to deliver His message to them.

In 5: 5 Jesus is "The Lion of the Tribe of Judah." Our Lord came from the tribe of Judah and is likened to a lion. Like a lion, He is strong and courageous, He devours his enemies and He always prevails over them. He prevailed with God as our Substitute by paying our debt. He prevails over the hearts of sinners whom He has chosen by saving them from their sin.

He is also called "the Root of David" in 5:5. In 22:16 He is also called "the Root and offspring of David." Jesus is the God from whom David obtained his life and He is also the Man who came from the root of David. As a Man, our Savior arose "as a root out of a dry ground" (Isaiah 53:2). Yet, He is the Root from which all his people draw their life. The Root of our family tree is Jesus Christ Himself.

In 5: 6 He is pictured as "a Lamb" standing "in the midst of the throne." That Lamb standing in the midst of the throne of God is Jesus Christ our Savior, who was slain for us from the foundation of the world (13:8). He is standing in the midst of the throne because He is the center of God's decrees and He is the One who executes all God's purposes. He alone is worthy and able to open the book of Divine predestination and carry out all of its decrees. Christ stands in the midst of the throne and of the twenty-four elders (the church of God) and the four beasts (the preachers of the gospel) as the Savior of all his people and the One of whom all his servants speak. The throne represents the glory and dominion of God; and Christ, as the Lamb of God, is the revelation and realization of God's glory.

In 13: 8, Jesus is the "The Lamb slain form the foundation of the world." God, knowing beforehand that we would fall into sin, purposed and decreed that Jesus Christ would be our sacrifice for sin before the world was even created; and God's elect are seen as being saved from eternity because they are in Him (Romans 8:28-31; Ephesians 1: 4). Everything that we experience day by day concerning God's redeeming grace was done for us in eternity before the world was made because God decreed it and purposed that Jesus Christ was the Lamb slain for our sins.

In 19: 11 the Lord Jesus Christ is called Faithful and True. This is a name that He is well deserving of for He is faithful and true in all things. He is Faithful to His people, to His blood covenant, to all of His promises, to His Father and to Himself. He is both the Truth and the True One. Jesus Christ is a true Friend and Brother (Proverbs 17:17), and a true Savior (1 John 1:9; 2:1-2).

In 19:13 He is the Word of God. "In the beginning was the Word, and the Word was with God, and the Word was God" (John 1:1). Christ is the Word by which God reveals Himself (Hebrews 1: 1) and through which the triune God performs all His works. He is the eternal, creating Word, by whom all things were made (John 1:3; Hebrews 11:2). He is the incarnate, revealing Word, by whom God is revealed to man (John 1:14, 18). And He is the almighty, saving Word (Hebrews 4:12-13), by whom God calls out and saves His people in regenerating grace.

In 19: 16 Jesus is the King of Kings and Lord of Lords. There is no king or god to whom He is subject. He rules over all others. The Lord Jesus Christ is the absolute, singular, and rightful sovereign Monarch of heaven and earth (Acts 2:32-36).

In 21: 5, 6 Jesus Christ states that He makes all things new. It is because of His sovereign grace that He makes all things new. "Therefore if any man be in Christ, he is a new creature: old things are passed away; behold, all things are become new" (2 Corinthians 5:17). In Heaven He makes all things new, supplying His people a new name and a new life, without the possibility of sin, sorrow, or death. When the old heaven and earth is destroyed by fire, He will create "a new heavens and a new earth, wherein dwells righteousness" (2 Peter 3:13).

In 22: 13 (also 1:18) Jesus Christ is the Alpha and the Omega. He is the "a" and the "z", the first and the last, the beginning and the end of all things. The whole of creation has its origin in Christ and shall find its consummation in Christ. Grace for everyday living begins and ends with Jesus. Every event of providence comes from Christ and shall glorify Christ. The entire Volume of Holy Scripture, from beginning to end, speaks of Christ. And in the salvation of God's elect Jesus Christ is the beginning, the end, and everything between (1 Corinthians 1:30-31). He is the complete, perfect and eternal revelation of God.

In 22: 16 Jesus is the Bright and Morning Star. He is the Light that shines in darkness, that shines in our hearts to give the light of the knowledge of the glory of God. He is the Day Star of grace, the Sun of Righteousness, rising over this sin-cursed earth, with healing in his wings. And he is the Star of that great eternal day yet to come.

In 22: 20 Jesus declares that He will surely come quickly. Soon he shall appear. Suddenly, without warning, the King of glory shall come again to destroy his enemies, save his people, restore his creation, and glorify his Father. "Then cometh the end," when He shall deliver up the kingdom, all the hosts of his elect unto God the Father, saying, "Behold I and the children which God hath given me!" And God shall be "all in all" (Hebrews 2:13; 1 Corinthians 15:24-28).

These are the ways in which the Lord Jesus Christ reveals Himself throughout Revelation. He is the theme of the book. His victory over His enemies is what the book is about. His help, aid and comfort to His church is what is demonstrated in this book. Through the two thousand years since its writing, Christians have found comfort in its words. Yes, the devil and his messengers, whether demons or worldly distractions or religious and political persecutors have had some authority over those who have stood firm in their love for Jesus, who have not left their first love, who have not taken the mark of worldliness and rebellion either in their minds or their works. But, who is victorious and who loses? Who has the aid and comfort of their Lord while in this world of tribulation and who enjoys everlasting life with the Savior? And who has their part in lake of fire which burns forever and ever?

So, How do we Properly Interpret Revelation?

So, how do we interpret Revelation correctly? How can I be sure that what you are saying is right? Everyone I know believes it is an end times book that chronicles the tribulation period. To reiterate what has been said many times throughout this book, the Bible clearly and without misunderstanding states that the second coming of Jesus occurs simultaneously with the resurrection from the dead and then – the very next thing in sequence - comes the end (1 Corinthians 15: 23,24). There can be no more time after the resurrection which occurs on the "last day." No if, ands, or buts, regardless of how many "prophecy experts" – who, in reality, are not prophecy experts, but are experts in Dispensationalism or Pre-Millennialism - declare otherwise.

Therefore, Revelation has a different meaning than what is the popular belief today. It is not a chronological record of the "tribulation period." Each successive chapter does not following the preceding one in time – especially if it is construed as happening after the resurrection. If studied with an open mind - not through a predetermined system of interpretation, but with a heart and mind that is sensitive to what God is revealing - it is not hard to see the same time frame – viewed from different angles - recurring throughout the book. It is a book of parables, if you will, a book of word pictures, of symbols that conveyed comfort and encouragement to those who received it originally. Those who originally read it would understand the symbols used while we today may have to work at getting the proper interpretation. Although the word pictures differ from each other, they show events that occur in the same time frame, only from different angles. To use the word that other commentators have used to describe Revelation, there are parallel scenes depicted, each concurrent with the others. The parallel scenes are from the first coming of Jesus through the second coming, with the final scenes in chapters 20 and 21 going beyond time into eternity.

The different scenes are as follows:

Chapters 1 – 3

Chapters 1 – 3 depict our Lord Jesus in the midst of the lamp stands. These lamp stands represent the seven churches to whom the letter is addressed. The letter as a whole is addressed to the seven churches in Asia, but each individual church is addressed in chapters 2 and 3. Since the number seven indicates completeness, the seven churches represent all the churches during the entire church age from beginning to end in their individual, distinctive characteristics. It shows the complete plan of God, in general principles, for the history of the world, especially that of the church. These events were beginning to unfold at that time – "the time is near" (1:3). The beginning of these events was not some 2,000 years off in the future. Jesus was right then and there walking among the churches. Yet, what we read in Revelation is still unfolding before our eyes. The events of Revelation continue today.

The Dispensational interpretation of this passage is that each individual church represents a different time period in the overall church age, each church age subsequent to the preceding one. In other words, the church at Ephesus represents the initial years of the church, followed by Smyrna, followed by Pergamos, on through Laodicia, which, according to them, represents the current years of the church.

This does not even begin to make sense. There are many inconsistencies with this doctrine, not the least of which is that to the church in Philadelphia Jesus revealed that they would be kept from the hour of trial which was to come upon the whole world. Dispensationalists and Pre-Millennialists take that word from our Lord to mean that the church is to be "raptured" prior to the "tribulation period." The obvious discrepancy is that this was spoken to the church they maintain represents the sixth period of church history. They insist that today we are living in the seventh age of church history, the Laodician church. How can there be seven "dispensations" of church history if the "rapture" occurs during the sixth? Why are we still here?

Another discrepancy in the Dispensational scheme of things, that were it not such a deplorable interpretation would be laughable, is the church of Sardis, the fifth of the churches to whom John wrote, of whom the Lord Jesus had nothing good to say, no commendations at all, represents the time of the Reformation, the time when the church awoke out of lethargy and rediscovered glorious Biblical truths. I think they got this one wrong, too.

What the seven churches represent is the conditions and circumstances that are evident in various churches throughout the entire church age. Just as there were seven churches during the first century, each different from the other, each with its own unique set of circumstances, so it will be until the Lord Jesus returns. At any given time throughout the centuries there are churches that manifest the identical or similar conditions as these seven. They are manifested simultaneously. There are rich churches, poor churches, missions minded churches, selfish churches, faithful churches, churches who allow heresy, dictatorial churches, churches who live by grace, all kinds of churches are evident in every city, town, and rural area in every nation at all times. The Lord has much to say to each individual church. Each message is tailor fit to that particular church and its unique set of circumstances. And the Lord's message to each church is meant for the churches today.

Chapters 4 – 7

Chapters 4 – 7 is a new scene and it is a vision of heaven and of the seals that are to be broken. It is obvious that chapter four begins a new vision. It is a natural division in Revelation. The scene is of the Lord upon His throne being worshiped by the multitude. The Lord is holding a book in His right hand. The book is sealed with seven seals, which the Lamb opens one by one. The hundred and forty four thousand are sealed and are standing before the throne.

This scene also begins with the first coming of Jesus and ends with His second coming. Jesus is worthy to take the scroll and open the seals because He had been slain and had redeemed people from every tongue and nation with His blood. He is shown as ruling in Heaven.

The first thing we notice in this scene is that the throne of God is at the very center of not only Heaven, but of the entire universe. This vision shows us that God is in control of everything that occurs in His universe. Nothing, not even our troubles and trials and tribulations are without His knowledge and direction. This knowledge should give comfort and assurance to all of His children in all circumstances of life, but primarily when we face adversity and Satanic oppression. The "all things" of 4:11 include our trials and sufferings, just as the "all things" of Romans 8:28 does. Nothing is excluded from His authority and dominion.

He is surrounded by a rainbow and twenty four thrones upon which are seated the twenty four elders. The rainbow that God gave to Noah as a covenant promise that He would never again judge the earth with water indicates that this rainbow carries the same meaning. God's judgment on sin has been satisfied in the death, burial, and resurrection of our Lord Jesus Christ. For believers, God's flood of punishing judgment against sin has been fulfilled in Christ Jesus. The covenantal rainbow is a promise for believers only, not unbelievers. The flood of God's judgmental wrath is (Romans 1:18) being revealed from heaven against them every day, and will culminate in the great outpouring of His fiery wrath on the great day of the second coming (2 Thessalonians 1:7-9).

The twenty four thrones and elders and the four living creatures - identified in Ezekiel 1 as Cherubim – are there for one purpose only – to praise and glorify the Triune God for all of His works of creation. Those works include the trials and tribulations of the seals that come upon God's people as a result of Christ going forth in the opening of the first seal.

He goes forth on a white horse – white symbolizing holiness and purity – to conquer sin, Satan, the world, and the flesh. This is His first coming, born to be a sacrifice for our sin and to "destroy the works of the devil." Chapter 5:5 tells us that the "Lion of the tribe of Judah...has prevailed"; 17:14 "the Lamb will overcome them". This is the identical rider who is mentioned in 19: 11 Now I saw heaven opened, and behold, a white horse. And He who sat on him *was* called Faithful and True, and in righteousness He judges and makes war.

The rider on the white horse is not the "anti-christ" as is represented by Dispensationalists and Pre-Millennialists. There is nothing in the description of this rider that would infer that; it is only their "system" that interprets it so. The rider on the white horse is none other than the Lord Jesus Christ, the King who conquers sin and rebellion through the gospel.

The scroll, with its seals, represents God's eternal plan, His purpose throughout eternity for the universe, but in particular, His plan for His people. As long as the scroll is unopened, God's plan is unfulfilled, unrevealed, unexecuted. When the seals are broken, God's plan is carried out in its entirety. The opened scroll provides protection for God's children when undergoing persecution and trials; it provides condemnation and judgment for those who persecute God's church and who are unbelievers; it provides victory over the enemies of Jesus and His people and eternal rewards for those who follow the Lamb.

The tribulation that occurs as the seals are opened are all part of God's plan for the spiritual enrichment of His people. As hard as it is to say this and to believe it – because in our humanity we all try to escape unpleasant circumstances - trials and suffering are designed by a loving Father in order to purify us from the stain and the seduction of the world. As we understand this fact, we can see more and more the faithfulness of God throughout history.

The red horse represents persecution against God's people, not war between nations. This is a logical deduction from the context. The gospel goes forth conquering souls for the kingdom of God, and whenever that happens, attacks against the followers of Christ occur. Persecution follows on the heels of the gospel message that effectively calls sinners to the Savior, that shines the light of Jesus Christ into darkness. We see this truth all through the Bible and in world history. The world will not tolerate exposure of its sins. It will fight back with all the venom and hatred of its god, Satan.

The word translated "kill" (Strong's #4969) in 6:4 means to butcher, slaughter, to maim violently. This, without a doubt, refers to unmitigated hatred and violence and cruel persecution to the point of a torturous death against those who have heard the good news of salvation in and through Jesus and only wish to share it with others so they can be saved. The "sword" (Strong's Concordance # 3162) used is a knife that was used for slaughtering animals to be sacrificed upon the altar, which in not the sword (Strong's Concordance #4501) of warfare used in verse 8.

As much as we would like to think that the gospel brings "peace on earth", it does not. It brings peace to those who receive Jesus, but not peace to those who reject Him or to the world in general. Jesus Himself said that He did not come to bring peace, but a sword in Matthew 10:34. Paul states that persecution will occur when one lives a Godly life.

2 Timothy 3: 12 Yes, and all who desire to live godly in Christ Jesus will suffer persecution.

The black horse follows closely behind the red horse. The black horse represents economic hardships that God's people suffer as a result of the persecution. Keep in mind that these "horses" were understood by the first century Christians who suffered in all of these ways because of the refusal to acknowledge any king other than Jesus. They were thrown out of homes and jobs and were unable to provide for their families in the manner they once were able to do. It has been so through the ages. Christians have always suffered economically when they stand for truth and against deception.

In America and most of Europe, countries that have a history of Christian belief, we may not see so much of this directed against Christians, but the direction the general thinking of the world and its politics is heading, do not be surprised if it does not occur again in our lifetime. However, in other countries that do not have a historical background of Christianity, Islamic countries for instance, or ones that have backslidden from Christianity into political atheism – communism - Christians are persecuted. Even in America if a Christian is true to his or her convictions and stands up for Christ, he or she very well could lose a job rather than cheapen their values and give in to worldly pressure. Christians, it seems, are the only fair game to be maligned, ridiculed, and oppressed without repercussion. No other group may be so treated without consequence. Christians, take heed and obey Christ rather than the world.

Matthew 5: 11 "Blessed are you when they revile and persecute you, and say all kinds of evil against you falsely for My sake. 12 Rejoice and be exceedingly glad, for great is your reward in heaven, for so they persecuted the prophets who were before you.

The fourth horse is the pale horse, sickly in color, indicates disease and death. Immediately behind him comes Hades, or the grave. Death kills and Hades accepts the bodies. But, this is not indiscriminate killing for they only have the authority – Divine permission – to kill part of the population, one fourth. God will allow no more.

Death and Hades have permission to kill using the sword (war), famine, pestilence (plagues or deadly disease) and wild beasts. This verse is closely related to Ezekiel 14: 21 For thus says the Lord GOD: "How much more it shall be when I send My four severe judgments on Jerusalem—the sword and famine and wild beasts and pestilence—to cut off man and beast from it?

God is not limited in the ways He allows death to come to man. We must never forget that He is in control of life and death. No one else.

When the Lamb opens the fifth seal, martyrs are heard crying out from under the altar for justice to be done upon those who were responsible for their deaths. This is not a scene of Heaven, but remember, it is a symbolic picture that John was given. All scenes in Revelation are symbolic in nature and must be viewed that way. The altar represents the bronze altar of sacrifice in the Old Testament temple. The blood from the sacrificial animals flowed under it. In this scene, the blood of the martyrs is seen flowing under the altar, for they were "sacrificed" for the sake of Jesus. They were slaughtered for Him.

They are heard crying out "How long, O Lord, holy and true, until You judge and avenge our blood on those who dwell on the earth?" They are not crying out for vengeance for their own sakes, but for the sake of God. They were slaughtered because of their faith in Jesus, and by killing them with such virulent hatred, their murderers have scorned the Almighty God. They, like Goliath the Philistine, have defied God. Unless God repays them in kind, His honor and righteousness will suffer. Those who have been faithful to their Lord unto death want Him to have all glory and honor, so they cry out for God to avenge Himself through avenging their blood that was shed for His sake.

When the sixth seal is opened, we see the judgment day. Again, we must be reminded of the fact that this is a vision, a symbolic representation of a reality. We must be reminded of these things because of the popular system of interpretation that has been so taught to modern Christians, and in many cases has been foisted upon us by well meaning but wrong teachers, that it is hard to see any other explanation. This is not a literal, actual episode that will occur in the future, but a symbolic vision.

John experiences in his vision an earthquake, the sun turning black, the moon becoming red as blood, the stars falling to earth, the sky being rolled up as a scroll, and the mountains and islands being removed from their place. The vision was real to John, but it is a symbolic representation of the precursor to the final judgment and the absolute terror and utter confusion it causes to the wicked who experience it. These judgments are God's response to the persecution of God's people.

Who are these wicked who experience this? 15 "And the kings of the earth, the great men, the rich men, the commanders, the mighty men, every slave and every free man..." The world that has mocked God and His Christ and that has persecuted and martyred His church will experience the complete outpouring of His wrath upon them. They will call out for the rocks and the mountains to fall upon them to hide them from the face of God and the wrath of the Lamb. The entire Godless world is in fear and trembling. They are fleeing from something far more terrifying to them than falling rocks and mountains. They are even crying out for death. God is moving against them and they cannot bear it. The ones who laughed at the possibility of hell, who made jokes about hell, who laughed at Jesus and His crucifixion, who scorned those who preached the gospel to them now realize how utterly foolish they were. They know that for them the opportunity for repentance and faith is gone. They have sinned away their day of grace. They realize their fate and are "scared as hell" over it.

But, the final judgment is not quite yet. The four angels who are about to unleash God's judgment are prevented from doing so until the servants of God are sealed in their foreheads thereby affording them protection from the coming final judgment. The sealing also certifies that those who are sealed are genuine in their faith, thereby being affirmed that they belong to God.

The number of those who are sealed are 144,000. Without giving a detailed explanation – there are many commentaries which will afford a more than adequate and satisfactory description of the reasons behind the symbolic meaning of the number – it represents the total number of the redeemed throughout the ages, both Old Testament saints and New Testaments saints. To make this passage literal – that there are merely 12,000 Jews from the tribes named – for some reason Joseph is named as a tribe rather than Ephraim and Manasseh as half tribes, although Manasseh is named as a tribe, and Dan is excluded altogether – does a great disservice to Biblical symbolism. First century Jewish Christians would understand the symbolism in that Rueben, Jacob's first born, was not mentioned first, but Judah, the tribe from which our Lord was born. Placing Judah first gives him the pre-eminence – because of his Son, Jesus – rather than giving it to Rueben. The meaning of this passage is that those who are sealed belong to Jesus the Lord. They are all His people, and they represent all of His people from all ages. To say that each tribe was limited to only 12,000 – not 11,900, not 12,100, but 12,000 exactly, not one more or less - to be sealed in and of itself indicates symbolism in the number. To say that they are "tribulation period" Jewish saints who evangelize the world is not an interpretation that the first century Christians would have understood.

The fact that the very next verse (verse 9) describes a great multitude that no man could number that included people from every nation, kindred and tongue gives force to the fact that the 144,000 do indeed represent all the saved from all time. Added to this brief explanation is the further mention of 144,000 in chapter 14:1 – 5, where John gives this commentary on them.

1 Then I looked, and behold, a Lamb standing on Mount Zion, and with Him one hundred and forty-four thousand, having His Father's name written on their foreheads. 2 And I heard a voice from heaven, like the voice of many waters, and like the voice of loud thunder. And I heard the sound of harpists playing their harps. 3 They sang as it were a new song before the throne, before the four living creatures, and the elders; and no one could learn that song except the hundred and forty-four thousand who were redeemed from the earth. 4 These are the ones who were not defiled with women, for they are virgins. These are the ones who follow the Lamb wherever He goes. These were redeemed from among men, being firstfruits to God and to the Lamb. 5 And in their mouth was found no deceit, for they are without fault before the throne of God.

These 144,000 are the ones who were redeemed "from the earth." They were singing a "new song" that no one except the redeemed could learn and sing. It is the song of the redeemed. It belongs to all redeemed of all ages. Their purity – given to them through the redemption in the blood of Jesus - is demonstrated in the word "virgin", and the fact that no deceit was found in their mouth and that they are faultless before the throne of God.

Compare: *Jude 24 Now to Him who is able to keep you from stumbling, and to present you faultless before the presence of His glory with exceeding joy, 25 To God our Savior, Who alone is wise, be glory and majesty, dominion and power, both now and forever. Amen.*

They have been made absolutely pure and undefiled by the Lamb. They faithfully follow Him through all circumstances of life, wherever He leads them. They are called "firstfruits" to God and the Lamb indicating that they represent all of God's people, not some "tribulation period" saint. These have been God's people from the beginning, with others added to their number as they came to faith in Christ.

They have been sealed in their foreheads by God, and that they are the entire church of God is verified in chapter *22: 3 And there shall be no more curse, but the throne of God and of the Lamb shall be in it, and His servants shall serve Him. 4 They shall see His face, and His name shall be on their foreheads.*

Those who have been sealed are protected by God from the judgments that are to come upon the earth, for their sin has already been judged by God in the crucifixion of Jesus. He bore their judgment and they are redeemed from the curse of the law, death.

The song they are singing is of salvation, praise, honor, glory, wisdom, thanksgiving, power and might that belong to God and to the Lamb who redeemed them. He has washed their robes white in His blood and has safely brought them out of "great tribulation", the sum total of all tribulation and persecution that the enemies of God and His people have used against them in an attempt to destroy them completely. They have endured persecution, but it has ended and now they are safe within the fold of the Good Shepherd where they will never again hunger or thirst, where the sun will not affect them again, and where their eyes are dried from all tears that have been shed because of pain and suffering and heartbreak over those who have scorned and blasphemed that name above all names. Never again will they suffer in any way. They are safe with their Lord forever.

Chapters 8 – 11

The next section is chapters 8 – 11 and it deals with the seven trumpets, sounding in answer to the prayers of the saints. These trumpets adversely affect the world. These trumpets sound in response to a world that has opposed Jesus and has persecuted His people. These trumpets do not sound only once, but again and again in every age. I know that there are many who take offense at the idea that God punishes the wicked by sending judgments upon them, but God is not merely a God of love, mercy, and grace, but is also a God of holiness who will not always allow sinful man to do as he pleases. His "wrath is (*present tense*) revealed from heaven against all ungodliness and unrighteousness of men, who suppress the truth in unrighteousness (Romans 1:18). God's wrath is constantly being revealed against sin, and its manifestation is explained in these trumpet sounds.

But, in all of these trumpets, God is calling sinners to salvation through repentance. Even in His wrath, He still extends mercy, ("in wrath remember mercy" Habakkuk 3:2) but sinners do not respond to His invitation. They still do not repent. 9: 20 But the rest of mankind, who were not killed by these plagues, did not repent of the works of their hands, that they should not worship demons, and idols of gold, silver, brass, stone, and wood, which can neither see nor hear nor walk. 21 And they did not repent of their murders or their sorceries or their sexual immorality or their thefts.

This shows the absolute hard-heartedness, arrogance and pride of sinful man. "If God is going to do this or allow this, I will not worship Him. I cannot believe in a God who does this." Their attitude is that they are teaching God a lesson by their response – or lack of an appropriate response – to His justified actions against their sin and arrogance. The sad reality is that they are stoking the fires of their punishment even hotter by their arrogant refusal to repent and receive God's mercy and forgiveness. The harder the heart, the hotter the flames of punishment.

As this section begins, there is silence in Heaven for about a half an hour. This is the silence of awe before the Almighty God.

Habakkuk 2: 20 "But the LORD is in His holy temple. Let all the earth keep silence before Him."

Zephaniah 1:7 Be silent in the presence of the Lord GOD; For the day of the LORD is at hand, for the LORD has prepared a sacrifice; He has invited His guests.

Zechariah 2: 13 Be silent, all flesh, before the LORD, for He is aroused from His holy habitation!"

The Lord is about to speak in judgment and all of Heaven is silent in anticipation of His actions. They are unable to speak or to even move about while waiting for the terrible consequences of the sins of the inhabitants of the earth to fall upon them. Reverent silence is the only acceptable reaction to the knowledge of forth coming judgment. Make no mistake about it. These trumpet judgments are in answer to the prayers of the persecuted saints. Seven angels are each given a trumpet, but before they sound their trumpets, another angel is given a vial of incense, which is mixed with the prayers of the saints. Since this vial of incense is given to the angel, it can be nothing other than the intercession of Christ for His saints to His Father. God sees and hears all that occurs on earth. He knows when His children are in tribulation and trials because of their faith, and He acts in response to it. Nothing escapes His sight. The vial is then cast to the earth, and the judgments begin.

The First Trumpet

There are two groups of judgments that occur. The first four trumpets harm the wicked in their physical beings while the last three trumpets harm them in their spiritual being. The first trumpet sounds and there is a outpouring of hail and fire mixed with blood that is cast down to the earth that results in a third of the trees and green grass being burnt up. This trumpet, which sounds throughout the time from our Lord's first coming to His second coming, most likely represents various disasters that afflict those who persecute the church that occur on dry land. Whatever these disasters entail, they include severe weather that destroys lands and buildings. Even as I write this, there is a 30,000+ acre fire raging in the Big Cypress Preserve, part of the Everglades just outside of where I live in Naples, Florida. It was started by a lightning strike. The smoke is drifting overhead and blocking out the sun. They are multiplied accounts of wild fires throughout America and the world that very well may be a result of this particular trumpet sounding. Think of the disastrous hurricanes of recent history; Ivan, Katrina, and Wilma, and the tsunamis and cyclones that strike Asia, of the terrible mudslides in rain-soaked California that destroys many homes. The news covers these events, but fails to credit the source of these events as God and the cause as man's rebellion against God and persecution of His church.

The Second Trumpet

The second trumpet sounds and what appears to John like a great mountain on fire is hurled into the sea. It was not a real mountain, but something that looked like a mountain. The symbolism is that God is causing terror to those who are unbelievers who make their living on the seas, or who sail the seas for pleasure. God is using maritime disasters as a tool to speak to those who reject Him, who foolishly think that they are the "captains of their own fate", who "sail their own ships." God is in control of all that happens upon this earth, not man. Puny man, arrogant man can do nothing to prevent the trumpets from sounding and working their designed destruction of killing one third of the sea creatures and ships, and turning a third of the sea to blood. The imagery is of destruction upon the sea, not a literal turning of water into blood. It is a vision, a word picture that conveys truth through symbols.

The Third Trumpet

The third trumpet sounds and it affects inland waters. In his vision John sees a huge fiery star falling from the sky that falls on rivers and streams. Hollywood has recreated similar scenes in movies where large meteors are heading toward earth with no possible way to avoid them. The screen is filled with terror stricken people screaming and attempting to escape, but how do you escape such a calamity? The scene John is seeing is one of total terror experienced by those who see it falling. This symbol is one that shows what God's judgments upon rivers do to men. Just recently the Red River flooded in North Dakota, Iowa, and parts of Minnesota that caused tremendous damage. There have been countless devastating floods that destroy towns and people. The name of the star is Wormwood, which symbolizes bitter sorrow and distress. This falling star that lands on the waters not only kills people, but destroys all that the water is used for, such as commerce and pleasure.

When Katrina broke the levy that held back Lake Ponchartrain from New Orleans, people were terrified, although the night before they were partying and laughing, completely disregarding the thought that disaster was imminent. Although unbelievers – and unfortunately many Christians also - absolutely reject the truth that God had anything to do with this flood that killed many people and destroyed a great portion of New Orleans, it was a result of this third trumpet sounding. But, man's rejection of truth does not negate it.

The Fourth Trumpet

When the fourth trumpet sounds, a third of the sun, moon, and stars are affected. Their lights do not shine for a portion of the day and night. How exactly this affects man is not clearly stated, but it cannot be overstated that the heavenly bodies do exert influence on life as we know it. When the sun is experiencing storms – sunspots – it drastically affects our earth. When the moon goes through certain phases, it affects certain men in various ways. Again, these events have occurred throughout the history of man and will continue to occur until Jesus returns and establishes the new heaven and earth.

John sees an eagle flying through the heaven announcing woe to the those who dwell upon the earth because the following three trumpets that are about to sound are far worse than the first four. These trumpets are not necessarily in succession as they sound through the ages, but only in John's vision do they follow successively, giving the impression of heightened drama and progressive terror as they follow one another in sounding.

The Fifth Trumpet

The fifth trumpet sounds and John sees a star fall from heaven to the earth. This is the same scene that Jesus described in Luke 10: 18...I saw Satan fall like lightning from heaven. Satan, because of his rebellion against God was cast out of Heaven to the earth. He was given the key to the bottomless pit, hell. This too, is under God's control in that Satan was given the key. It is not his to use as he sees fit, but it belongs to God. God allows him to open the pit as He sees fit. Satan and all he does is only by God's permission. John sees smoke arise from the pit as it is unlocked. The symbols indicate that Satan incites evil in the world by filling it with the wicked influences of demons. He fills it with hatred for God and His people. This great smoke is the darkness that blinds the minds of men so they cannot see the truth. The smoke is so thick that it blots out the light of the sun.

2 Corinthians 4: 3 But even if our gospel is veiled, it is veiled to those who are perishing, 4 whose minds the god of this age has blinded, who do not believe, lest the light of the gospel of the glory of Christ, who is the image of God, should shine on them.

He fills the world with sin and the sorrow, pain and death that results from rebellion against God. This scene describes in detail the terrible darkness that results from rejecting the truth of the gospel. Romans 1 gives the horrible consequences of failing to worship the Creator and instead worshiping the creation. The moral decay that precipitates God's unleashing this trumpet judgment is that men suppress the truth – they hold down truth – they hide it so that others will not hear it and believe it (Romans 1:18), then they do not glorify God, they are unthankful, they profess themselves to be wise, and they worship created things rather than the Creator. God allows them to reap the rot and rancid decay of this satanically inspired "wisdom" by giving them the desires of their evil hearts. They fulfill the lusts of their hearts, engage in vile passions, dishonor their bodies with each other, engage in flagrant homosexuality, and as a result of these choices, they reap a reprobate (debased, worthless) mind that is so proud and self-centered that they think any action or attitude they decide to take is good and profitable for their soul.

Out of the smoke come an army of locusts. Unlike the locusts that plagued Egypt and those that Joel 1 speaks of, these did no damage at all to vegetation, or to those who have been sealed by God in their forehead, but attacked only men who did not have the seal of God in their forehead. Like the locusts in Joel 1 that laid waste and withered all the trees and green vegetation of the land, these demonic locusts are laying waste the souls of those who refuse to obey the gospel of Jesus Christ. They turn the lives of men and women into a living hell. They strip away all regard for God and His word, His Son, and the salvation He offers to them through Jesus. They are completely withered spiritually. The graphic description of these demons portrays a picture of utter hopelessness and dreadful terror in the hearts and souls of those they attack. These people who have turned their back on the Lord Jesus now seek death but they are unable to die. Death flees from them like they have fled from Christ. This is the fulfillment of Proverbs 1: 24 – 31.

24 Because I have called and you refused, I have stretched out my hand and no one regarded,

25 Because you disdained all my counsel, and would have none of my rebuke, 26 I also will laugh at your calamity; I will mock when your terror comes, 27 When your terror comes like a storm, and your destruction comes like a whirlwind, when distress and anguish come upon you.

28 "Then they will call on me, but I will not answer; They will seek me diligently, but they will not find me. 29 Because they hated knowledge and did not choose the fear of the LORD 30 They would have none of my counsel and despised my every rebuke. 31 Therefore they shall eat the fruit of their own way, and be filled to the full with their own fancies.

What a terrible price to pay for the foolishness of pride and arrogant disregard for Christ. Those who reject or neglect the wisdom of God in order to obtain the wisdom of the world will be terrified when their day of reckoning comes. God will not heed their cries for mercy. Their day of grace is far spent. They will reap what they have sown. These demons will destroy all ability in those they attack to repent and come to the light of salvation that produces joy, peace, righteousness, holiness and gives true wisdom and understanding. The king that rules over these demon locusts is named Abaddon and Apollyon, which means destroyer. Once people have been stung by them, their soul and all capacity for spiritual discernment is destroyed. They are "past feeling" and "have given themselves over to lewdness, to work all uncleanness with greediness" (Ephesians 4:19) because of "having their understanding darkened, being alienated from the life of God, because of the ignorance that is in them, because of the blindness of their heart" (Ephesians 4:18). God will no longer offer His gift of salvation to them. They are true reprobates. These demons have been stinging humans over and over again throughout the ages and will continue to do so until the Lord Jesus returns and destroys them.

The Sixth Trumpet

The sixth trumpet sounds and a voice is heard speaking from the horns of the golden altar. It gives the order for the four evil angels that have been bound at the river Euphrates, the eastern boundary of Roman civilization, beyond which were barbarians, to be loosed so they can work their destruction upon the world. They plunge the world into war. In the symbolism we see that the Euphrates is dried up (Revelation 16:12) so the barbarian hordes could make war on the civilized Roman Empire. This is not like the war that proceeds from the fourth horseman, which is sent by God as a warning to repent. The symbolism of the fourth seal includes believers as victims of it, but this war is the sum of all wars that has been waged in the history of mankind, and it is sent in particular to unbelievers as a stern warning to repent and punishment for their actions against the church of Jesus Christ. God has heard the voices cry from under the altar, and Christ has mixed His intercession for them with their prayers, and these wars of terrible consequence through the years are in answer to those prayers.

John sees a great army assembled and he hears the number of them: 200 million soldiers. This number, too, is symbolic of a huge number, of the total of warriors in all wars. It is not, as some imagine, the army of China. This is not one battle, but the sum total of all wars. Yet, it may be that the symbol points more in particular to the horrible wars, with their engines of war that have the ability to cause more damage than wars of years ago, that will be waged toward the end of time just prior to the second coming of our Lord Jesus. This is indicated by the words of verse *15: So the four angels, who had been prepared for the hour and day and month and year, were released to kill a third of mankind.* A certain year, month, day and hour has been reserved for the loosing of these four angels. Yet, the scene is not limited to the end time wars because God has always been in charge of war and peace, therefore, the start of all war and the end of all war is in His hands and controlled by His will. Those who die in war and survive the conflict is in His hands. He allows only a third of mankind to be killed, although instigated by demonic angels and started by demon controlled men.

All of these trumpets have been sounding since the first coming of the Lord Jesus Christ and will continue until His second coming. They are sounded as a warning to unbelievers in answer to the prayers of His persecuted church. God's people are precious to Him; He sees their suffering and their tears and hears their cries; He will not allow the world to hurt them without avenging them. *"Vengeance is Mine...I will repay."*

He repays them by allowing the demons of war to inflict physical, emotional, mental and spiritual agony upon them. War causes the unsaved – not all unsaved, however - to suffer in all of these ways because they do not see that one purpose of war is to call them to repentance. Though God's people do not seek war or the suffering it causes, they do not suffer in the same way as the unsaved do. They realize that although instigated by demonic forces that control ungodly men, God is still in control of even war. Yet, in spite of His warnings through the trumpet blasts, mankind in general does not repent, but continues in them, even to the point of blaspheming the God who has the power to end their misery.

The Angel and the Book

An angel comes from Heaven to the earth clothed with a cloud; he has the countenance of the sun, a rainbow over his head, and legs like pillars of fire. He is a giant angel that places one foot on land and the other in the sea. His appearance indicates that He is a direct messenger of Christ. The rainbow represents God's covenant faithfulness to His people, the clouds symbolize impending judgment, and the brightness of his face shows God's holiness. He is holding a little book in his hand, which we will get to shortly. He shouts with a loud voice and seven thunders answer. John is about to write down what the seven thunders say when he is instructed not to reveal the content of the thunders, but to seal them so they remain unknown. Why was John not to reveal these thunders? Because the secret things belong to God and Him alone.

Deuteronomy 29: 29 "The secret things belong to the LORD our God, but those things which are revealed belong to us and to our children forever...

There are things at work in our universe and world and lives that belong to God and are for His eyes and knowledge only. Man does not like that fact; he wants to have all knowledge of everything and feels God is holding out on him if there is something he cannot attain. This is the first lie Satan told man, and he is still telling it.

The angel raises his right hand to heaven and swears that time will be no more. The final judgment is about to happen. God's people are about to see the culmination and fulfillment of all of their prayers and the unsaved, who have "sown the wind" are about to "reap the whirlwind" (Hosea 8:7). They are about to reap the crop of hatred and destruction they have sown against God and His church to a much larger degree than they ever expected. When the seventh trumpet sounds – this is the "last trumpet", the "eschatos trumpet" – it brings to fruition the mystery of God. To reiterate what has been previously stated, there can be no trumpet that sounds after the "last trumpet" which resurrects the dead, so the first six trumpets that sound in Revelation cannot possibly be after the "rapture." The Dispensational and Pre-Millennial interpretation just is not sound theology. This seventh trumpet very clearly shows the second coming and the judgment that is meted out simultaneously.

The mystery of God to be fulfilled when the seventh trumpet sounds is his plan to unite all things in heaven and earth under Christ's headship as is stated in Ephesians 1: 9 Having made known unto us the mystery of his will, according to his good pleasure which he hath purposed in himself: 10 That in the dispensation of the fulness of times he might gather together in one all things in Christ, both which are in heaven, and which are on earth; even in him:

Until the seventh trumpet sounds and brings in everlasting joy and glory for His people and everlasting shame and contempt for the unsaved, Jesus is working all things for the good of His people here on earth. In part this "mystery" includes the unrestrained expression of God's wrath against those who reject His Lordship over them and who persecute those who do live for God's glory. His wrath is display in the trumpet and the bowl judgments.

Before we see the judgment of the seventh trumpet, there is an interlude, not of time, not in the chronology of the execution of these trumpets, but it is meant to show God's comfort and protection for His children through these judgments. It is a parenthesis that depletes no time during these trumpet sounds, but it shows how God is dealing with His church at the same time He is dispensing judgment against the ungodly.

How can that be? How can it be that only the unsaved, those who have rejected God's provision of salvation and have been instrumental in persecuting the church be the only ones who suffer these judgments when both are alive on earth at the same time? I'm not sure that I buy that. Do you really not understand? First of all, what does verse four say? It very clearly says that the only ones to be tormented by these locusts were "only those men which have not the seal of God in their foreheads."

Those who were afflicted by the two hundred million warriors and their horses still did not repent of their sins. This clearly indicates that only those who were not "sealed in their foreheads" by God are part of this judgment. If that is not enough to convince you that God protects His people from these judgments that fall upon man throughout the course of history, then go back to Exodus and reread the account of the confrontation between Moses and Pharaoh. For the first few plagues that came upon Egypt, even Israel suffered through them. Then, beginning with the plague of the flies in Exodus 8, God protected Goshen where Israel lived from the remainder of Egypt which suffered the more severe plagues.

I'm sure you have noted that the judgments of Revelation closely parallel the judgments against Egypt. Those judgments against Egypt were sent by God in response to Israel crying out against the persecution they were suffering at the hands of the Egyptians. God heard their cry and delivered them from their tormentors and sent His punishment upon them. While God was judging them with these plagues, He was also revealing Himself to them and to His people. All could see His mercy extended to Israel. The Egyptians had ample opportunity to repent, but they did not. God allowed them to reap the result of their idolatry, their pride, arrogance and self-sufficiency, and their persecution of God's people.

God has not changed the way He protects His people through the judgments He sends on those who, like the Egyptians, think they are above His authority and reign. Many of God's people enjoy good health and satisfaction with their lives even though they may not have all the financial amenities that the unsaved have. A personal example. I have never enjoyed financial success or the so called "better things" in life, but I have enjoyed excellent health and have always had my needs met and beyond. I have enjoyed the best things in life; knowing the Savior personally, a Godly wife and family, ability and opportunity to serve the Lord, understanding of His Word, knowledge of everlasting life.

This is just one small example of how God protects His people while the unsaved, although accumulating much of what the world offers, still are not satisfied. They always seek more, and when they do not attain it, or when they lose some of their wealth – as has happened in the past year or so – they go completely to pieces emotionally and mentally, and many times physically. The world is all they live for, and when it is taken away through God's judgments, they cannot handle it. They seek death rather than living with loss. Not in all cases, but many. We have seen examples of this, also. And yes, it is God's judgments that we are seeing against those who seek only wealth and power, who deny the God who gives them all they have.

The Apostle John approaches the angel and requests the book that is in his hand, and the angel gives it to him with the instruction that he should eat it. The book would be sweet in John's mouth, but bitter in his stomach. The scroll is God's Word, as Psalm 119:103 describes "How sweet are Your words to my taste, s*weeter* than honey to my mouth!"

If the scroll is sweet in his mouth, how does it turn bitter in his stomach? The bitterness is symbolic of the antagonism and persecution that God's people must endure. The salvation message is the sweetest ever heard, but upon receiving God's Word and ingesting it, making it an integral part of your life, there will be those who persecute you. The first horseman, Christ, goes forth preaching the gospel and conquering sin and its destructive influence, and is followed immediately by the second horseman of persecution and slaughter. Those who follow Jesus will experience the blessedness of salvation, of forgiveness, but also must bear the cross. John was in exile because of the Word of God and he was writing to persecuted Christians in the seven churches. The same standard is in place for today's Christians. Jesus still demands that His disciples "take up the cross." Cross-bearing can be a bitter experience.

Measuring the Temple

In John's vision, he is given a measuring rod and told to measure the temple of God, the altar, and those who worship there, but he was not to measure the outer court of the temple because it had been given over to the Gentiles, and they would trample the temple for a period of forty two months. What is this measuring about? What does it signify?

To help us understand this better, we need to jump forward to chapter 21 and consider a few verses there. First, *verse 9 "...Come,*

I will show you the bride, the Lamb's wife." 10 And he carried me away in the Spirit to a great and high mountain, and showed me the great city, the holy Jerusalem.

One of the seven angels who pour out the bowl judgments takes John to show him "the bride, the Lamb's wife", which is none other than the church, the redeemed of all ages. The next sentence tells us in no uncertain terms the symbol in Revelation that pictures the church. The angels "showed me the great city, the holy Jerusalem." The new Jerusalem is the church, not a literal city. The church is described as a beautiful city. It had twelve gates upon which were written the names of the twelve tribes of Israel. Since our Lord was born of the tribe of Judah of Israel and He called Himself "the Door" in John 10, the only way to obtain salvation, it is not too hard to see that this picture in Revelation 21 is confirming that entrance into the new Jerusalem, the church, can only come through Jesus. Israel gave us the Savior, He gives us eternal life.

The city has twelve foundations upon which are written the names of the twelve apostles. Again, this is not hard to understand. Ephesians 2 gives further amplification of this symbol.

19 Now, therefore, you are no longer strangers and foreigners, but fellow citizens with the saints and members of the household of God, 20 having been built on the foundation of the apostles and prophets, Jesus Christ Himself being the chief cornerstone, 21 in whom the whole building, being fitted together, grows into a holy temple in the Lord, 22 in whom you also are being built together for a dwelling place of God in the Spirit.

The church is built upon the foundation of the apostles and the prophets, Jesus Christ being the chief cornerstone. The entire building, the temple, the church is formed and fit together as a habitation for the Living God. Since the foundation of the new Jerusalem is shown as bearing the names of the apostles, is it so difficult to understand that the new Jerusalem is exactly what the angel said it was, the church, the bride of Christ, and not a picture of Heaven?

Hebrews 12 explains even further that the heavenly Jerusalem is the church. *22 But you have come to Mount Zion and to the city of the living God, the heavenly Jerusalem, to an innumerable company of angels, 23 to the general assembly and church of the firstborn who are registered in heaven...*

The writer of Hebrews equates the heavenly Jerusalem, the new Jerusalem with the general assembly and the church of the firstborn who are registered in heaven. Their names are recorded in the Lamb's Book of Life. You are come, he writes, to the heavenly Jerusalem, i.e. the church, the redeemed, those who have eternal life. It is not Heaven itself, but is a group of people comprised of believers who are called the heavenly Jerusalem, the place where God dwells.

Back to Revelation 21. In verse 16, the angel measured the city, just like John was told to do to the temple here in chapter 11. The temple of God is the church and the new Jerusalem is the church. These are the same ones who are sealed by God in their foreheads. What the measuring signifies is that the church is set apart from the rest of the world by God. It is sanctified and holy. The world is ungodly. It is not measured with the temple. They have the mark of the beast. It is profane and not to be included with God's people. God's people are not to mingle with the world. They are to have no part with it. Because God has set apart the church from the world - the Gentiles - it will be trampled underfoot by the ungodly. It will be persecuted by them. This is the bitterness in the stomach that John experience when he ate the scroll.

Remembering to whom John wrote and why he wrote to them, this is another word from our Lord to them to give them comfort in their persecution. Jesus explicitly tells them that they are special to Him, that He dwells with them, that they are sanctified and holy regardless of what the rest of the world thinks or does. The church is protected by God, they are safe from His judgments while they fall upon the ungodly. They may suffer in this life, but they are eternally secure.

The Two Witnesses

These two witnesses, again, represent all believers of all time. In every scene where we see Godly people being persecuted it is not difficult to see that they represent the church. We just saw the temple being trampled underfoot, and in this scene we see the same type of persecution occurring. Because of current teachings that linger in our minds and taint our perception, we must remind ourselves of the situation in the first century and the reason for this revelation of Jesus Christ that was given to the seven churches. Christians were being persecuted and martyred for their faith, so God gives many word pictures of what they were enduring for His sake, and what the final result would be. The final result is always victory for God's people and agonizing defeat for their enemies. Each of these word pictures tell the same story. It does not change.

The two witnesses represent the church as it preaches the gospel fulfilling its commission to make disciples. It is seen robed in sackcloth – humility – as it ministers to those in need of truth. Jesus sent out his disciples two by two and this vision continues that mandate. As the message is preached, persecution occurs, as is shown by the red horse. As they are persecuted, they pray as is shown in the opening of the fifth seal, and God answers them by the trumpets. Judgments fall upon those who are responsible for persecuting the church. Fire proceeds from the mouth of the two witnesses and devours their enemies just like it happened with Jeremiah.

Jeremiah 5:14 Therefore thus says the LORD God of hosts: "Because you speak this word, behold, I will make My words in your mouth fire, and this people wood, and it shall devour them.

They have the power to shut up the heavens so it does not rain, just like Elijah did, and turn water into blood, just like Moses did. God still sends drought and water plagues in answer to the prayers of His persecuted saints. His methods have not changed. He does not change. Most people, including many Christians, are in the habit of attributing natural disasters of any kind to some imaginary female figure they call "Mother Nature." However, it is Father God who is in charge of these events. Need I say that there is no such entity as Mother Nature? She?? is a very poor substitute for the eternal, omnipotent God who rules over all. People just do not like to admit that there is a God who punishes those who reject Him and His message of repentance and salvation, who carelessly and maliciously hinder His work by attacking His people, the church.

Anyone who would harm or attempt to destroy the church should be extremely careful in how they approach God's people, for in a very real sense, the church is still a powerful entity when it prays in the fullness of the power of the Holy Spirit. The church does not pray for retaliation for the sake of revenge, but it prays for the holiness of God to be realized in the world, and God answers that prayer. His glory is His main concern and should be the church's.

These two witnesses are identified as the two olive trees and the two lamp stands that stand before the Lord of the whole earth. In Zechariah 4 we get an idea of what these witnesses represent in John's vision. Zerubbabel is identified by the angel who spoke with Zechariah as the one charged with the rebuilding of the temple, who in verse 14 is said to be standing before the Lord of the whole earth. He was the governor of Israel. In the preceding chapter, Joshua the high priest is shown standing before God. In Revelation 11, the two witnesses are those who worship God and are involved in His work of building the kingdom of God as opposed to the two beasts in Revelation who persecute the church, ungodly government and false religion.

They witness for a period of 1,260 days, the same amount of time that the holy city was given over the Gentiles for them to trample it. It is the same period of time in which these events occur, from the first coming of Jesus to His second coming. The very clear teaching in setting the time for the trampling of the city and the preaching of the witnesses is that time is limited. Time will not continue without end. When the gospel age ends, so does the world. It will be on the "last day" in which will sound the "last trumpet" which will kill the "last enemy", death, when the dead are raised - the saved to forever be with the Lord, and the unrepentant to everlasting destruction from the presence of the Lord.

Toward the end of the age, Satan will have been released from his chains that have bound him in respect to his ability to deceive the nations, and he will have waged war against the saints and have put to silence their witness. This is the apostasy, the falling away that 2 Thessalonians 2: 3 says must occur before the Lord returns. The greater part of humanity, although having had the gospel preached to them, turn away from truth and choose the lie of the devil. Why do they believe this lie? Because they have pleasure in their unrighteousness (2 Thessalonians 2: 11,12). This is the battle of Armageddon. It is a spiritual battle, one that is bent on destroying every vestige of truth. Not every Christian will have been killed or silenced, but the church as a whole will have been destroyed in their ability to publicly preach the gospel. As the witnesses are silenced, killed, the world will rejoice that they no longer will have to tolerate "hell-fire and damnation" preaching. They will think that they have been proven correct in their rejection of God, Jesus, and the preaching that dared to say that they "must be born again." The "born againers" are no more. They now have freedom from the "narrow-mindedness of preaching" that tormented them for so long, telling them that they are not good enough to go to heaven, that they cannot save themselves but need a substitute to pay for their sin.

Are we not at this moment seeing more and more intolerance toward Christians and Bible preaching that condemns sin as unholy and demands repentance in order to enter the kingdom of God? It has always been so in the struggle the church has waged throughout her history, but at this time, it is intensifying. Governments – even our own in America - pass laws that hinder the free proclamation of the gospel for fear of offending certain groups who are allowed to practice whatever abomination they desire. Need I enumerate them? You know what is now allowed that at one time – in the not too distant past – were not even whispered about, but now is proudly proclaimed as "my right."

However, the church only lies dead for three and half days, a very short amount of time.

The bodies of the witnesses begin to stir as they lie in the streets. God has breathed new life into them. The church has been publicly vindicated by God. The world who had been rejoicing in the death of the church is now terrified as God brings the church to life again. God calls and the church rises into the clouds to meet their Savior and God. Every eye is beholding this event and they quake with fear. The earth shakes violently, cities crumble, people are killed. These are the events that immediately precede the judgment of the second coming. The church was right after all and the world was wrong. But it is too late for them to now repent.

Not all of the wicked are killed in the earthquake and those who remain, it is said that they "gave glory to God." It is the terror of the moment, not repentance, that causes them to cry out to God. The "last trumpet" is about to sound.

The Seventh Trumpet

This section also ends in the final judgment with the kingdoms of the world becoming the kingdoms of God and of His Christ, and Christ reigning forever and ever. The nations, the unsaved, are judged and those who fear God are rewarded. That this is the final judgment of God against sinners there can be no doubt. This is the trumpet that calls forth the dead from their graves. This is the trumpet that sounds on the last day that defeats the last enemy. Jesus is returning to earth accompanied by His holy angels. Those who have died in the Lord are with Him, and those who are alive have risen to meet Him in the air as He descends to the earth. It is the day of final victory for the saints and final defeat for the enemies of God. As this last trumpet sounds forth there is a shout of victory in Heaven, "The kingdoms of this world have become the kingdoms of our Lord and of His Christ. And He shall reign forever and ever."

Now, it is not in question as to whether our Lord has been reigning over the kingdoms of the world or not. Not at all. This trumpet does not signal the beginning of God's reign. God has always reigned over the affairs of men – it just has not always been evident to all. Now it is manifest so that every man, woman and child is fully aware that there is a God who is alive and well and is in charge of all things. Many think because of the form and manner of world affairs that God has lost control or that Satan is in control or that man is in control of what occurs. Nothing is further from the truth. When the day of the Lord's return and He judges sinners once and for all, there will be not a doubt. It will be apparent to all. The world's system and its rulers will be toppled and they will bow the knee to Jesus and confess with their mouth that Jesus is Lord. All opposition to Him is forever abolished. It will be crystal clear to everyone that Jesus is the Supreme Ruler of the universe.

The twenty-four elders, who represent the redeemed of the ages sing a new chorus.

11: 17 "We give thanks to you, Lord God Almighty, who is and who was, for you have taken your great power and begun to reign. 18 The nations raged, but your wrath came, and the time for the dead to be judged, and for rewarding your servants, the prophets and saints, and those who fear your name, both small and great, and for destroying the destroyers of the earth." (ESV)

I used the English Standard Version for this passage because the NKJV and the KJV seem to be the only translations that includes the words "and is to come" after "who is and who was." All other translations omit these words because He no longer "is to come." This IS His second coming. We know this is a vision of His second coming because the twenty-four elders are clearly stating that the time has arrived for the dead to be judged and for the Lord's servants to be rewarded, and for the destroyers of the earth to be destroyed. Those who have aided in the destruction of the order that God intended for this earth will meet their God and all of their arrogance and pride will be crushed under the feet of Jesus.

The temple is opened in Heaven and John sees the mercy seat. Remember again, this is not a picture of Heaven, but a vision of the reality that for God's people, they are to experience mercy as they have never known before. They will have it in its entirety. Nothing will be withheld from them. They will enjoy God's presence intimately and eternally. And the reason for this is because of the sacrifice of Jesus in payment for their sins. Grace, through the covenant of His blood, is fully realized.

On the other hand, the same mercy seat that gives eternal joy and intimate knowledge of God to His people gives judgment and punishment to the unsaved. This is seen in the thunders, lightnings, earthquakes, and hail that proceeds from it. God's mercy has been rejected and now those who have rejected it are themselves being rejected by God as we have previously seen in Proverbs 1.

Chapters 12 – 14

Chapter 12 begins a new major division in Revelation, one that concentrates on the spiritual conflict that empowers false religions and governments to persecute the church. The two beasts, the dragon, Babylon, and those who take the mark of the beast are the predominant characters in this vision. We see their opposition to Christ and His church, and we see their ultimate destruction.

This revelation of our Lord Jesus Christ in His power over all that offend Him and His people gives comfort and encouragement in times of battle fatigue and weariness. Although it must endure persecutions of all kinds – physical, emotional, mental, and spiritual – the church is triumphant in her war with her enemies.

It is important to understand that Satan's primary focus for destruction is Christ. He has attacked Christ since the beginning of time, not just since His birth. In fact, his rebellion against God and His Anointed began before time, in eternity. Satan is seen in John's vision as a fiery red dragon who is standing before the woman who is clothed with the sun and has the moon as a footstool and is wearing a crown of twelve stars. She is about to give birth to a child. The dragon has seven heads, each with a crown, ten horns, and his tail drags a third of the stars of heaven to the earth. His purpose is to devour the child who is about to be born to the woman the very moment He is born. The dragon, Satan, knows very well that the child who is to be born is none other than the Redeemer, the Promised Seed of the woman who will crush his head, completely stripping him of his power over the nations to deceive them and over individuals who place their faith in Him. So he attacks with full fury and venom in an attempt to destroy Him completely. However, the Child is born and is snatched away from the dragon's attempt and is taken to God. The dragon fails in his attempt to kill the Child. But, the dragon is not thwarted – he now directs his hatred against the woman, but the woman escapes to the wilderness where she is protected and nourished by God for 1,260 days.

Again, the symbolism of this vision is not hard to understand. The time period of 1,260 days is identical to other specified periods of time we have seen in these various visions. It extends from the first coming of Jesus to His second coming. The woman in the vision is the church. Although to the world the church is of no consequence and to be openly vilified both physically and verbally, to the Lord she is absolutely beautiful, resplendent in glory, as is signified by the description given her in this passage. Her Child is the Lord Jesus Christ, the One who is to rule all the nations with a rod of iron (Psalm 2:9).

Why is the period of time from the first coming of our Lord to the second coming numbered as "three and a half years" or "1,260 days" or "time, times, and half a times"? These are all the identical length of time. This time reference would bring to the mind of those reading or hearing this vision the account of Elijah in 1 Kings 17 and 18 when God sent him to the wilderness to hide from Ahab. God providentially cared for Elijah while Ahab was persecuting those who followed Jehovah. Ahab and Jezebel were idolaters who tried to destroy believers and rid them from Israel. This account is also mentioned in James 5:17. If we compare Revelation 12:6 with James 5:17 we will readily see that the Holy Spirit had Elijah and Ahab in mind with this reference to nourishing through three and half years.

The dragon attempts to usurp the authority of the Child, who he knows is destined to rule the nations. He does this by "deceiving the nations" (Revelation 20:3) and getting them to follow him instead. His deception began with Cain and has continued from then. He has been successful, for he is called "the god of this world (age)" in 2 Corinthians 4:4. Before Christ, he was able to deceive entire nations, but now he is limited in his ability because he has been bound by the gospel that has gone into all the world. But, he still is a powerful foe, and Christians are exhorted to "submit to God and the devil will flee from us" (James 4: 7).

But, what does all this mean? Well, like the other symbolic visions that John has seen, it shows God's protection through Satan's persecution of the church. The woman, the church, is hidden in the wilderness and is fed and protected from the dragon. From the very beginning of human history, since the initial revelation of the coming Redeemer who would crush the head of the serpent (Genesis 3:15), Satan has sought to destroy God's people. Cain killed Abel, the Godly line of Seth intermarried with the ungodly line of Cain, the world became filled with violence and God sent a flood to destroy it and begin humanity again with Noah and his family. Abraham, Isaac, and Jacob met with tremendous adversity but they prevailed because the hand of God was upon them to protect them. In Egypt Israel was persecuted and enslaved until Moses led them out from bondage and into freedom. When Israel entered Canaan they again met with hostility and war. All throughout the Old Testament Israel was led astray by worldliness and idolatry, but God providentially cared for His chosen seed, protecting and nourishing the people through whom His Son would be born.

When Jesus was born in Bethlehem according to the Scriptures again Satan, in the form of Herod, tried to kill Him, but as we know, he was unsuccessful,. In the persons of the Pharisees and Sadducees Satan again attacked the Lord, thinking by crucifying Him they would defeat Him. Think again! The crucifixion of Jesus and His subsequent resurrection was the ultimate crushing of the head of the serpent, for it gave eternal life to those who trust in Him. It was the payment in full for their sins and iniquities that had separated them from God. God was satisfied with the sacrifice of His Son, and His wrath was turned away from them.

In every generation of the church since the beginning, the devil has continued to attack her since he could not destroy Jesus. But God has borne her on eagles' wings away from his most direct and damaging attacks. He has faithfully fed her with manna from His Word. The flood of lies, innuendoes, delusions, false religions, worldly philosophies, political promises of utopia, and theories of so called science has been hurled at the church, but true believers have always rejected these as from Satan and has refused to trust in them.

Yes, the church has been attacked in the most severe manner, but no, she has not been permanently damaged by the attacks. She has always persevered. Others, however, those who are Christian in name only, have been deluded into believing these lies and have been sucked into a false sense of security, thinking that "all paths lead to God" and other such nonsense. The unbelieving world has swallowed the entire flood of lies Satan has generated. They think they are so wise in their philosophy and ways, but as Romans 1 states, they have become fools in their wisdom. The true church has undergone severe attacks and has always triumphed over them and will do so until the Lord returns in glory. God always protects His people.

Since he was not successful in attacking the church, Satan directs his poisonous venom against "the rest of her offspring", which is individual Christians. They, too, are protected by God from the onslaught of the devil. God gives us wisdom to reject temptation and choose holiness. When we "acknowledge Him in all our ways", "He directs our paths" away from that which displeases Him.

Yet, many times we are drawn away and enticed by worldly influences and we sin. James speaks directly to this in his first chapter. Temptation gives birth to sin and sin brings forth death. Every time. Yet, God protects us in this also. How? We may very well suffer from our waywardness and deliberate sin, yet we do not suffer the full punishment for our sin. Jesus has absorbed the punishment for us in His sacrificial death on the cross. His broken body took the blows that we deserve, thereby "protecting" us from the devil's plan to have God so angry with us that He destroys us since he, Satan, is unable to do so. Satan's plan is again thwarted. His design to destroy Jesus, His church, and individual Christians is foiled.

Since he cannot destroy Christ or His church by deception, temptation or sin, Satan chooses outright persecution by two beasts, one political and the other religious. Through the ages there have been numerous governments who have persecuted the church in an attempt to totally annihilate it. This is what the first century Christians were facing in Rome. The Roman empire worshiped Caesar, and when the Christians refused to do so, they were persecuted, killed, thrown to lions and made sport of in Roman coliseums.

The First Beast – Ungodly Governments

The vision of the first beast that arises from the sea is the beast of anti-Christian government. This beast is a monstrosity in its appearance and devastating in its power. It has seven heads and ten horns. There are crowns on its horns. On its heads are names of blasphemy.

It has the appearance of a leopard with feet like a bear and a mouth like a lion. The dragon gives power to the beast so it can fulfill his will. The beast roars out blasphemies against God. The unbelieving world worships the beast. It has a head that apparently dies and is brought back to life again. What does all this mean?

This beast that arises out of the sea is very closely attuned to the previous beast that comes out of the abyss in chapter 11. It is the representation of the dragon in a form that humans can see and understand. The "sea" represents humanity, and this beast arises from the nations and governments of the people of earth. This beast is empowered by Satan to do one thing and one thing only – to persecute God's people, and thereby persecute Christ (Acts 9:5). Whenever there are governments who persecute God's people simply because they are Christians it is the embodiment of this beast that is doing so. It has seven heads, demonstrating different forms and varieties of manifestations. It has appeared as Egypt, Philistines, Babylon, Medes and Persians, Greece, Rome, atheistic communism, dictators of Third World counties, and in modern Europe and America as extreme liberalism who believe that there should be no restraints placed upon ungodliness. Lawmakers and judges who take away freedom of religion and replace it with freedom from religion and who sanction all manner of ungodliness are the present day manifestation of the beast. It is important to see that this beast wears its crowns on its horns, not its heads. The horns represent its power, and its power, Satan, wears the crowns. The power that sustains these godless governments, their ideas and authority, is derived from none other than the dragon. They may not realize it and certainly do not like to be so designated, but any government who takes away the freedom to worship God and evangelize in His name and punishes those who do is a form of the beast that is represented in this passage. It is one of his seven heads.

The head that was wounded and healed, I believe, has a historical reference to the Roman Empire, which particulars the first century Christians were well aware of, when Nero, who was a persecutor of Christians committed suicide. He had some Christians crucified, others covered with tar and oil and burned, others nailed to trees and others thrown to lions – all so the heathen Romans would be entertained. After his death – for a season - there was little trouble for the church, and later Domitian gained the throne and reestablished persecution.

The beast has power for forty two months, the same length of time as we have noticed before. It is again to be stated that this represents the time from the first coming of Jesus to His second coming. By mentioning again this time frame, the first century Christians would know that this was the time in which they were living, and they knew from the description of the beast that the power behind Rome was the devil himself. They would also realize that he is a defeated foe and through persevering they would gain the ultimate victory. Although more and more we are witnessing a hatred and disgust by the world for Jesus Christ and His church, we need to be aware that the beast has power only for a while. The worst thing governments can do to Christians is to kill their bodies, but have no power over their souls. Jesus instructs us to continue to preach His word regardless of the persecution involved, even to a martyr's death.

Matthew 10: 27 "Whatever I tell you in the dark, speak in the light; and what you hear in the ear, preach on the housetops. 28 And do not fear those who kill the body but cannot kill the soul. But rather fear Him who is able to destroy both soul and body in hell.

God is to be feared more than those who "breathe out threatenings" and who are allowed by God to inflict bodily harm on believers. He is the ultimate authority in the universe, and He will judge those who reject Him and refuse to honor and worship Him.

The Second Beast – False Religions and Philosophies

The second beast arises from the earth. It has only two horns, like a lamb, but it speaks like a dragon. It exercises the authority of the first beast and performs miracles when in its presence so the masses are deceived into worshiping the image of the first beast which he has made to speak and to come alive. Anyone who will not worship the image of the first beast, he orders to be killed. He then orders everyone without distinction of class or race to be marked in their forehead or right hand as a sign of loyalty to the first beast. Whoever did not receive the mark was forbidden from buying or selling or conducting any type of business. The mark, or number, of the beast is 666.

What does this mean? This second beast is false religion and philosophies. These have always been a snare to God's people. This beast appears to be a lamb, it appears to be gentle and loving, but it conceals the hideous monster that deceives people. So many false religions and false philosophies have the appearance of peace and tranquility and wisdom and intellectual correctness, but they are nothing more than the roaring of the dragon. Many could be enumerated, but I will forego the listing of these false religions. You know who and what they are. Any religion or philosophy that does not honor and glorify Jesus Christ is included in this depiction of the beast. This beast arose from the earth. James 3:15 tells us that wisdom that confuses and is envious and self-seeking and lies is from the earth. It is not to be trusted. It is demonic, of the devil.

James 3: 15 This wisdom does not descend from above, but is earthly, sensual, demonic.

This includes aberrations of sound theology, of the "faith once for all delivered to the saints" (Jude v. 3) as has been previously discussed, especially in chapter three. It includes all the false religions that have been perpetrated upon mankind from the beginning. Any religion that does not have Jesus Christ, His eternal oneness with the Father, His essential Godhood, His virgin birth, His sinless life, His sacrificial death, His burial, His resurrection, His ascension, His Lordship and eternal rule over all of creation, His second coming in power and glory, His judgment of all who reject Him and His eternal fellowship with all who receive Him, His eternal glory and worthiness to be worshiped as their central theme is a false religion and is to be shunned. It emanates from the second beast.

This beast causes all, small and great, rich and poor, free and bond from all nations and nationalities to receive a mark on their foreheads or right hands. The number of the beast is 666, the number of a man. There are so many thoughts on what this number means, but the context is relatively clear on this. The context is dealing with the false religions and philosophies that come from the second beast which arises from the earth. Again, James tells us that this wisdom is earthly, sensual, full of lies. Man's religions and philosophies are exactly that. Man is the one who carries out these insidious philosophies that damn the souls of those who believe them. They are the ones who take the mark. Unregenerate man thinks he is so smart and wise, so he develops his own religion and follows it straight to hell. Man is the one who kills for the purpose of destroying Christ and His people. 666 is the mark of unsaved, unrepentant mankind who fulfill the demands of the dragon by believing and implementing his lies and causing others to believe them also. This beast glories in these rebellious men, for they have sold their souls to him. As a reward he promotes them in the world as they adhere to his thoughts and deeds. They are successful in commerce, politics, and education. They can buy and sell, for they have the worldly means to do so. The dragon speaks through their so called wisdom and they obey. They have rejected God and His wisdom, so He has allowed them to reap what they have sown. They have temporary power, but that power will fail and destroy their very souls.

The mark is on the forehead or the right hand. Since God seals His servants on the forehead to set apart those who are His and afford them protection, so this second beast – in the form of a lamb – outwardly impersonating the Lamb of God – making others think that they are following a true savior – cause those who buy into his lies a mark on their forehead or right hand, thus setting them apart as followers of the dragon, the devil, and he rewards them with worldly gain. So many cults and false religions are prevalent today and to their disciples, they appear as a lamb, as a peaceful, loving lamb that is harmless and cuddly and not capable of harming anyone. But, in reality, they are disciples of Satan. He has marked them as his own. This marking by the beast has been ongoing throughout church history. It is not for a singular, particular point in history, especially in some "tribulation period" yet to come. The mark distinguishes those who receive it as worshipers of the beast.

*Revelation 14: "If anyone **worships the beast** and his image, and receives **his mark on his forehead or on his hand,** 10 he himself shall also drink of the wine of the wrath of God, which is poured out full strength into the cup of His indignation. He shall be tormented with fire and brimstone in the presence of the holy angels and in the presence of the Lamb. 11 And the smoke of their torment ascends forever and ever; and they have no rest day or night, who **worship the beast and his image, and whoever receives the mark of his name."***

That's clear, is it not? What does the mark signify? It means that those who receive it belong to the beast, just like a brand or mark on a slave or cattle shows that they belong to someone. It means that they are in the service of the one whose mark they bear. Christians are sealed with the mark of the Holy Spirit, so we are His servants. We belong to God. Those who are sealed with the mark of the beast belong to him. On the forehead the mark signifies those who have the mind of the beast, those who think what the dragon spues out is truth. They think his thoughts and speak his words. They follow his philosophy of life. The mark on the hand designates those who work for the beast, who take action in his name. Both persecute the church. One through what they say and write, the others through what they do. The beast uses both intellectual and physical persecution in an attempt to achieve his end.

Those who do not receive the mark of the beast, who instead follow Jesus Christ may not be as worldly successful as those who do follow vain philosophies and worldly endeavors, and thus cannot "buy and sell" as others can, but they have the presence and the power of the Almighty God at work in their lives and eternal life to come. Is it worth having worldly power and wealth and recognition if it means eternal damnation?

In chapter 14 we see three different scenes. The first scene begins in verse one, and it is in Heaven. It shows the 144,000 who have the name of the Lamb and His Father on their foreheads. This is the same group that was seen in chapter seven. In chapter seven they were surrounded by the enemies of the church while they were still on earth, but in this vision, they are in Heaven and are singing a new song along with the four living creatures and the twenty four elders. We must note that although they have been persecuted and martyred by the dragon and the two beasts, not one of them is missing from the tally. Every single soul of the 144,000, which represents the entire body of the redeemed of all ages, is present to engage in the worship of the Lamb. All are safe and secure in Heaven. "None of them is lost" (John 17:12).

Heaven's chorus is singing and it is a song that only the redeemed may sing, those who have been "redeemed from the earth", for only they have experienced salvation. It is a song of the Lamb and of His salvation and of His glory. They are virgins - spiritual virgins – they have not been defiled by the dragon or the beasts. They have remained faithful to their God in the midst of tribulation. They have not chosen the path of least resistance during their pilgrimage on earth. They have not given in to the lure of worldliness and the desire for acceptance by others, but have faithfully proclaimed the gospel of Jesus Christ. They, like Moses, chose to suffer affliction with the people of God rather than to enjoy the pleasures of sin for a season.

To show that these 144,000 are indeed the entire assembly of the saved from all ages, they are called "firstfruits to God", "redeemed from among men." These are the chosen by God who have been separated unto Him from among all other men on earth. James 1:18 calls those whom God has "brought forth (given birth to) by the Word of Truth", "firstfruits." They have been set apart by God from all others as His own special possession. In the Old Testament, the firstfruits of the land, whether man, animal, grain, fruit, or vegetable, belonged to God, and must either be sacrificed to Him or redeemed by a substitute. He claimed them as His own. They represented the best of the land. In like manner, the church, God's firstfruits among men, are the best of humanity, not because of any inherent goodness, but because He has chosen them for Himself from among all others. His election of them has made them "firstfruits." Since they were "redeemed from among men", they are the full amount of those elected by the Father for salvation. They are not "special Christians", somehow more spiritual than others, super saints, more in tuned with God than other Christians. They all have the Father's name written on their foreheads. They were all singing the song of redemption.

The second scene begins in verse six, and it takes us from the Heavenly scene of verses 1 – 5 back to earth. This vision does not follow the Heavenly scene chronologically, for it takes us back to view what is transpiring on earth just prior to the second coming and final judgment. Three angels are about to speak, and their messages are a final warning to those who dwell on earth. The first angel proclaims the "everlasting gospel" to them that they should fear God, give glory to Him and to worship Him who made the heavens and earth and the sea and the springs of water. The people to whom the message is addressed evidently have never given a serious thought to God and His worthiness to be worshiped and feared. They have been too consumed with their own lives and what they want out of it to give Him a second thought or even a first thought. Here is judgment about to fall upon them and they are just "eating and drinking, marrying and giving in marriage."

This scene reminds me of a trading card I had in the 1950's. It pictured a man falling from a high building, and as he is falling head first toward the street below, he is smiling and saying, "I'm still OK." The world is falling head first toward certain destruction and it is laughing and smiling all the way thinking that they are still OK.

The second angel speaks and cries out that "Babylon is fallen." That seductive worldliness that lured so many to itself has been judged and found guilty, and sentence has been passed by God. Spiritual fornication has been totally destroyed in God's judgment. That which the world has worshiped and substituted for God has been crushed by the Lord Jesus. No more does it call out to the simple to turn in to her and enjoy worldly pleasures (Proverbs 1).

The third angel cries out with a loud voice that those who have chosen the world over the Lord Jesus Christ will have the wrath of God poured out in full strength into their cup and they will drink it all. There will be no more offer of mercy. They have chosen and now they will receive the just recompense of their error. There are no more chances for repentance. The first angel offered it, but they refused. It is now eternally too late. They have chosen to worship the beast and now they must suffer with him. It is a never ending punishment with fire and brimstone.

It is not just those who actively take part in the persecution of the church who are in view here. It is everyone who has refused the offer of salvation whether they have been vociferous in their denial of Christ or merely indifferent toward Him. Jesus clearly stated in Matthew 12:30 that "he who is not with Me is against Me." Anyone who has not taken a stand with Jesus has taken the mark of the beast and will be dealt with according to the cry of the third angel.

Again we see the final judgment. The patience of the saints is rewarded. They are blessed and they enter their rest and their works follow them to Heaven. They may have had very trying times on earth. They may have suffered persecution and even martyrdom, but now they have been rewarded by their God. They are in His presence forevermore, never again to shed a tear or experience any fear or suffer in the least. In John's vision he sees two harvests; one harvest is of God's people and the other is of the wicked.

The Lord Jesus is seen sitting on a white cloud. He is wearing a crown of gold and is holding a sickle in His hands. He thrusts His sickle into the earth and His chosen ones are taken from the earth to Him. He has come for His own and received them unto Himself. Don't forget. This is not a literal sickle and reaping. It is the second coming of our Lord symbolized by this vision.

There is another reaping in this vision. It is of the wicked. An angel thrusts his sickle into the earth and the "vine of the earth" is reaped and its grapes – the wicked - are thrown into the "winepress of the wrath of God" where they are squeezed until they the blood that comes out of the winepress flows for almost 200 miles at a depth that reaches to a horse's bridle. Again, this is not literal, but it is a picture of complete and hopeless destruction in punishment of the wicked. It is a symbol of an absolute crushing of their hopes and dreams to be their own gods and to design their own world in which they rule according to their wicked desires. It is a vision of the crushing and breaking – but not the total destruction - of the very bodies that they used to fulfill their own sinful purposes, never thinking they would ever come to this place of judgment. They have come to the end of their pleasurable earthly existence and have met their eternal Judge.

Chapters 15 & 16

These two chapters are the beginning of a new division of Revelation. The bowl judgments are announced in chapter 15 but not actually poured out until chapter 16. These seven judgments will be the conclusion of God's dealing with the wicked while still on the earth. Before we witness the outpouring of the finality of the wrath of God upon humans on the earth, there is a prelude of praise that ascribes righteousness and glory to God for all of His marvelous works. The redeemed are seen standing beside a sea of glass in Heaven, playing harps, and singing the song of Moses and of the Lamb. Just as Moses and Israel gave God the glory for His triumph over Pharaoh and Egypt at the Red Sea, so the redeemed give glory to God for His triumph over the dragon, the two beasts, and Babylon. They praise the righteousness of God in the judgments that He pours out upon the unrepentant world. God is holy and just and righteous in all that He does. God's glory is seen in these seven bowls about to be poured out full force.

The tabernacle in Heaven is seen opening and seven angels with God's seven last judgments upon the wicked are seen leaving the tabernacle in preparation to pouring them out. The bowls are full indicating that the judgments are fierce and unable to be avoided. The tabernacle is full of smoke, hiding the mercy seat from view, so that no one can mitigate these judgments or intercede for those for whom they are intended. God's mercy has reached its limits and now there is nothing but wrath that proceeds from Him.

The Seven Bowls of Wrath

The vision John sees next should fill every unrepentant heart with terror, for the voice of the Almighty God – who they have scorned and rejected – thunders from the throne room and calls for the seven angels to pour out His wrath upon those who have had many opportunities to repent but have deliberately chosen to ignore and scorn the God who is calling them. These bowls of wrath, in many respects, remind us of the plagues of Egypt sent to punish those who hardened their hearts against God and refused to obey Him. Yet, God's outpoured wrath has not been limited to the Egyptians, but has been manifested throughout the ages, but especially so since the first coming of our Lord Jesus Christ.

In the times "of ignorance", the days in which men fashioned gods of their own liking and desires of wood and stone, silver and gold, the days in which nations were formed from one blood and shown where they were to live and not pass over (Acts 17:26, 29), God has overlooked – He did not bring immediate judgment to those who so lived. But now, Paul emphatically states, God commands all men in every nation to repent. Repentance is not optional. It is commanded by God. Why is He commanding repentance now? Because He has appointed a day in which He will judge the world in righteousness by Jesus Christ who He raised from the dead. Failure to repent brings devastating consequences. Eternal consequences.

Acts 17: 30 Truly, these times of ignorance God overlooked, but now commands all men everywhere to repent, 31 because He has appointed a day on which He will judge the world in righteousness by the Man whom He has ordained. He has given assurance of this to all by raising Him from the dead."

The judgments of these first six bowls are not the final judgment, but they are sent because men have failed to obey God's command to repent as Paul preaches in Acts 17. He sends immediate judgment upon them as they scorn His commands and make light of His mercy and longsuffering with them. These judgments are prior to His final judgment. These judgments have been being sent by God throughout the ages when God's patience has run out with unrepentant sinners. They are sent out but men still will not repent. They have become even more stiff-necked against God.

Not all of these judgments are sent against every unrepentant person. Whoever disregards the warnings of the trumpets, meets with the bowls of wrath. Some have the first bowl, the painful sores as their judgment. This judgment is the same one that God told Israel through Moses in Deuteronomy 28: 27 that anyone who did not obey God and His commandments would suffer. In fact, in Deuteronomy 28 we can see God judging those who turn their back on Him just like we do in Revelation. Many have been judged and have died and entered hell by disease and physical afflictions by our Lord. Please listen carefully. Not all disease and physical maladies that cause death are bowl judgments, but many are. Do not for one minute believe the argument that God has nothing to do with sickness and disease that His mercy and longsuffering has no end. He does judge sinners here on earth if they harden their hearts beyond remedy.

For believers, their physical pain and disease is never a bowl judgment. God disciplines us in order to conform us more to the image of Jesus Christ through suffering and pain, but it is never a wrathful punishment. This bowl judgment, as verse two says, is only for those who bear the mark of the beast and worship him. Those who have deliberately chosen to follow the Satanic plan rather than God's commands, who have refused God's offer of salvation through the blood of Jesus are open to be recipients of this bowl.

God uses the sea to send other unrepentant sinners to hell. All disasters at sea are meant to warn the ungodly to repent, but having not repented, many maritime disasters have been God's judgment upon sinners to take them out of this world. This is the second bowl.

The third bowl judgment also involves water, but it is poured out upon fresh water, rivers and fountains, springs, that which is used for drinking and irrigation for edible plants and vegetables. When these waters are rendered undrinkable, in the vision turning it to blood, many die from it. Notice that the angel in charge of this bowl cries out to God that His judgments are righteous. A voice from the altar reiterates the righteousness of God's judgment in this bowl. Whatever this bowl includes – it may be more than drinking water - the ones who die because of this bowl are the ones who have shed the blood of the saints; they have received what they have sown. In the opening of the fifth seal, the souls of those who had been martyred were seen crying out from under the altar for God to avenge their blood, and now He is doing it again in like kind to those who are guilty of the blood of the saints and prophets. Again, this is demonstrating that these bowls have been poured out again and again through the ages. Those who persecuted the prophets and shed their blood had this bowl poured out upon them during their lifetime, and through the various times of persecution, the same bowl has rendered the same judgment upon the persecutors.

The fourth judgment bowl is poured out upon the sun causing it to burn hot and scorch those upon whom it shines. It brings to mind Nebuchadnezzar's oven in which he meant to burn Shadrach, Meshach and Abednego. Instead, it burned and killed the soldiers who threw them into the fire. The same furnace killed the ungodly but did no harm to God's children. Do God's principles work in the same way today? Quite obviously they do. The scorching sun burns the unsaved, and instead of repenting, they blaspheme God the more. It is not hard to see how this bowl has affected the world in which we live. So many heathen countries have suffered extreme heat and drought while others have enjoyed the blessing of rain and fruitfulness. God sends this judgment on those who do not worship Him, but instead blaspheme Him and become even more adamant in their rejection of Him.

The fifth bowl is specially designed for the beast and his seat of power. Every world power that has persecuted the church has come to nothing, and usually in a very painful, humiliating way. Egypt persecuted Israel and had to suffer the death of every one of their firstborn when the angel of death passed through the land. Then their military force was drowned in the Red Sea. The blood of Israel and the honor of God was avenged upon them. Babylon suffered a humiliating defeat at the hands of the Medes and Persians when they thought they were undefeatable. They were busy partying and getting drunk and desecrating the gold and silver utensils from the temple in Jerusalem when they were destroyed militarily and politically. The Medes and Persians were conquered by Greece and Greece by Rome. Moral cancer rotted Rome and it slowly died a painful, lingering death. Each and every one of these political manifestations of the beast was filled with darkness – they had their own gods they worshiped and they blasphemed the God who created them. The light shined upon them – they had the witness of the truth

- they had many opportunities to choose to follow the true God – but they rejected Him and chose the painful death they died. None of them repented of their persecution of God's people and of their blasphemy against God.

I know that there are many whose patriotism will not allow them to believe this, but America is teetering very close to the edge of the cliff of destruction by the imminent pouring out of this bowl. The precipice into which we are sliding ever so surely is one from which we may not escape. On 9/11 some preachers publicly stated that it was a judgment from God and they were ridiculed and scorned by the media and even by other Christians. Were they so far from the truth? America is choosing a path that is anything but righteous, anything but holy, anything but God fearing and God honoring. Many leaders in all branches of the government are more concerned with their "political future" than they are in doing what is right. They wet their fingers and hold them in the wind to see which direction it is blowing before they decide how to vote on any given issue. I will not elaborate the decisions that are plaguing and ruining this country. You know what they are. Righteousness, which exalts a nation, is being cast aside, and sin, which is a reproach to any people, is being promoted so as to make those who choose perversity feel like they are an important part of society.

Christians are being silenced on every front in favor of appeasing those who out rightly reject Christ and a holy life. Christians are being targeted as intolerant, unforgiving, and unwilling to allow people to do whatever they decide is right for them if they speak out against sin and immorality. Anyone with any moral standards at all is attacked whenever they speak out against unrighteousness and moral perversity. What is the difference between America today and Rome of yesterday? Rome had its gods of hedonism, pleasure, power, materialism, gold, silver, wealth and education for the sake of intellectual superiority. It reveled in the destruction of the gospel by torturing and killing Christians who preached truth. America has not yet reached the depths of debauchery that these other former world powers have, but we are heading in that direction along with much of Europe. Does God have to pour out the fifth bowl upon us? If He does, it will be too late. Repentance will not be possible. The trumpet is sounding now. It is not too late to repent right now, but if the bowl is poured out...

The sixth bowl is poured out on the Euphrates. The Euphrates was the northeast boundary of the Promised Land. In Genesis 15:18 God told Abraham that He would give Abraham's descendants all the land from the "river of Egypt to the Euphrates." Everything beyond the Euphrates, therefore, represents that which is not included in the covenant, wickedness and worldliness. When the bowl is poured out on the Euphrates, it dries up and the "kings of the east", the ungodly world, Babylon, Assyria and beyond attack the Promised Land. The vision represents Satan, the dragon and the ungodly governments, the beast, and false religions making war on the church, the covenant community, those who have a relationship with God.

Demonic forces, represented by the three frogs, are behind this attack on all that is Godly and good. These frogs are loathsome, abominable and repulsive. They speak all that is hateful and despicable against Christ and the church. They are the influence behind the attack. This is the battle of Armageddon. This is not, contrary to popular belief and visions of Hollywood, a literal battle comprised of literal armies gathered together in the literal valley of Megiddo in order to despoil Christ of His authority and power. It is a Satanic attack on the church who wields Christ's power – through the gospel – here on earth.

Again, I must remind you, that this is a vision that portrays a spiritual truth. It is not literal as defined by so many. It is literal in that the truth it portrays through symbolism will occur as it is seen in the vision. How do you know you are right in what you are saying when so many others see it differently? Because it all fits together perfectly. It all corresponds with other Scriptures. There are no discrepancies in this interpretation. It honors Jesus Christ. It is about Him.

This battle takes place during the three and half days of Revelation 11 when the bodies of the two witnesses lay in the street. It is the same time as loosing of Satan for a little while in Revelation 20. It is the time when Satan's power against the church it at it zenith. The church is in desperate need of intervention by God. It has become practically helpless against the beast and false prophet who are empowered by the dragon. Just when it seems there is no hope for rescue, when the Satanic forces are about to completely destroy the church and its witness, Christ will suddenly appear and will deliver His people.

This battle has its precursor in Judges 4 and 5 where we see Israel being tormented and persecuted by her enemies, this time the Canaanites under the rule of King Jabin. The Canaanites have decimated Israel and have oppressed them cruelly for twenty years. Israel was so in fear of the Canaanites that they hid themselves and did not even walk on the public roadways (Judges 5:6). The Canaanites were a powerful enemy militarily. They mustered 900 chariots of iron while Israel did not even have a sword or a spear (5:8) with which to defend themselves. Israel is in a heap of trouble. But God is in control of the entire situation. He is about to act in their behalf.

Deborah was the judge at that time. God spoke through her to Barak to assemble his army to fight with the Canaanites led by Sisera, the commander of their army. God Himself would fight against the Canaanites and would bring victory to Israel. The battle was fought at Megiddo, and the Canaanites were sent running for their lives. Judges 5:20 states that "they fought from the heavens; the stars in their courses fought against Sisera." God did indeed intervene on Israel's behalf and gave them a glorious victory over their enemy.

Armageddon symbolizes each time the church is oppressed, when the need is great because there is no strength left to resist the attacks of an overpowering enemy, and God intervenes to defeat the enemy miraculously. When God's power is suddenly manifest to defeat those who oppress His people, that is a shadow of the final Armageddon. He did it when He the angel of God killed 185,000 Syrian soldiers in one night. He will do it again at the end of this age. In 2 Chronicles 20 when Jehoshaphat was facing a great multitude from Moab and Ammon and other nations that he could not defeat with his army, Jahaziel, the prophet, told him in verse *15 "Thus says the LORD to you: 'Do not be afraid nor dismayed because of this great multitude, for the battle is not yours, but God's...17 You will not need to fight in this battle. Position yourselves, stand still and see the salvation of the LORD, who is with you, O Judah and Jerusalem!' Do not fear or be dismayed; tomorrow go out against them, for the LORD is with you."* God intervened and completely decimated the enemy of Israel without Israel lifting a sword. This is the sixth bowl of judgment that is poured out on the unbelievers.

The bowls are bowls of wrath are poured out upon those who will not repent of their various sins. The seventh bowl is poured out and we see the incredibly vivid description of the terror of the final judgment. God's patience has reached its end and He now judges Babylon, that worldly system that has brought so much wealth and prosperity and pleasure to those who have taken the mark of the beast and has caused so much suffering to God's people. Babylon is absolutely crushed and ruined beyond all recognition and repair. All that gave satisfaction to the ungodly is destroyed. The world mourns and cries out in agony over her defeat.

John sees the bowl emptied into the atmosphere. The entire planet is affected by this bowl of wrath. Life on earth is over. God's voice emanating from the throne pronounces that "It is done!" God's wrath that He has held in check for all the ages has been released to work its punishment on all those who have rejected Him to gain the pleasures of the world. The judgment day is here. John experiences lightening flashing, thunder crashing, great noises thrashing through the air and an earthquake such as had never been witnessed before. Babylon, the anti-christian world system is broken apart. The nations lay in ruin. All that had oppressed God and His church is completely and utterly destroyed forever. It will never be heard from again. It has experienced the extreme fierceness of the wrath of God. Every island flees away, mountains are demolished and great hailstones – each weighing one hundred pounds falls upon men who are still blaspheming God. Throughout eternity in hell they will blaspheme and curse the name of the Lord Jesus Christ. The anger they felt toward Him on earth continues forever, tormenting their souls and bodies without end.

Chapters 17 – 19

The last few verses of chapter 16 give a summary of the destruction of Babylon. These next chapters give the details of that destruction and the reasons for it. We have seen the punishment of those who take the mark of the beast, and now we will see, in symbolism, what happens to Babylon, the beast from the sea, the false prophet, and in chapter 20, which we have seen in part in a previous chapter, the destruction of the dragon, Satan. The first century church undergoing severe persecution needed to know that those who were hatefully attacking and martyring them would have the vengeance of God executed upon them, that God was not unaware of what they were enduring. Through the years, this same message has been needed by other Christians going through persecution by governments and false religions and worldly minded entities. This message has brought comfort to God's people through the years. God knows all about it and will avenge them.

One of the seven angels who had the bowls called to John to come so he could see God's judgment on the harlot who was riding on the scarlet beast, the one who arose from the sea, the one with seven heads and ten horns, the one who was full of blasphemy.

There are many contrasts to be made as we look at this passage. The harlot is the world's imitation of the church, the true bride of Christ, for it attempts to impersonate the description of the church in chapter 12. The church is clothed with the sun, the moon was under her feet and she had a crown of twelve stars on her head. Her exquisite beauty and composure comes directly from God, for her adornment is God's creation. She has the beauty of the bride. The harlot has manmade and earthly adornments, objects that man values, but things that God does not think of as worth anything – purple and scarlet cloth, gold, jewels and pearls. Her attraction is not true beauty, for she is not a bride, but a prostitute. She only has painted beauty that wears off. These are things that are included in the list of 18:12,13 as merchandise that God destroys that causes the world to weep and wail.

The woman of chapter 12, the church, is great with Child. She is about to give birth to a Son. The woman of chapter 17 is a prostitute, one who seduces the "kings of the earth" and all of mankind, but has no desire or even ability to bring forth a child. She only wants the pleasure without the pain or responsibility of bearing a raising a son. She sees her fornication as a money making proposition, one that brings her power and fame.

The woman of chapter 12 is being persecuted by the woman of chapter 17. The prostitute is jealous of the bride, for the bride has something of lasting value while she does not. The woman of chapter 12 flees to the wilderness where God cares for her and feeds her and gives her drink. He provides complete nourishment for her. The harlot in chapter 17 is also seen in the wilderness where she evidently has chased the church and is seen drunk with the blood of the saints whom she has persecuted and martyred.

The world has attempted by the power of the dragon to be a substitute for the church. It gives momentary pleasure but not lasting joy. It gives temporary power but not eternal security. It gives gold and silver that will decay but not true riches that are laid up in Heaven. It has its own gods – the devil, the serpent, the dragon, the political beast and the false prophet. The world would deny that they worship Satan and accept as truth his policies, for it wants to believe that it is in control of its own destiny, that it is making its own decisions without any outside influence, that it is providing for itself. The church, however, knows that she worships the true God, the Creator, the One who provides daily nourishment for our souls and our bodies.

Worldliness, which rides on the back of the beast, is deception personified. It has absolutely nothing of value to offer anyone, yet most people are intoxicated by it – they are like drunkards who lose all sense of perspective - and adopt its values as their own. They are like men who constantly enter the brothel to engage in sexual immorality with a prostitute. They are deceived by her. They get no love, nothing of lasting value, only the deceit of whoredom. The beast, empowered by Satan, supports and encourages Babylon and all of its worshipers. It gives gifts to them, trinkets that have no lasting worth, that are destined to be destroyed with the passing of time and on the great Day of judgment.

This worldliness, this Babylon, is symbolic of everything in every age that would deceive, lure, entice, seduce and lead people away from the true God, giving them the sense of well-being - just like the drunkard is secure in his drink, even when he regurgitates it all and passes out from it. It is the substitute god that the dragon has produced. Babylon of old was a center of commerce and industry that afforded worldly success and pleasure. It was to Babylon that Israel was taken as captives for seventy years. Israel had failed to keep their covenant with the Lord, so He gave them the desires of their hearts, but not in the manner they would have chosen. He gave them worldliness but not the pleasure and self-autonomy they sought. Many Christians today seek worldly success and go to Babylon for fulfillment of their desires, but they do not get what they seek. They are severely disappointed with the results. It causes much pain and confusion and loss of perspective – just like the drunkard. Anyone who chooses worldliness over Godliness will not be pleased with their choice, but will suffer the consequences of that decision. God is not mocked. Whatever we sow, we reap.

John is amazed when he sees the harlot with the name "Mystery, Babylon the Great, the Mother of all Harlots and of the Abominations of the Earth." Everything that is abominable and seductive has been born of Babylon. It began with Babylon of old when Nimrod led his people to build a tower that reached into the heavens so they might "make a name for themselves." Assyria followed with its capital city of Nineveh, then along came Babylon again with Nebuchadnezzar. The Medes and Persians came next, followed by Greece, followed by Rome. All of these empires personified the beast, but none of them continued. They all met with death in one form or another. What causes amazement to those whose name is not recorded in the Book of Life is that the beast always comes back to life after suffering death. The dragon will give life to another power so it can assume the form of the beast. In our lifetime Germany was incarnate in the beast, but it was killed. Japan took the body of the beast, but it too was killed. Russia, another embodiment of the beast, for "an hour", died.

The beast is not manifest only in major world powers, but in every government that is anti-christian and takes action to silence the gospel and those who preach it no matter how influential on the world stage it is or is not. Throughout history, every manifestation of the beast perished. It died and is no more. Each time the beast dies, it goes into perdition, hell. The beast, the angel tells John, "was, is not, and yet is." It had life, died, and will be back again. It continues to be "resurrected" - the fatal head wound is healed - in another nation, yet it maintains the same essence, the same power and authority. This beast will continue to reappear until the day it is judged and found guilty and has its sentence of eternal punishment passed upon it.

The beast has seven heads and ten horns. The seven heads represent every major world power that has existed in the past and will exist in the future. In John's day it represented Rome, which is explained in verse 9. Rome is the city of seven hills. It was the seat of anti-christian persecution, of seduction and enticement, of worldliness and compromise. The harlot sat upon these seven hills. The ten horns are ten kings who had not at that time received their power. These ten horns represent all of earth's major players in commerce, art, education, industry, science, government, and all other categories that support and give aid to the beast. Anything that promotes itself over Christ is included in these ten horns. These ten horns are all those who give allegiance and support to the beast. They have their power for but one hour, and very short amount of time. They make war against the Lamb and His flock, but they are soundly defeated by the Lamb, for He is the King of Kings and Lord of Lords. How foolish of them to trade away eternity for one short hour.

All throughout history this has been the overriding theme. The beast makes war on the saints, and for a short amount of time, it appears to be victorious, all seems to be going well. It is enjoying its drunken seduction with the harlot; it thinks nothing can go wrong, that its luxurious playtime will continue indefinitely. Like Judas Iscariot who thought more of thirty pieces of silver than he thought of Jesus, it dies a horrible death because the Lamb is vastly more powerful and has infinitely more power than it does. The Lord Jesus is ever revealing Himself as the King of Kings and Lord of Lords. He will not allow any other power to usurp His authority and glory. Every world power that exalts itself over the Lord Jesus Christ is doomed to meet with the same fate. It will perish into perdition.

There comes a time when worldly minded people, those who have supported the beast, who have supported the anti-christian culture, who have been "in lust" with the world, turn against the harlot, and condemn and hate the worldliness they have desired and engaged in. They begin to see that the luxury and pleasures and culture of the world is absolutely worthless. They see that it has gained them nothing. They, in disgust and revulsion, like Judas Iscariot, throw down their "thirty pieces of silver" which they have taken to themselves in exchange for what would have saved their souls. But, again, as like Judas, it is too late. Their choice is made and the result is set in stone. The temporary pleasures of sin and worldly choices always bring devastating consequences. This is how it always is: the treasures and pleasures of the world allures and attracts people, they harden themselves against God and His message of redemption, they themselves are hardened by God (verse 17 "fulfill His purpose") against ever receiving salvation, and when it is too late, they realize how foolish they have been and become disgusted with their lives and choices they have made. This scene has been played out multiplied millions of times throughout history, yet no one, it seems, has learned from the mistakes and soul damning errors of others. People continue to do things in what they believe to be their own way – not realizing that it is the way of the beast - and reject the offer of free grace.

In chapter 18, Babylon is the theme. An angel announces that Babylon has fallen. It has not fallen in actual time, but in God's plan, it has, so that makes it as good as done. It is no wonder that God has caused it to fall. Look at the description of Babylon. It is the "dwelling place of demons, a prison for every foul spirit, and a cage for every unclean and hated bird!" It is the garbage dump of the earth. There is nothing good or worthy in it or about it. It is a scene of vomit and drunkenness and fornication and mountains of filth and garbage and rotten stench. It stinks to high heaven. Demons and every kind of foul spirit and carrion eating birds has made Babylon its abode, and are so sickened by it that even they consider it a prison from which there is no escape. There is nothing attractive about it; yet, it has been the desire of the world. Worldly people have literally sold their eternal souls to purchase a dwelling within its city limits in order to obtain a small portion of the temporary riches that are available only in and through her.

The angel issues a stern warning to God's people to "Come out of her, my people, lest you share in her sins, and lest you receive of her plagues. For her sins have reached to heaven, and God has remembered her iniquities." This warning to come out of Babylon is for all Christians from every period of time. Every day of every year Christians are seduced and enticed to go to Babylon and partake of its delicacies. It just looks so good to the eyes and it pulls at the heart and mind to "try it; you'll like it." But it is not so. It brings forth punishment and death. Anyone who shares in the sins of Babylon will also share in its punishment.

The angel continues that Babylon should receive exactly what she has rendered to God's people. She is to be repaid double what she has given. What is it, the same amount or double the amount? The "double" that she is to receive is the "double", the same amount, of what she has done. For every sin of pride and arrogance, she is to receive the same amount in torment and sorrow. The torment and sorrow is the "double", the opposite, of the pride and arrogance she exhibited. This is God balancing the scales of His justice. She glorified herself, was presumptuous, and was boastful; she had said in her heart, "I sit as queen, and am no widow, and will not see sorrow." Because of her arrogant boast that was within her prideful heart, she will experience the plagues of God in one day – death, mourning and famine. She will be burned with the fire of an all consuming jealous God (2 Thessalonians 1:7,8; Hebrews 12:29) – for strong is the God she has ignored, ridiculed, and rejected. God's final judgment has fallen upon her, and she has fallen forever.

As Babylon is judged, those who have profited from her weep and wail and lament in torment and agony of soul over her. Gone is their profit. Gone is the fruit of their greed. Gone is their luxurious lifestyle. Gone is the delight of their fornication with her. All of it is gone. She has been incinerated by the wrath of the holy Almighty God. All the kings, the mighty men of earth, the men of great worldly influence, the men of wealth, the merchants who have peddled the wares of Babylon, not caring who they cheated and stole from, or who they sold their worthless products to as long as they made an obscene profit from them, stand from a far and watch the fire and smoke of the destruction of Babylon ascend into the heavens.

The list of the products sold by the merchants show – in order – the value placed upon them by the merchants and those who desired them and paid for them. Gold, silver, precious stones and pearls.

This is what the harlot adorned herself with in chapter 17, thinking that these objects – dug from the earth – added beauty and desirability to her. But none of these hold true value. They all perish with the using and time. None of them will endure the judgment. They will be burned up with the fire that falls from Heaven that consumes Babylon. Then more of the apparel of the prostitute is mentioned as wares sold by the merchants of Babylon; fine linen, purple, silk and scarlet. More of what the world values, but all it does is hang on the outside of the body. It does nothing at all for the soul, which is worth more than the combined treasures of the world according to Jesus.

The list continues with other products used in luxurious lifestyles; articles that cater to the construction of luxury dwellings and business outlets; woods, ivory, bronze, iron, and marble. Next in value are spices, ointments and perfumes – all things to make the body look and smell appealing – just like the harlot (Babylon) of Proverbs 7: 6 – 21 (read this passage to understand just how insolent the harlot is, and how utterly foolish is the person who is seduced by her). Next in the list of wares is luxurious food stuff – wine and oil and fine flour and wheat. Not just necessary food, but gourmet food and wine that contributes to gluttony and sinful lifestyles, none of it necessary to maintain life. It is expensive food and wine that is served only in the finest of restaurants and only to the rich who can afford it. The least valuable in the merchant's list of goods is the bodies and souls of men. That which is worth more than the accumulated wealth of the world, the souls of men, is also that which is least esteemed by those who would gain wealth.

Although John's vision was based on current circumstances in the first century Roman Empire, the details of the vision have been prevalent in every age since then. Worldly men and women desire that which brings them money and fame and influence. It is to be stressed that when Babylon is judged and it collapses, which it surely will, then everything that the world desires perishes and they are left with absolutely nothing. No wealth, no health, no fine foods or clothing, no influence, no education, no recognition. Nothing. This collapse of Babylon has happened time and time again with each empire that has fallen. The wealth of the merchants of each nation that has been judged by God and has been cast aside has also been "burned up." The merchants have all wailed and bemoaned their losses.

Even as I write this, the economic situation of the world is perilously close to collapse. Thousands of Americans have lost jobs and homes and retirement income. General Motors and Chrysler are filing for bankruptcy, and the news today was that California has no money. Whoever heard before of governments laying off workers? Who would have ever thought that two major auto makers would be bankrupt? The government is taking over banks that have failed. China owns much of America's credit. But, I know that there are many who will just not acknowledge the relationship between the economic situation we are in and the judgment of Babylon. Why do so many think that America is exempt from God's judgment? Any nation that blatantly and arrogantly promotes extreme godlessness like abortion on demand, homosexual marriage, materialism, hedonism, anti-christian rulings by courts, political correctness that attempts to silence the free proclamation of the gospel for fear of offending those who are ungodly is asking for God to judge them. Yes, there are many other nations who are godless, but they, too, are being judged.

Reread your Old Testament to see how many times God had to deal harshly with Israel because of their refusal to live according to God's commands, because of their compromise with surrounding nations and because they adopted their idols and lifestyles. It is not un-American or unpatriotic to say such things, but it is very patriotic to mention these things. If one is aware of why a disease is spreading but withholds the information, he is to be blamed for the deaths of many. God told Ezekiel to blow the trumpet to warn when there was trouble in Israel. Anyone who denies these truths and does not warn others does not care a whit about their country or fellow citizens. God will forgive and restore if there is repentance.

Although there have been many economic collapses throughout the ages, there is the final judgment on Babylon that is yet coming, and when it does, Babylon is forever done. Six times in verses 21 – 23 the words "not…anymore" are used to announce that Babylon and its activities and its values will never be heard from again. They cease to exist forever. The city is gone, its music, its craftsmen and workers, its millstones – food production and industry, no more marriage, and no more light – only darkness. This darkness is the darkness of eternity for all who have rejected the Lord Jesus Christ. And when this is announced, God's people are told to "Rejoice over her, O heaven, and you holy apostles and prophets, for God has avenged you on her!" in verse 20. The prayers of all of God's people from the beginning of time have finally been answered in full. God has avenged the blood of the martyrs on those who were responsible for shedding that blood.

John receives a new vision beginning in chapter 19. The hallelujahs are ringing through Heaven for three distinct reasons. First of all, the great multitude of Heaven is shouting "Hallelujah" because salvation and glory and honor and power belong to the Lord God Almighty. God's power and glory and honor and salvation have been seen in the righteousness of His judgments that He has poured out upon the harlot who had done so much damage to the earth through her fornications. He has avenged the blood of the saints which she has shed. The long awaited vengeance has been fulfilled. God's people cry out "Hallelujah" on this account.

The second chorus of "Hallelujah" is because of the smoke of the destruction of Babylon is rising forever. Her eternal torment is her just recompense. The multitude in Heaven rejoices. As hard as it may be for some to accept and believe this, God's people – all of them – will rejoice when God's punishment comes to unbelievers, even to family members who have rejected Jesus and chosen the mark of the beast. We will be in our new bodies where sin cannot influence us ever again. The love of our God and love for our God will be foremost. He will be our joy throughout endless ages. We will despise all that caused us grief and suffering and pain and torment and sin in this life, and we will not regret – not even for one moment – the destruction of all of that and those who rejoiced in sin.

The third chorus of "Hallelujah" from the great multitude in Heaven is because "the Lord God Omnipotent reigns!" The marriage of the Lamb has come and the bride is ready for her Bridegroom. The bride is clothed in "fine linen, clean and bright." The fine linen represents the righteous deeds of the saints." Our works have followed us into eternity (Revelation 14:13). This feast is not just for the week that accompanied a Jewish wedding, but it is forever. This is the fulfillment of everything God has done for His people since before time began. He chose us in eternity past. During the Old Testament times He announced the wedding to come; when Jesus took on flesh, the engagement took place; the dowry was paid on Calvary; and now the Heavenly Bridegroom has come to claim His bride, the church and we shall forever enjoy His presence and fellowship. The gospel has been realized to its fullest degree. Needless for the angel to say – I think John probably understood this – "Blessed are those who are called to the marriage supper of the Lamb." No matter what their earthly life was like, no matter if it was one of sheer suffering and poverty, now they have eternal riches and peace and glory.

John's next vision goes backward in time from the eternal bliss of the redeemed at the marriage supper to the moments just before the final judgment on earth. Babylon, the harlot, has been judged, and now we will witness the final judgment of the beast and the false prophet. John sees Heaven opened and the Lord Jesus Christ sitting upon a white horse. He is called Faithful and True and His name is "The Word of God." He is wearing many crowns and a robe that has been dipped in blood. His eyes were a flame of fire and a sharp two-edged sword is proceeding out of His mouth. He has come to judge righteous judgment and to make war on His enemies, those who do not obey the gospel.

He had a name written that no one knew except Him. A name reveals a person's character. God changed Abram's name to Abraham denoting that he would be a father of many nations. God changed Jacob's name to Israel, meaning that he would be a prince with God. The name that only Jesus knew signifies that those He was coming to judge had no clue as to His real character. They always thought He was someone to mock and to blaspheme, that His name was a swearword. But, they were about to find out more than they ever thought possible, yet they will never understand any more about Him than His judgment upon them. They will only understand Him as the One who strikes the nations with the sword of His mouth and who disciplines them with a rod of iron, the King of Kings and Lord of Lords, the One who treads the winepress of the fierceness and the wrath of the Almighty God. Not one of them will ever "know His name" as He lovingly and graciously reveals Himself to His people throughout eternity.

Before the beast and false prophet are destroyed by the sword from the mouth of Jesus Christ, an angel calls all the birds that fly through the heavens to gather together to feast on the flesh of all those who are gathered together to do battle against Jesus and His church. Compare this verse to Deuteronomy 28:26. I must, again, reiterate that this is not a battle between literal armies as has been taught erroneously, but it symbolizes that final defeat of all of the enemies of Jesus Christ and the church when He comes again. The destruction of the political beast and all false religions are set in stone. So much so, that in the vision John sees, carrion eating birds are called to ready themselves prior to the actual destruction of the two beasts. Are there going to be literal birds eating literal flesh? No. It is a vision of the reality of the total destruction of all of the enemies of Jesus Christ.

When Satan is loosed from his restraint for a season just prior to the second coming (see chapter 20), (also reread the comments on the sixth bowl judgment) he mounts an all out attack against the church. He gathers governments, false religions, and those who have taken the mark of the beast, all those who worship the world and all that it offers against the church in an attempt to once and for all kill the church. This is the battle of Armageddon. It is not a nuclear war. It is not Russia invading Israel. It is not China attacking anyone. It is not the armies of the world gathering in the Valley of Megiddo to try to prevent the Lord Jesus from returning. I've heard all of these "explanations." It is not a literal battle. The battle of Armageddon is this final spiritual battle that ends with the utter defeat of all of the unsaved when the Lord Jesus Christ returns, taking fiery vengeance upon them (2 Thessalonians 1: 7-10).

John sees the beast and his armies assembled against the church for their final assault in order to rid the world of these "born againers." There is a very important issue concerning this battle that needs to be understood. The Bible gives absolutely no description of this battle. It is stated that the armies are assembled to do battle, and the next phrase is that they are defeated. Therefore, as I have stated before, to assign to it some other literal meaning will be - at best - very poor speculation. It is not a long, protracted battle. It is over before it begins. The beast and false prophet are captured and thrown alive into hell, then those who took his mark and worshiped the beast were killed.

Again, do not think that the beast and the false prophet are two individuals. They represent the anti-christian governments and false religions. Why is it said, then, that they are thrown into hell alive? Because their defeat is so thorough and instantaneous that their influence on the earth, their ability to deceive and to persecute Christians are forever over. They have not one lick of power left when the Lord Jesus Christ comes back to earth in power and glory. All of their influence over others goes straight to hell along with these leaders and kings and politicians who have resisted the gospel and tried to prevent it from being preached. Jesus has the power and the authority and all ability to do as He sees fit, and He sees fit to send them to their eternal punishment. The birds completely stuff themselves with the flesh of those who have been killed by the sword from the mouth of Jesus. This symbolic language is another picture of the judgment day.

Under the influence of the Holy Spirit, John describes first of all in chapters 15 and 16 the defeat of the men and women who have taken the mark of the beast. Babylon's destruction is described in chapters 17 and 18. We see the beast and the false prophet being defeated by Jesus in chapter 19. Every single enemy of the church has been thrown into hell by the Lord Jesus Christ at His coming to judge. Although each of these enemies have been viewed separately – in different chapters – they each have their separate histories so to speak - they are all destroyed simultaneously when Jesus returns. To repeat, Revelation is not a chronological treatise. It is parallel in its accounts, repeating the same events from different angles and with different characters playing the lead part.

The only enemy of the church yet to be seen defeated is the dragon, Satan. His demise is next.

Chapters 20 – 22

The final section is chapters 20 – 22. It most definitely begins a new section where we see Satan's punishment beginning with his binding for a thousand years so he can no longer deceive the nations. In chapter 12 Satan is cast out of Heaven to the earth where he rages against God's people because he knows his time is short. The parallels between chapters 11-13 and 20 are worthy of mention here, for if we see and understand them, the message and meaning of Revelation is much clearer. Chapter 19 ends with the final judgment, and chapter 20 goes back to the first coming of our Lord Jesus Christ just as chapter 11 ends with the final judgment and chapter 12 begins again with the first coming of Jesus.

The first parallel we see is that in chapter 12 Satan is cast down to the earth and the Christ is born, crucified, resurrected and ascended back to Heaven. Satan's power could not prevail against Michael and his angels, and Christians overcame him by the blood of the Lamb. He was greatly weakened in his abilities. In chapter 20, his power is limited in that he can no longer deceive the nations. The nations no longer hold power over the church, but the church is victorious over the nations through the preaching of the gospel. Every nation, kindred and tongue has heard the gospel and have those who have been redeemed by the blood. This is also the first horseman going forth and conquering through the gospel message.

The second parallel in chapter 12 is that there is a long period of time – 1,260 days – in which the church ministers the gospel and is nourished and protected by the Lord "from the presence of the serpent." God greatly limits the influence he can exert on the church in her gospel calling. She makes disciples of all nations. Yet, he does persecute her, but through the persecution, the gospel abounds (Acts 8:1-4). In chapter 20, Satan has been bound and cast into the bottomless pit so he can no longer deceive the nations, and the gospel is freely preached to all nations. The souls of the redeemed are reigning with Christ in Heaven, and those redeemed who are still alive are overcoming the devil by the power of the Holy Spirit through the blood of Jesus.

At the end of the age, for a brief period of time just preceding the return of our Lord Jesus Christ, Satan is given freedom to severely persecute the church and deceive the nations once again. This is seen in chapters 11:7 and 13:7. He makes war with the saints. The parallel is seen in chapter 20:7-9. He gathers all his armies together with the beast and false prophet to war against the church to silence her forever, but he is met with destruction at the second coming of Jesus, the fourth parallel between the chapters we have been considering.

When we see these four events that are God's design for the ages, we can see that what is portrayed in Revelation through these visions given to John show us again and again these four events in order; the first coming of Jesus, the binding or hindering of Satan for "a thousand years" in respect to the gospel message being preached to all nations, Satan being loosed from his chains of restraint for a brief period of time, then the second coming and the day of judgment.

In the chapter entitled The Millennium, we discussed this passage in detail, so I will not do so again. I will, however, add a few more comments regarding the binding of the serpent for the thousand years. We must – again I say it – remember that this is a symbolic vision that John is seeing. It is not a literal dragon that is literally bound with a chain and thrown into a literal abyss. Under this symbolism, what would the first century Christians who received this letter from John understand it to mean?

They were living in a day of extreme persecution and of spiritual darkness. Rome had more idols than could be counted. It was a time of abominable, filthy, heathen celebrations that ignorant, deceived, superstitious, hopeless people engaged in. There were relatively few Christians churches that were preaching truth and shining light into this sin darkened environment. This had been the history of the world until Jesus was born. Entire nations had been enslaved by Satan and his blatant hatred of truth and love of idolatry. Paul, preaching to the citizens of Lystra who began to worship him and Barnabas after they had witnessed the healing of a crippled man, said in Acts 14: 15 and saying, *"Men, why are you doing these things? We also are men with the same nature as you, and preach to you that you should turn from these useless things to the living God, who made the heaven,* the earth, the sea, and all things that are in them, 16 who in bygone generations **allowed all nations to walk in their own ways.**

Previous to the coming of Jesus, God allowed people to practice idolatry – He did not judge them immediately - but now the True Light had come into the world, and God now commands that all men everywhere repent. There is no excuse for not repenting. It was in this world of idolatry and darkness that the Christians of the first century were living, so they would see symbolism in a much different light than we who are living in the twenty first century who have been exposed to Christian teaching for two thousand years. Those Christians who had heard of Jesus through the preaching of the apostles would quite naturally wonder when God would overturn their situation of living with such idolatry and persecution. They had undoubtedly heard the prophecy of *Psalm 2: 7 "I will declare the decree: The LORD has said to Me, 'You are My Son, today I have begotten You. 8 Ask of Me, and I will give You the nations for Your inheritance, and the ends of the earth for Your possession.*

Also, *Psalm 72: 8 He shall have dominion also from sea to sea, and from the River to the ends of the earth. 9 Those who dwell in the wilderness will bow before Him, and His enemies will lick the dust. 10 The kings of Tarshish and of the isles will bring presents; the kings of Sheba and Seba will offer gifts. 11 Yes, all kings shall fall down before Him; All nations shall serve Him.*

This symbolism of the binding of Satan is the answer. He will no longer be allowed to deceive entire nations as he had done in the past. Why? Because Jesus had come to set men at liberty from the enslavement of sin. There are numerous passages that deal with the fact that the gospel is for all nations and that Satan can no longer deceive the nations because Jesus has come. Look for them and study them. They are in both the Old Testament and the New Testament. It is in that sense and that sense only that Satan is bound. He still exerts much influence on the world and especially on those who have rejected the gospel of Jesus Christ. He still holds sway over the beast of ungodly governments and over the false religions of the day and over those who have taken the mark of the beast. He is also influential in the lives of those Christians who do not live in obedience to the Lord Jesus. But, he cannot deceive entire nations. He is bound in that regard.

While Satan is bound and the gospel is producing souls for the Savior, in Heaven the souls of those who were slaughtered for the sake of the gospel are reigning with Jesus. Many of those who are being saved are also being persecuted and beheaded because of their love for the Lord Jesus and their commitment to Him. They refuse to worship the emperor, and as a result are slaughtered. In order to comfort those who are facing such persecution, our Lord Jesus gives this vision to them of what is happening with those who have been sacrificed for the cause of the gospel. They are reigning with Jesus in Heaven. Not just for a few moments, but for "a thousand years." Their suffering may be short lived but their reigning with the Lord is eternal, beginning with their death, and continuing forever.

The popular system of belief has this reigning with Christ as occurring on earth during what the proponents of this system describe as the Millennium. They have Christ – sitting on David's throne in Jerusalem - and the tribulation period Jews as the ones who rule and reign on earth. Well, there's just a whole lot of problems with that. Where, exactly, does Revelation tell us that this reigning is taking place? First of all, it takes place where the thrones are. Throughout Revelation thrones are only seen in Heaven. Show me any passage in Revelation where it is stated without misunderstanding that there are thrones on earth. Can't do it? Didn't think so. Thrones are seen only in Heaven throughout Revelation.

Secondly, the thousand year reign occurs where the "souls" of the martyrs are. John emphatically states that he sees souls, not bodies. And it is the souls of those who have been beheaded that he sees. There is nothing at all that can be construed as referring in the least to the resurrection of the bodies of the saints who have been martyred. It is only during the period of time – this thousand years - between the first coming of Jesus and the second coming of Jesus that the souls of those who had been martyred reign with Jesus. Why? Because at His second coming, their souls and their bodies are reunited and both body and soul live with Jesus for eternity.

Thirdly, this reigning occurs where Jesus is. Where is Jesus? In Heaven. And, as Acts 3:20 states that Jesus must stay in Heaven until He returns and makes all things new. So, during the period of time between His first and second comings, He is in Heaven, and so are the souls of those who have been martyred for the sake of the gospel.

What exactly are they doing in Heaven? They are worshiping and praising God for His righteous judgments. They are living with Jesus, free from all that causes pain and sorrow. Everyone who had not worshiped the beast (20:4) is there, not just those who have been martyred.

For comments on the first resurrection, refer back to the chapter entitled The Millennium. No more comments are needed in this chapter.

As we have seen already, at the end of the age, just before Jesus returns, Satan is loosed from his chains that have hindered him from deceiving the nations, and again he is granted that power for a short amount of time only. He gathers the forces of Gog and Magog for a final attack on the church. They are symbolized as gathered in the Valley of Megiddo, for this final battle. Comments have already been made as to the background of this battle known as Armageddon. This just verifies what I have been saying all along that the visions John sees are parallel, not chronological. The events repeat themselves through Revelation.

Who are Gog, Magog, Meshech and Tubal? I remember quite vividly, as I am sure many of you do, that it was taught – especially in the late 60's – that these names were directly translated as Russia and Moscow and other Russian cities, and that they were going to invade Israel, but Israel would defeat them and kill so many of them that it would take seven months to bury the dead. This novel scenario was picked up by many preachers and echoed from the pulpits of thousands of churches. It made for sensational preaching, but it was wrong. I remember as a young man when I first heard that thinking, "Wow! That's pretty neat. How did he figure that out?"

That "interpretation" was taken from Ezekiel 38 and 39, although that passage was misinterpreted by them. Now, Gog, Magog, Meschech and Tubal are mentioned in those chapters, but this prophecy has nothing to do with modern day Russia and Israel, hence, neither does the Battle of Armageddon in Revelation. But it does build on the history of the Jews during the time of Antiochus Epiphanes, the Syrian, the arch-enemy of the Jews, the one who was responsible for the last persecution that Israel endured under the old dispensation. The Seleucid Empire included modern Afghanistan, Iran, Iraq, Syria, and Lebanon, together with parts of Turkey, Armenia, Turkmenistan, Uzbekistan, and Tajikistan. It included the cities of Meshech and Tubal. This empire was established under Seleucus, one of Alexander's generals, after the death of Alexander the Great. Without getting into the historical details, Antiochus, the Syrian, ruled this empire at a later date, and he invaded Israel – in fulfillment of Ezekiel's prophecy - and we have all heard of his desecration of the temple when he sacrificed a pig on the altar. Since this persecution of God's people was the last under the Old Testament, although it occurred during the 400 year interval between the Testaments, it is the likely episode that helps us interpret this vision in Revelation, which is the final attack against the church before Jesus returns.[15]

The armies of Gog and Magog during the attack under Antiochus Epiphanes would have been huge, so they could very well be used as a symbol for the worldwide aggression against the church in this final confrontation. Gog and Magog, the nations in "the four corners of the earth" in verse 8 do not mean the furthest nations in distance, but simply refers to the entire world. So, the entire world of wickedness is gathered to do harm to the church.

Do we not see this in part today? More and more – it seems like it occurs each and every day - Christians are being attacked and silenced. The world simply hates Jesus and all those who love Him and stand up for Him. But in the final days before He returns, this hatred will be at its zenith, far worse than we can imagine now. The world thinks it is winning this battle against truth and righteousness, but in the end, it loses big time. Fire comes down from Heaven, the fiery vengeance of 2 Thessalonians 1, and consumes those who are gathered against Christ and His church, casting them into hell where they are tormented day and night forever. The devil is also cast into the lake of fire and brimstone where he also is tormented day and night forever. The beast and false prophet are described as being there, but they are cast there together. It is said that they are there because their destruction has already been described by John, not because they preceded him there. There is only one final judgment of all who have opposed Jesus, not several.

Further details of the judgment are described in the next few verses concerning the great white throne judgment. The second coming of Jesus coincides with the destruction of the current heavens and earth. This is described in 2 Peter 3:10 as the dissolution of the elements, in Matthew 19:28 as the regeneration, in Acts 3:21 as the restoration of all things, and in Romans 8:21 as the deliverance from the bondage of corruption. At the same time, the resurrection occurs, the one and only general resurrection, and all stand before God.

The Dispensational, Pre-Millennial description of the great white throne judgment is that only the unsaved will be there, that Christians will never see the great white throne, that if you are there, you are lost. But, that does not measure up to this passage. It fits their system perfectly, but not the Biblical system. The verses state that the dead, small and great – in other words, everyone who has died – stood before the great white throne. Books were opened, including the Book of Life, and everyone was judged according to the entries of those books. Anyone whose name was not found in the Book of Life was cast into the lake of fire. The very strong implication is that there were people present at the great white throne whose names were found written in the Book of Life who were not cast into the lake of fire.

John's final vision is of the new heaven and new earth. The old heaven and old earth "fled away" in chapter 20 and now the new heaven and earth appear. This is what nature itself has longed for, the restoration of the original creation. If we look at how Genesis describes the original creation, we can better understand the new creation. God created the original heaven and earth and He restores it in Revelation. The sun, moon and stars are created in Genesis to give light to the earth, but in Revelation, there is no need for the sun or moon for the Lamb is the light. Paradise was lost in Genesis and restored in Revelation. Genesis shows man hiding from God and Revelation shows man having fellowship with God, for God is dwelling with His people. In Genesis the way to the Tree of Life was guarded by cherubim and in Revelation the way is clear for all to eat of it.

There is no more sea which represents the turmoil and unrest and conflict between people and nations. If you have ever been on the sea when it is angry and its waves are restless because of a storm, as I have been, then you can certainly understand this symbolism. It is the sea that gives birth to the beast; the roaring, raging sea of sinful humanity. The universe is now at peace. No more sea. No more sin.

John sees the holy city, the New Jerusalem coming down from Heaven. It had the appearance of a bride ready for her wedding. There is no doubt at all that this city is the symbol for the church. It is called holy. It is totally consecrated, set apart for God. It is likened to a bride. It pictures a permanent residence as opposed to a tent, a temporary place to live. It portrays a large number of inhabitants, safety and security. The city is seen coming down from Heaven. The church is Heavenly since it is "born from above."

The church now experiences no more weeping, no sorrow, no pain, no death. Why? The former things are all passed away and all things are new. No one or nothing that offends or causes sin or sorrow or pain or weeping will ever be allowed to show itself to the church again. Ever. Sin is gone. What man has attempted to achieve on his own, namely, Paradise on earth, is here, but not because man achieved it, but because God did it.

That the New Jerusalem is indeed the church and not Heaven itself is seen next. The angel told John to (verse 9) *"Come, I will show you the bride, the Lamb's wife." 10 And he carried me away in the Spirit to a great and high mountain, and showed me the great city, the holy Jerusalem, descending out of heaven from God, 11 having the glory of God..."*

The angel told John to come and see the bride, the Lamb's wife, and he was shown the holy Jerusalem. The city is equated with the bride, the church. The church is the dwelling place of the glory of God. He dwells with us. It is a place of holiness and communion with God. Babylon, the impersonator of the church, had its worshipers and its "glory", but it was the glory of earth, which is destroyed in the fiery second coming of Jesus.

The church is portrayed as a place of rarest beauty; pure transparent gold, sparkling light like precious stones, twelve gates each - of single pearl, twelve foundations – each of precious stone, its height, length and width were identical, showing its perfection in all respects. It is illumined by the glory of God, and there is no temple, for the Lamb Himself is the temple, the center of worship. Jesus, the Light of the world, the One who shows us the Father and provides the salvation necessary to see the Father and have fellowship with Him, is the source of light. Without Him, there is no light, and the church would not be the church. In the church, there is no more night, for Jesus is constantly with us to give us light. The wall surrounding the church provides absolute and eternal security to all within it. The gates are always open for anyone from any nation to enter at any time, for there is never night there, so there is no need for the gates to ever be shut.

(Later insert. I just got back from a church service in which the preacher applied this description of the church to Heaven to show how blessed our loved ones who have died are and something of what they were experiencing. He spoke of diamond studded walls, literal streets of gold, drinking from the transparent sea before the throne of God and of literal mansions that are 1,500 miles high. UMMM...I don't think that in Heaven neither God nor the redeemed will give a hoot about diamond studded walls and 1,500 mile high mansions, or anything that holds earthly value now. The description of the New Jerusalem in terms of earthly value is designed to show men the eternal value of salvation. The church is where true value lies, not in things the people of earth value.)

From the throne of God flows the river of the water of life. This is the symbol of eternal life. No one outside of the church has access to this river and therefore has no eternal life. How does Jesus describe eternal life?

John 17: 3 And this is eternal life, that they may know You, the only true God, and Jesus Christ whom You have sent.

No one outside of the church knows Jesus Christ and the Father. Knowing the Father and the Son equates to eternal life. The fact that the river flows from the throne reveals that eternal life can only come from God. He has provided eternal life for us through the blood of Jesus Christ. This is a large flowing river with trees of life full of fruit lining the banks. Super abundant access to eternal life. Our salvation can never run out. It is eternal.

The throne of God and of the Lamb is within the church showing the absolute Lordship of Jesus Christ over His church. But no one with the church is obstinately opposing His sovereignty over them for they all willingly submit to Him and His decrees. He is the Lord who provided salvation for everyone whose names are written in the Lamb's book of life.

The angel has a few closing comments for John, namely that these things that John has just seen, must shortly come to pass. They must begin occurring now. Jesus reiterates that He is coming quickly - suddenly. There will be little if indeed any time at all to prepare when the time is upon us. Therefore, keep the words of this prophecy. Those who keep it will be blessed and will be ready when Jesus does return. They are the ones who are righteous and holy now and will continue to be so throughout eternity. They are the ones who keep His commandments, who have the right to enter into the city and be partakers of the tree of life.

Those who do not keep the words of this prophecy are the ones who are unjust and filthy now and will continue to be so throughout eternity. They are the dogs, sorcerers, sexually immoral, murderers, idolaters, and liars. There are no second chances after the Lord Jesus returns. What a person is when He returns is what they will continue to be forever.

Anyone who ignores this warning, this word of truth from the lips of the three witnesses to its veracity – John, the angel, and Jesus Himself – if it is pooh-poohed away or if its message is changed in anyway – subtracting from it or adding to it - that person will not have a part in the Book of Life. They will be forever condemned. As with the entire Word of God, it must be received as from God Himself. It is not to be trifled with or sensationalized beyond what it is inherently. It is God's message to the world.

The last words of our Lord Jesus Christ are the words that give us hope, that are what has kept Christians through the years going in the midst of tribulations and trials, looking forward to the day when we see Him face to face. It is a promise the world cannot match; its fulfillment holds greater expectation for Christians than any promise of worldly wealth or prominence could possibly hold. *"Surely I am coming quickly."*

And the redeemed answer, *"Even so come Lord Jesus."*

Summary of Revelation

We have seen the seven divisions of Revelation that are apparent within the book itself. It is not to be read as a chronological unveiling of events, but as an overview of time from the first coming of Jesus until His second coming seen from various points of view. Revelation deals with Jesus and His workings with His people and His opposition and war with those who oppose Him. It is a revelation of Jesus, not of some supposed "anti-christ."

That these sections run concurrently with each other is also indicated by the time designation within the sections. Forty two months, twelve hundred and sixty days, time and times and half a time, or three and a half years, are equivalent to the other. The trumpets and bowls of wrath are identical in its series of judgments. In each section we see the second coming of our Lord in judgment.

But, there are two major divisions of Revelation. In chapters 1 – 11 we see the antagonism of unbelievers against believers. The world attacks the church, God's people, but God defends them and gives them victory. In chapters 12 – 22 the real power struggle is seen as Satan attacks Christ, and because he could not defeat Him, he centers his fury on His people, the church, through persecution by governments and false religions and through seduction by the world. The spiritual struggle of God's people is intense, but they are victorious through the blood of the Lamb.

Not only are there readily seen divisions in Revelation, there is also a unity that is unmistakable throughout the entire book. In chapter 1, Jesus reveals Himself in various ways, such as holding the seven stars in His right hand and walking among the seven golden lamp stands, as being the First and the Last, dead and alive forevermore, a sharp two-edged sword coming out of His mouth, eyes a flame of fire, feet like burnished brass, the Faithful Witness, holding the keys of death and the grave, the Firstborn from the dead, and Ruler of the kings of the earth. In chapters 2 and 3, He repeats these designations of Himself to the seven churches as they have the need to understand and experience Him. He personally reveals Himself to each church as fits their need.

The fulfilling of the mission of the church and the subsequent hatred by the world is portrayed in the next section of chapters 4 – 7. The mission of the church of Jesus Christ is to bring His light to the sin darkened world. When the church attempts to do that, the world attacks the church. The Light shines in the darkness in chapters 1 – 3, and the darkness fights back in chapters 4 – 7 through the opening of the seals. The world may appear to be winning, they may temporarily impede the progress of the church, but John 1: 6 assures us the darkness cannot overcome the church of Jesus Christ. The trials and tribulations that the church encounters are meant to purify her. Many are the Scriptures that tell us of the cleansing action of trials in our lives. The corporate body also needs them to keep it purified. When Christ goes forth riding His white horse in 6:2, He goes forth to conquer, and as a result, Satan fights back. Jesus said as much in Matthew 10.

34 "Do not think that I came to bring peace on earth. I did not come to bring peace but a sword. 35 For I have come to 'set a man against his father, a daughter against her mother, and a daughter-in-law against her mother-in-law'; 36 and 'a man's enemies will be those of his own household.'

The second, third, and fourth seals show all of the trials, persecutions, and troubles that come upon the church as a result of the conquering gospel of Christ of the first seal. The fifth seal shows the souls of the martyrs awaiting the final judgment of the sixth seal. Although persecuted and martyred for the cause and name of Jesus Christ, victory for the Lord's people is imminent. The church is about to emerge from this great tribulation, the sum total of all of her persecutions and trials, triumphantly. Her consummation is pictured in 7: 9-17.

9 After these things I looked, and behold, a great multitude which no one could number, of all nations, tribes, peoples, and tongues, standing before the throne and before the Lamb, clothed with white robes, with palm branches in their hands, 10 and crying out with a loud voice, saying, "Salvation belongs to our God who sits on the throne, and to the Lamb!" 11 All the angels stood around the throne and the elders and the four living creatures, and fell on their faces before the throne and worshiped God, 12 saying: "Amen! Blessing and glory and wisdom, Thanksgiving and honor and power and might, Be to our God forever and ever. Amen." 13 Then one of the elders answered, saying to me, "Who are these arrayed in white robes, and where did they come from?" 14 And I said to him, "Sir, you know." So he said to me, "These are the ones who come out of the great tribulation, and washed their robes and made them white in the blood of the Lamb. 15 Therefore they are before the throne of God, and serve Him day and night in His temple. And He who sits on the throne will dwell among them. 16 They shall neither hunger anymore nor thirst anymore; the sun shall not strike them, nor any heat; 17 for the Lamb who is in the midst of the throne will shepherd them and lead them to living fountains of waters. And God will wipe away every tear from their eyes."

    The light affliction of the tribulation is not to be compared with the eternal weight of glory that is ours in Heaven. Although not pleasant while enduring it, the tribulation of God's people will pass, never to be seen again when Jesus returns. The redeemed are clothed in white robes because they have been washed clean in the blood of the Lamb. Forever they are before the throne of God, enjoying fellowship with their Lord to the fullest measure possible.

    In chapters 8 – 11 we see judgment meted out against those who persecute believers in answer to their prayers. Much of what we believe to be "natural occurrences" are really God dealing with the unbelieving world in response to how they treat Christians. God is constantly dealing with wrong doing against His people. His trumpets of judgment run concurrently with the opening of the seals of persecution. It is not difficult at all to recognize God's hand upon the land (earthquakes), the sea (hurricanes, tsunamis), rivers (floods, pollution, water shortage because of drought), in the heavens (excessive heat and cold), the evil influence of demons, war, and the fear of final judgment as His judgment against those who deny Him and are hateful and antagonist toward His people. He will not be mocked by anyone and He will avenge His own. Throughout history there is a record of God dealing in this way.

These trumpets are not the final judgment, but they are a precursor of the final judgment. They destroy only a third part of nature and of men. They are warnings sent by God for men to repent, but they do not. They still prefer their sin, pride, arrogance, murders, sorceries, sexual immorality, and worship of demons over repentance and salvation through the blood of Jesus. Man knows best. Or so he thinks. Even with the hand of God against him, man remains stiff necked and unrepentant.

While these judgments are falling, the church is safe and secure. Christians are still witnessing for their Lord, still being persecuted, still being faithful to Christ. And they remain faithful to the end, right to the final judgment when "The kingdoms of this world have become the kingdoms of our Lord and of His Christ, and He shall reign forever and ever" (11: 15).

The twenty four elders cry out in verse *17* *"We give You thanks, O Lord God Almighty, the One who is and who was and who is to come, because You have taken Your great power and reigned. 18 The nations were angry, and Your wrath has come, and the time of the dead, that they should be judged, and that You should reward Your servants the prophets and the saints, and those who fear Your name, small and great, and should destroy those who destroy the earth."*

The church has been rewarded for their faithfulness to Christ through persecution and hateful attacks and martyrdom. They are rewarded through answered prayers that send judgment upon unbelievers and in their eternal reward.

With the beginning of chapter 12 we can see the underlying cause of such hatred and animosity and murderous intent of unbelievers toward believers. We also see the outcome of those who refuse to repent in spite of the trumpet judgments. In the first eleven chapters we see the symptoms, so to speak, of what lies under the surface. We see the church being the light of the world, shining in the darkness and being hated and despised on account of the light. Many are martyred because of their witness to the light and against the darkness. They pray, and God answers by judging those who oppress them by sending His answers in the form of disasters of every imaginable kind upon them while His people are triumphant through it all, still maintaining their faithfulness to their Lord Jesus Christ who washed them white in His blood.

We now readily see that these outward manifestations of the hatred of the world against the church are a result of the hatred Satan has toward Christ, and the resulting spiritual battle. Unregenerate man is but a puppet in the hand of Satan, doing what he desires them to do, and displaying hatred and spewing venom at the children of God. The dragon uses governments and religious organizations – false religions – to persecute true Christians. In John's day, the persecution came from Rome and from Judaism and also from the false religion of emperor worship.

Through the years the persecution of God's people has come from many other governments and false religions. Most recently, of course, it has come from communist governments who do all they can to eliminate the truth of the gospel which condemns them and their atheistic doctrines, and from the false religion of Islam, which is filled with volatile hatred toward Christianity and Jews and all others who do not accept their counterfeit belief system. Any religion that is bent on killing those who do not accept their beliefs is a false religion. True religion – Christianity – is one of love and of grace toward those who are unbelievers or skeptical and who need to investigate it further. Christianity understands that not everyone will accept its tenets, but leaves the disposition of unbelief in the hands of God. Christianity is merciful to unbelievers, not condemnatory, unlike all false religions which want to force those who do not believe as they do into their belief system, or to destroy them completely. These "beasts" are used by Satan in an attempt to destroy God's work and God's people. But, he is unsuccessful and will remain so. He may win a few skirmishes here and there, but the "battle is the Lord's" and He is victorious.

There are five enemies of the church who are mentioned. The dragon - Satan, the beast from the sea – governments, the beast from the earth – false religion, the great harlot, Babylon – worldliness, and those who accept the mark of the beast – men who refuse to accept Christ and do His work but instead do the work of Satan. Every one of them are defeated and hurled into the lake of fire where they will remain, tormented day and night forever.

Although their destruction is shown in separate accounts, it all occurs on the "last day." It of necessity must be so. In our Lord's parable of the wheat and the tares, He emphatically declares that judgment against (all things that offend) the world, the flesh, the devil, and all workers of iniquity will occur when the angels separate the ungodly from the Godly and cast them into the lake of fire.

*Matthew 13: 40 Therefore as the tares are gathered and burned in the fire, so it will be at the end of this age. 41 The Son of Man will send out His angels, and they will gather out of His kingdom **all things that offend**, and those who practice lawlessness, 42 and will cast them into the furnace of fire. There will be wailing and gnashing of teeth. 43 Then the righteous will shine forth as the sun in the kingdom of their Father. He who has ears to hear, let him hear!*

God, in mercy, pours out His judgments upon the earth so that perhaps some will turn in repentance to Him. However, Revelation makes it clear that unregenerate man is head strong and hard hearted and will not repent of His horrible sins of worshiping demons and idols, and of their murders and sorceries and of sexual immoralities and of blasphemies against God. Even after suffering the outpouring of the bowls of wrath, man still continues to think that he knows best and refuses to acknowledge that God is Lord instead of himself. He will not turn to the Living God in repentance. Along with the destruction of those who take the mark of the beast is also the destruction of worldliness, governments that persecute God's people and all false religions. It all ends in final judgment.

Wherever God's people are being the "light of the world", there will be enemies of God attacking them. The world, controlled by Satan, hates the church as Jesus said it would because it hates Him. As incredible as it is, the world does not want to have its sins and faults exposed so they can repent and have eternal life; no, it would rather remain in darkness and wickedness and perish eternally. Who in their right mind would exchange heaven for hell? Who in their right mind would choose to "enjoy the pleasures of sin for a season" and suffer in hell eternally rather than choosing to "suffer affliction with the people of God", as Moses did (Hebrews 11:25), and enjoy "pleasures forevermore" at the right hand of God (Psalm 16:11)?

The hatred may not be an active manifestation as is shown in our word pictures of Revelation. It may be a passive hatred, but it is hatred none-the-less. Whoever is not for Christ is against Him. There is no third choice. Passive neglect is identical to active rejection in God's eyes.

Hebrews 2: 3 how shall we escape if we neglect so great a salvation...

There are so many who, knowing the truth of Jesus, just do not take the time to worship Him. They are too busy with their own projects that they deem far more important than God. So many people busy themselves with work, arts, projects, entertainment, sports, pleasure, and leisure in an attempt to avoid God. They have been told that they must give an account to God – and many know that to be true - but they do not want to do so. They believe that if they busy themselves with other things that God will forget about them if they are not actively conscious of God and His demands. If they can avoid God now by being busy, then God will overlook them and give them a free pass. Out of sight, out of mind.

But, God is not like man in that He forgets those who forget Him. God will not overlook anyone. Everyone will give an account regardless of how much they attempt to avoid God now. God is not mocked. God has decreed that every knee will bow and that every tongue will confess that Jesus Christ is Lord to the glory of God the Father. Why would anyone who has heard these sobering words still think that they are exempt from fulfilling them? Anyone who neglects and rejects Him now will be rejected by God eternally. When Jesus returns, there is no second chance. God's final judgment, which will be decreed at the second coming of our Lord Jesus, has eternal ramifications because time ends at that moment and eternity begins for everyone.

Author's note: When I first began this chapter, in all honesty, I did not have an adequate understanding of every detail that I included in this chapter. I just knew that the popular interpretation was not correct. As I studied the passages, more and more was revealed to me. This chapter alone took me almost a full year to finish. I had to wrestle the Pre-Millennial boogie man all through it. Brain washing and indoctrination is hard to overcome. It was not my intention when I began to give as much explanation as I did. *(I know. Many of you think I did not give enough detail, and others think I gave way too much because you think I got is all wrong.)*

My original intent was to give a paragraph or two on each major division of Revelation – only what I wrote in the Summary of Revelation - thereby demonstrating the error of futurism and Pre-Millennialism and giving the original Scriptural sense of the passage as would have been understood by the first century Christians who received it. It was never my intent to attempt to interpret every single phrase and word in Revelation. That is impossible for anyone to do anyway. There is obviously so much more that could and probably should be said in this brief commentary, but, as Pilate said, "What I have written, I have written", and it will have to suffice for now.

Chapter Nine

Conclusion

The Pre-Millennial and Dispensational view of Scripture is a mirage. It is not real. Like the weary, thirsty desert traveler who is crawling the last few feet to what he thinks is an oasis with palm trees and a spring, so are those who believe in the "two staged second coming of Jesus" and a future "tribulation period" which they define as the "seventieth week of Daniel", that occurs after the resurrection and "the rapture" and a future "millennium" of a literal one thousand years, which also occurs after the resurrection and second coming of Jesus. When the time of the second coming occurs, it will not be according to what they have espoused. Their minds have been trained by well meaning teachers of the Pre-Millennial system to "see" these things where they are not. It is a false image – one that is not really there.

When I was in the Navy, I was a radarman. At times the radar repeater showed a false image. It was a reflection of wave perhaps, or just a figment of its own imagination. Whatever it was, it manifest itself as a true image, but it was not. It was false. It was not there regardless of what the screen showed. No matter how much the Captain insisted that it was real because the repeater showed it – and he did on one particular occasion – it did not make it so just because he wanted it to be. The same is true of Pre-Millennialism. It is a false image. When we are told something repeatedly we begin to believe it as true whether it is or not. There is no doubt that this system is the most popular among evangelicals today, but it does not make it true simply because the majority of teachers are teaching it and the majority of Christians are believing it. Like our friend in the desert who believes with all his heart he is seeing an oasis, it is still a mirage, a trick of the mind.

Or, let me give an opposite illustration using my Navy experience again. This time, instead of a false image, on one occasion, the Captain came running into CIC (combat information center) and yelled, "Ehrlich, how far is that thing?" I asked him, "What thing?" "That thing" he replied as he grabbed me by the shirt collar and escorted me to the porthole. There was a large – very large – white light shining down on our ship hovering about 200 yards off our port side. But, there was nothing showing up on the radar scope. It was definitely there – the entire ship's crew saw it - but it was hidden from our radar. This is exactly what has happened in regard to the truth of the second coming. The truth is right before our eyes, yet, because our "radar" is tuned to the Pre-Millennial frequency, we cannot see it. When it does become apparent to us, we wonder – like my Captain – why it is not visible to our "radar". Why did we not see it immediately? Why did I think I saw something that really is not there? Why doesn't everyone see the truth? *(The object that was over our ship appeared 100 miles or so off the coast of south Florida as we were heading to the now infamous Guantanamo Bay. Our radio crew heard reports that it was seen up and down the east coast from Maine to Florida. I believe it was in either late 1966 or early 1967).*

Another example to illustrate seeing things that are not really there is a stage magician or illusionist. Through sleight of hand and misdirection, he gets the audience to believe that he is doing one thing when he is actually doing something entirely different. He misdirects our attention to something else. To those who are convinced of the legitimacy of Dispensationalism or Pre-Millennialism, this may sound unduly harsh and cruel and unchristian, but I will give my observation anyway. I believe this was the intent of the original perpetrators of this system. They used theological "sleight of hand" and "misdirection" to cover up their real intent of seducing the unstable to become followers of themselves and also to make a name for themselves. It was about them, not Jesus. This is seen in the study of their theological journeys. Once they began their deceptive teachings, they very well may have begun to believe what they were teaching. But, as my chapter on the origins of this system shows, they were men who desired to have their own way regardless of church teaching or of what their worthy contemporaries thought of them. I am not the judge in these matters. I am not attempting to be one; I am merely stating what I have observed. However, it is apparent to me that intent to deceive and promote self lies at the foundation and core of Dispensationalism.

The simplicity of the second coming of Jesus has been pushed aside in favor of a very complicated and complex system devised by man. It was at a time when many cults were forming in both Europe and America, when so many people were having "extra revelations" from whom they imagined to be God. As much as those who believe in Dispensationalism and its less radical brother, Pre-Millennialism, do not want to believe or even to consider this truth – the fact that this system had its birth during the time period when many cults were also being born – should definitely give us pause and put everyone on alert. When so many other deceptive and devious systems were forming, why do I believe that this one is somehow from God and all the others are from the devil? Does it not make more sense to realize that all of these "extra revelations" originated with the same source?

What the Lord and His apostles taught – and what the church through the first eighteen centuries taught – is that the second coming of Jesus Christ is on the last day, at the last trumpet, and defeats the last enemy – then comes the end. This is simple. It is not complicated or complex. The truth of the Scriptural second coming of Jesus is there for all to see. It is not hidden from our view, but it is in plain sight. It is not masked from our radar, nor does Scripture use sleight of hand or misdirection. It is a matter of do we want to believe it or not? Do we want to risk the ire of those who teach the popular Pre-Millennial system?

The details we believe concerning the second coming of Jesus should not be the basis of whether we think a person is saved or not. What is important is that we know Him as our Lord and Savior and are watching and waiting for His return as He promised.

END NOTES

[1] The complete text of Lacunza's book may be downloaded free of charge at www.lacunza.org

[2] Should you care to read any of his writings they may be found on the world wide web at http://www.sacred-texts.com/swd/index.htm Be prepared to shake your head is disbelief. Get a clothes pin for your nose, because this stuff really stinks.

[3] This information comes from ICR monograph 27 found at www.i-c-r.org.uk

[4] I cannot give credit for this quote. I failed to write it down and cannot find it. Sorry. It is a legitimate quote. This attitude demonstrates the cultic nature of Irving. "I am right; you are wrong."

[5] Dr. Martyn Lloyd-Jones *The Church and the Last Things*, 137

[6] Dr. Martyn Lloyd-Jones *The Church and the Last Things*, 138

[7] Dallimore, *Forerunner of the Charismatic Movement*, 166–68.

[8] J.N. Darby, *The Hopes of the Church of God* (London: G. Morrish), p.106

[9] Fuller, "The Hermeneutics of Dispensationalism," 40–46.

¹⁰ Ryrie, *Dispensationalism Today*, pp.44-45

¹¹ L.S. Chafer, "Dispensationalism," Bibliotheca Sacra 93 (1936):93 Chafer's Systematic Theology makes the point that in the Old Testament men were justified by the Law, while in the New Testament faith was without works

¹² Bass, *Backgrounds*, 39.

¹³ Blaising, Craig, "Development of Dispensationalism by Contemporary Dispensationalisms," 254

¹⁴ http://poweredbychrist.homestead.com/files/cyrus/Schofield.htm#_edn6

¹⁵ Many are the internet sites that give this historical background. I am also indebted to William Hendrickson's "More Than Conquerors" pages 193, 194 for getting me to think along these lines. He credits E.W. Hengstenberg, W. Fairweather, and A.H. Sayce for his information.

Appendix A

This is Margaret MacDonald's handwritten account of her 1830 revelation as it appears in Memoirs of James & George MacDonald, of Port-Glasgow. It is also recorded in many other works.

"It was first the awful state of the land that was pressed upon me. I saw the blindness and infatuation of the people to be very great. I felt the cry of Liberty just to be the hiss of the serpent, to drown them in perdition. I repeated the words, 'Now there is distress of nations, with perplexity, the seas and the waves roaring, men's hearts failing them for fear — now look out for the sign of the Son of man.' Here I was made to stop and cry out, <u>'O it is not known what the sign of the Son of man is; the people of God think they are waiting, but they know not what it is.</u>' I felt this needed to be revealed, and that there was great darkness and error about it; but suddenly what it was burst upon me with a glorious light. I saw it was the Lord Himself descending from Heaven with a shout, the glorified man, even Jesus; but that all must, as Stephen was, be filled with the Holy Ghost, that they might look up, and see the brightness of the Father's glory. <u>I saw the error to be, that men think that it will be something seen by the natural eye; but 'tis spiritual discernment that is needed, the eye of God in His people.</u> Many passages were revealed, in a light in which I had not before seen them. I repeated, 'Now is the kingdom of Heaven like unto ten virgins, who went forth to meet the Bridegroom, five wise and five foolish; they that were foolish took their lamps, but took no oil with them; but they that were wise took oil in their vessels with their lamps.' 'But be ye not unwise, but understanding what the will of the Lord is; and be not drunk with wine wherein is excess, but be filled with the Spirit.' This was the oil the wise virgins took in their vessels — this is the light to be kept burning — *the light of God — that we may discern that which cometh not with observation to the natural eye. Only those who have the light of God within them will see the sign of His appearance. No need to follow them who say, see here, or see there, for His day shall be as the lightning to those in whom the living Christ is.*' Tis Christ in us that will lift us up — He is the light — *'tis only those that are alive in Him that will be caught up to meet Him in the air.* I saw that we must be in the Spirit, that we might see spiritual things. John was in the Spirit, when he saw a throne set in Heaven. — But I saw that the glory of the ministration of the Spirit had not been known....I said, Now shall the people of God have to do with realities — now shall the glorious mystery of God in our nature be known — now shall it be know what it is for man to be glorified. *I felt that the revelation of Jesus Christ had yet to be opened up — it is not knowledge about God that it contains, but it is an entering into God* - I saw that there was a glorious breaking in of God to be. I felt as Elijah, surrounded with chariots of fire. I saw as it were, the spiritual temple reared, and the Head Stone brought forth with shoutings of grace, grace, unto it. It was a glorious light above the brightness of the sun, that shone round about me. *I felt that those who were filled with the Spirit could see spiritual things, and feel walking in the midst of them, while those who had not the Spirit could see nothing* — so that two shall be in one bed, the one taken and the other left, because the one has the light of God within while the other cannot see the Kingdom of Heaven. I saw the people of God in an awfully dangerous situation, surrounded by nets and entanglements, about to be tried, and many about to be deceived and fall. Now will THE WICKED be revealed, with all power and signs and lying wonders, so that if it were possible the very elect will be deceived. — This is the fiery trial which is to try us. — It will be for the purging and purifying of the real members of the body of Jesus; but Oh it will be a fiery trial. Every soul will be shaken to the very centre. The enemy will try to shake every thing we have believed in — but the trial of real faith will be found to honour and praise and glory. Nothing but what is of God will stand. The stony-ground hearers will be made manifest — the love of many will wax cold. I frequently said that night, and often since, now shall the awful sight of a false Christ be seen on this earth, and nothing but the living Christ in us can detect this awful attempt of the enemy to deceive — for it is with all deceivableness of unrighteousness he will work — he will have a counterpart for every part of God's truth, and an imitation for every work of the Spirit. The Spirit must and will be poured out on the church, that she may be purified and filled with God — and just in proportion as the Spirit of God works, so will he — when our Lord anoints men with power, so will he. This is particularly the nature of the trial through which those are to pass who will be counted worthy to stand before the Son of man. There will be outward trials too, but it is principally temptation. It is brought on by the outpouring of the Spirit, and will increase in proportion as the Spirit is poured out. The trial of the Church is from antichrist. It is by being filled with the Spirit that we shall be kept. I frequently said, Oh be filled with the Spirit — have the light of God in you, that you may detect satan — be full of eyes within — be clay in the hands of the potter — submit to be filled, filled with God. This will build the temple....Jesus wants His bride. His desire is toward us. He that shall come, will come, and will not tarry. Amen and Amen. Even so come Lord Jesus."

Breinigsville, PA USA
03 November 2009
226942BV00003B/4/P